To my wife Maha
and to our children and their families
Stefan and Kristina Ateek and their daughter Lisa,
Sari and Tanory Ateek and their son Naeem,
Nevart and Richard Willborn

Contents

Foreword

What do I see and hear in the Holy Land? Some people cannot move freely from one place to another. A wall separates them from their families and from their incomes. They cannot tend to their gardens at home or to their lessons at school. They are arbitrarily demeaned at checkpoints and unnecessarily beleaguered by capricious applications of bureaucratic red tape. I grieve for the damage being done daily to people's souls and bodies. I have to tell the truth: I am reminded of the yoke of oppression that was once our burden in South Africa.

I see and hear that ancient olive trees are uprooted. Flocks are cut off from their pastures and shepherds. The homes of some people are bulldozed even as new homes for others are illegally constructed on other people's land. I grieve for the land that suffers such violence, the marring of its beauty, the loss of its comforts, the despoiling of its yield. I have to tell the truth: I am reminded of the bitter days of uprooting and despoiling in my own country.

I see and hear that young people believe that it is heroic and pious to kill others by killing themselves. They strap bombs to their torsos to achieve liberation. They do not know that liberation achieved by brutality will defraud in the end. I grieve the waste of their lives and of the lives they take, the loss of personal and communal security they cause, and the lust for revenge that follows their crimes, crowding out all reason and restraint. I have to tell the truth: I am reminded of the explosive anger that inflamed South Africa, too.

Some people are enraged by comparisons between the Israeli-Palestinian conflict and what happened in South Africa. There are differences between the two situations, but a comparison need not be exact in every feature to yield clarity about what is happening. Moreover, for those of us who lived through the dehumanizing horrors of the apartheid era, the comparison seems not only apt, it is also necessary. It is necessary if we are to persevere in our hope that things can change.

Indeed, because of what I experienced in South Africa, I harbor a vast, unreasoning hope for Israel and the Palestinian territories. South Africans, after all, had no reason to suppose that the evil system and the cycles of violence that were sapping the soul of our nation would ever change. There was nothing special or different about South Africans to deserve the appearance of the very thing for which we prayed and worked and suffered so long.

Most South Africans did not believe they would live to see a day of liberation. They did not believe that their children's children would see it. They did not believe that such a day even existed, except in fantasy. But we have seen it. We are living now in the day we longed for.

It is not a cloudless day. The divine arc that bends toward a truly just and whole society has not yet stretched fully across my country's sky like a rainbow of peace. It is not finished, it does not always live up to its promise, it is not perfect—but it is new. A brand new thing, like a dream of God, has come about to replace the old story of mutual hatred and oppression.

I have seen it and heard it, and so to this truth, too, I am compelled to testify—if it can happen in South Africa, it can happen with the Israelis and Palestinians. There is not much reason to be optimistic, but there is every reason to hope.

Naim Ateek gives voice to this hope by calling for a theology and a practice of nonviolent justice and love. He examines a past filled with injustice and pain, but he also looks forward with hope to a future that might truly reflect the dream of God for the Holy Land. We need voices like his to call us to seek reconciliation and to live in justice and love.

Archbishop Desmond Tutu
Cape Town, South Africa

Preface

This book picks up the struggle for justice and peace from where it ended in my first book, *Justice, and Only Justice*.[1] Tragically, justice as expressed in United Nations Resolutions 194, 242, and 338 has not been achieved so far, and the peace we desire still seems remote. Thus, we still need to return to the roots of our faith as believers to address themes that exacerbate enmity rather than transform it. Our God-given mandate is to see that an enduring peace is achieved in the Middle East.

The conflict over Palestine has become highly charged and divisive not only for the people of the land who have been scattered, with many clustered in crowded refugee camps, but also for millions of people who live thousands of miles away. This book, therefore, attempts to strike at the heart of the conflict and address the major obstacles to peace in a lucid and straightforward manner. These obstacles include the difficult issue of the Jewish character of the state of Israel, the enigma and problematic of Zionism, as well as the seemingly intractable questions of Jerusalem and the Palestinian refugees. The book seeks to engage, educate, and challenge the readers regardless of which side of the conflict they take. The book ends on a hopeful note with a vision of peace for all the people of the land—Israelis and Palestinians alike.

It is important, however, to state in the beginning that I, the author, am an Arab Palestinian Christian and a citizen of the state of Israel and that I have lived most of my adult life under the Israeli occupation. I am writing from my perspective as a Christian, and the solutions I propose are based on faith in the God of love and peace, justice and mercy, liberation and reconciliation.

Although written from this particular perspective, I hope many Muslims, Jews, and secular people will also read this book. Ultimately, the proposed solutions are meant for all the people of the land, whether Israelis or Palestinians. It is also hoped that people of other faiths will be stimulated by the book's critiques of various interpretations of the Bible. I have also emphasized the major principles on which a just peace can be built, and these are not limited by a single religious tradition.

Palestinian liberation theology, as other liberation theologies, begins with its context and takes that context very seriously. The Palestinian context continues to be one of occupation and oppression. Many people believe that since the state of Israel has been successful in establishing a strong and viable state, it might be open to resolving the conflict with its neighbors. Unfortunately this has not happened: today violence still spills forth, and the whole region cries out for a peaceful solution to the conflict.

Because the region in turmoil is known by many as the "Holy Land," it is not surprising that scripture is often referred to—by both Jews and Christians. Because this is so, I intentionally address a number of biblical and theological themes that have direct bearings on the conflict itself and any potential solution. Such themes include a theology of God and the land, violence and nonviolence, the politics of Christian Zionism, as well as a number of related themes.

Finally it is important to point out that life in the Middle East does not draw a line between politics and religion. The two are closely intertwined, and have been so from time immemorial. Religion can be a source of tremendous spiritual strength, but religion, when misused and translated into action by people of power, can also become a deadly weapon.

God is very much present to the people of this land and is continuously invoked by Jews, Muslims, and Christians. It often seems that each of our religions has created God in its own image to serve its own needs; perhaps this is why it seems that at times God is part of the problem rather than the solution. How then can we speak of God and God's authentic word for us as we struggle for justice and peace? Such are the challenges of this book as it addresses the politics of the Israel-Palestine conflict.

Jerusalem
May 15, 2008

"Nakba, Arabic for catastrophe, refers to what happened to the people of Palestine as a result of the establishment of the state of Israel on their land. It is not the establishment of Israel itself that is called Nakba, but the effect which this event had on the Palestinian people." May 15 marks the Nakba day for the Palestinians and Independence Day for Israel. Only when justice is done and Palestinians can celebrate their own independence will a comprehensive peace be felt throughout the land. As long as one side celebrates while the other mourns, no authentic celebration or peace is possible.

Acknowledgements

Due to Sabeel's busy programs in Jerusalem and travel requirements for meetings and conferences, the writing of this book is long overdue. In order to expedite the process, I left Jerusalem with my wife, Maha, and spent several months in Pasadena, California, where, with the help of many friends, I was able to complete the first working draft. Help from friends came in various ways. Before we arrived in California, the Episcopal bishop of Los Angeles, the Right Reverend Jon Bruno, Canon Lydia Lopez, and my son, the Reverend Sari Ateek, made arrangements for our stay. The Reverend Canon Denis O'Pray and the Vestry of the Church of Our Savior in San Gabriel donated the use of a beautiful house next to the church. Furniture for the house was provided when an elderly woman, a member of St. James Parish in South Pasadena, passed away and willed her furniture to the church. Through the kindness of the Reverend Anne Tumilty and the Vestry of St. James, this furniture was given for our use. The Reverend Bud Williams generously provided a car. Thanks also to Bob and Maurine Tobin, who stepped in at Sabeel during my absence in Jerusalem.

I would like to express my thanks to all those who provided financial, material, and moral support for the writing of this book. Specifically, I want to thank the presiding bishop of the Episcopal Church, the Most Reverend Katherine Jefferts Schori, the Reverend Canon Brian Grieves, the Reverend Ed Bacon, Randi and Doni Heyn-Lamb, Sandy and Sue Smock, the Reverend Darrel Meyers, Joan B. Darby, the Reverend Stanley and Jeanne Fowler, Edward Gaffney, Donald L. Gibbon, and Helen Chapin Metz.

For help with research and editing of the book in the United States and Jerusalem, many thanks to Matt Hamsher, Chad Cain, Tanory Ateek, and Cathy Nichols. In Jerusalem, David Hosey, a mission intern with Global Ministries of the United Methodist Church, spent many hours assisting with editing the manuscript. I am very much indebted to Cedar Duaybis for her invaluable help. Without her meticulous review of the chapters and her pertinent suggestions it would have been very difficult to finalize the book. I am indeed grateful for her patience, dedication, and the generous giving of her time.

Additionally, I would like to express special thanks to the Reverend Canon Richard Toll, coordinator of Friends of Sabeel North America (FOSNA), and to my brother, Saleem Ateek, for their constant encouragement and support throughout the process. Sister Elaine Kelley, FOSNA administrator, was also a vital part of this project.

I especially want to thank Sabeel board members Samia Khoury, Cedar Duaybis, and Jonathan Kuttab. Thanks are also due to the entire staff and volunteers of Sabeel in Jerusalem and Nazareth and to all those who make the work of Sabeel possible. Of course, none of this would have been possible without the loving support of my wife Maha.

I am also grateful to Susan Perry, senior editor of Orbis Books, for her support and patient guidance. I thank Orbis Books for its support and for agreeing to publish the book.

I thank God for all those who might not be mentioned here by name but who supported me faithfully through their thoughts and prayers. To all these and many others who contributed in various ways, I am deeply grateful. I am thankful for all who share in a passion for justice and peace for all the people of the Holy Land, and for the Palestinian Christian community that has persevered through such adversity and provided inspiration for much of the material in this book.

It is only through the grace of God that I was able to finish the task.

PART I

RECAPPING HISTORY

Chapter 1

The Birth of Sabeel

"To give light to those who sit in darkness and in the shadow of death, to guide our feet into the way of peace."
—Luke 1:79

I returned to Nazareth in Israel in 1966, having completed my undergraduate work and theological training in the United States. On October 20, I was ordained a deacon in the Anglican Church by Archbishop Campbell MacInnes at Christ Church, Nazareth, where I had grown up. It was a very moving and meaningful experience for me after having been abroad for seven years. Especially inspiring were the Arabic words inscribed above the altar:

> The Spirit of the Lord is upon me,
> because he has anointed me
> to bring good news to the poor.
> He has sent me to proclaim release to the captives
> and recovery of sight to the blind,
> to let the oppressed go free,
> to proclaim the year of the Lord's favor. (Luke 4:18)

I was excited to begin my ministry in the church and to become immersed in the service of Christ. Yet in spite of the importance of this event, my joy could not be complete without the physical presence of my father.

On Israel's Independence Day in 1958 the Israeli military governor had allowed the Palestinian Arabs living in Israel to move around without permits. My father took advantage of this temporary freedom to rent a pickup truck and take all of his children back for the first time to see our home in the town of Beisan, the home from which we had been forced out nine years earlier. Even today I clearly remember how we were not allowed even to look inside our home. The three houses built by my father that made up our home had been divided into smaller units, each occupied now by a Jewish immigrant family. It must have been very difficult for my father to see our home occupied by Jewish immigrants who had come from North Africa while he, the rightful owner, was prevented even from entering them. A few days after this traumatic experience, my father suffered a stroke from which he never fully recovered, leaving him unable to walk or speak clearly.[1]

Shortly after, when I was ready to begin my studies in the United States, my entire family came to see me off at the Lydda Airport (Ben Gurion). My mother brought my ailing father to the airport so that he wouldn't continue to look for me or wonder where I had gone. My father knew that I wanted to study for the ministry and that I was determined to return to serve God in my own country and among my own people. Sadly, my father died a year later.

All these memories crossed my mind during my ordination in 1966. I believed that my father was there with me in spirit, proudly blessing me as I took my ordination vows to faithfully serve God. Indeed, the words of Jesus Christ spoken in the synagogue in Nazareth centuries before and inscribed in beautiful calligraphy above the altar were both inspiring and empowering. My fervent prayer on that day was to be guided by the Spirit for an enriched ministry to God's glory and honor.

Seven months later, on Trinity Sunday, May 21, 1967, I was ordained as a priest at St. John the Evangelist Church in Haifa. I still remember it was a *khamseen*, one of the hottest days of the year. The weather was hot and the political climate was even hotter. The Israeli army stood on one side of the border, and the armies of Egypt, Syria, and Jordan were amassed on the other as they prepared for war. On June 5, approximately two weeks later, the 1967 war broke out. Israel's preemptive strike swept through the Arab armies in an impressive victory that resulted in the occupation of the rest of Palestine, including the West Bank, East Jerusalem, the Gaza Strip; parts of Jordan; and large territories from Egypt and Syria. The war had changed the map of the Middle East.

TWO PIVOTAL EVENTS

Two events impacted my ministry politically and theologically and contributed to the emergence of a Palestinian theology of liberation. The first was the 1967 war. I was at home in Shefa-Amr washing my car when my mother called to say the war had begun. For the next few days, like many others, I was glued to the radio (we had no televisions at the time). And, as the saying goes, the first casualty of war was the truth, which was washed away by a wave of propaganda. It later became clear that the Israeli army had destroyed the Egyptian Air Force and was able to march unhindered through Sinai. Vast Arab territories were captured by Israel and thousands of people were killed. Instead of redressing the 1948 injustice, the war further exacerbated matters.

The war brought back my childhood memories of the 1948 war, although at that time I was too young to comprehend the enormity of the tragedy. Now, as an adult, I relived the past in the lives of the people who lived in the occupied territories. Hundreds of questions rushed at me, ranging from politics to religion, from international responsibility to humanitarian anguish and need. I became keenly aware of the depth of the injustice committed against the Palestinians and also the foolishness and futility of war in resolving the conflict. Although I felt deeply about the importance of justice and peacemaking, I was conscious of my own inadequacy. I felt the need for peace in my guts, agonized over the injustice, and prayed to God for an end to the injustice and the oppression. Everywhere I went the topics of justice and peace were on the menu. People asked questions—political and theological—and I spent many hours in discussions and debates. The political situation that was the heart of the struggle became our daily ration of food.

Unclear about what to do, my immediate response was to immerse myself in the pastoral, educational, and ecumenical ministry of the church. Indeed, the war sharpened my awareness about the importance of being involved in the work of justice and peace. At the same time, I was conscious of my immediate pastoral responsibilities. Whenever possible my sermons included an emphasis on justice, but it was not always the central theme. I gained tremendous insight from the political and religious discussions in the Shefa-Amer community, and these discussions developed my understandings of the issues of peace, social and political concerns, and our Christian responsibility of involvement.

For the next thirteen years, I was a priest, pastor, teacher, and counselor, helping people deepen their love of God and of each other. Over time my ministry transcended the denominational boundaries of my small parish as I started to bring Christians of various denominations closer to each other. When I moved to serve the church in Haifa in 1972, this ecumenical dimension became an essential part of my expanded ministry and flourished in new and exciting ways. For the first time, clergy of all the denominations in the area were meeting regularly for prayer and study, and working together we were able to initiate programs in the community that brought Christians together. It was wonderful to see the churches come alive as clergy exchanged pulpits and people's faith was deepened through interdenominational Bible study and other gifts of the Spirit.

Although I was grateful to God for what was happening in the ecumenical ministry in Haifa, something seemed to be missing. Trusting the Holy Spirit, I left Haifa with my wife Maha and our two little boys, Stefan and Sari, and returned to the United States to begin graduate studies in Berkeley, California. This is when I first began to articulate a Palestinian theology of liberation. Although I was not sure where God was leading me and how this theology would be used, I felt a deep satisfaction and comfort that God was guiding me. In 1985, after I completed my doctorate in theology, I was transferred from Haifa to St. George's Cathedral in Jerusalem to serve its Palestinian congregation. This transition set my face directly toward the work of justice and peace.

The second event that defined my path was the *intifada*.[2] Twenty years had passed since the 1967 war and a viable solution was not yet in sight. In 1979 President Jimmy Carter had successfully brokered a peace treaty between Israel and Egypt. A treaty with the strongest Arab state in the Middle East ruled out the possibility of another war. Israel could now afford to ignore Syria and keep the Golan Heights under its control. In fact, in 1981, in a clear violation of international law, Israel belligerently annexed the Syrian territory. At the same time, it accelerated its consolidation of the West Bank (including East Jerusalem and the Gaza Strip) by confiscating additional Palestinian land and by building and expanding settlements. So long as the United States was on its side, Israel did not really care what the rest of the world thought or did.

In 1979 the U.N. Security Council issued Resolution 446 condemning the building of settlements, but Israel was not deterred. Neither the Arab countries nor the international community was able to stop Israeli expansion, and the U.N. resolutions went unheeded. At that time, newly arrived in Jerusalem, I witnessed firsthand the escalating violence of the Israeli army against the Palestinians. In those days, the Palestinian people had no access to weapons and arms. Although they were trapped by the ferocious and brutal fist of the Israeli army, their resistance was largely nonviolent.

At that time Yasir Arafat and the main Palestine Liberation Organization (PLO) leadership were based in Tunis and the PLO was still considered a terrorist organization. The Israeli government outlawed contact with any of its members. Hamas did not yet exist, and most of the Palestinian people were supportive of the PLO, considering it their sole legitimate representative. Palestinians were united by strong feelings of nationalism based not on religion but their identity as Palestinians, an identity that embraced love of people and of the land. As the Israeli oppression worsened and the international community stood inept and crippled before Israeli power, all flickers of hope were extinguished. With nowhere else to turn, the Palestinians turned to themselves, and on December 9, 1987, the *intifada* erupted, affecting the whole of the Palestinian community in the occupied territories.

The *intifada* was a spontaneous uprising of the whole Palestinian community both on the West Bank (including East Jerusalem) and in the Gaza Strip. Palestinians—men and women, young and old—rose up in solidarity with one another with one clear message: the illegal Israeli occupation of their country must come to an end. Palestinians from the various political factions came together to cry out that they wanted to live in freedom in their own state—not under the domination of a foreign state. The *intifada* was a nonviolent uprising that Israel was unsuccessful in crushing. Its foundation was patriotic and nationalist and was not based on religion.

The first *intifada* still stands as one of the rare moments in Palestinian history when the nonviolent power of the people was exhibited at its best. It continued for the next five years until the Oslo Peace Process came into being. In many ways, the *intifada* established the capability of the Palestinian community to resist nonviolently the occupation of their country. In retrospect, it is unfortunate that the Palestinian leadership was unable to capitalize on and nourish this type of resistance. Israel, which tried to present the *intifada* as a violent struggle, reacted to it as such, yet it is recorded in history as a profound illustration of the resilience of the Palestinians and the power of nonviolence in resisting an oppressive power.[3] While the *intifada* did not achieve its goal, it will always stand out as a bright mark in the history of the Palestinian struggle.

These two events—the 1967 war and the first *intifada*—set the stage for what was to come. The former showed the expansionist policies of the Israeli government on the one hand, and the futility of war and violence to redress injustice on the other. The latter pointed toward the way of nonviolence as the only way to resist the occupation, and clearly showed that the Palestinian people, both Muslim and Christian, were capable of such an undertaking.

THE EMERGENCE OF HAMAS

As a popular uprising the *intifada* expressed the will of the people. One of its important demands was to recognize the PLO as the only legitimate representative of the Palestinian people. Until then, Israel and the United States had refused to recognize the PLO and had tried unsuccessfully to create an alternative, but the Palestinians were solidly behind the PLO with Arafat as its leader.

As the *intifada* heightened, two words were heard on the Palestinian streets. "Hamas" stood for "The Movement of Islamic Resistance" and "Hamam" for "The Movement for Christian Resistance."[4] Some Palestinians, including myself, immediately suspected that Israel was attempting to interject religion into the conflict in order to shatter the national unity and solidarity of the Palestinians. Having failed to create a political substitute for the PLO that was acceptable to Palestinians and unable to crush the *intifada*, Israel cleverly stirred up religious rivalries.

Many of us immediately saw this as a trap. I remember vividly calling one of my friends in Bethlehem and pleading with him to do everything he could to stop the emergence of a Christian resistance movement that would be based on armed struggle. We were grateful to God that the Palestinian Christian community promptly suppressed Hamam and that it never saw the light of day. However, Hamas found fertile soil among some Palestinian Muslim groups who were already predisposed to such an idea. Religious slogans for the liberation of Palestine began to appear more frequently under the permissive guise of the Israeli soldiers. Indeed, religion was a potent force that could rally Palestinian Muslims and generate religious fervor. The implied message became clear: if Palestinian nationalism failed to achieve the liberation of Palestine, Islamic nationalism inevitably would. The emerging new slogans were religiously partisan—"Palestine is Islamic," "Jerusalem is Islamic," "Islam is the answer"—rather than the more religiously inclusive slogans that emphasized the nationalist character of Palestine.

Hamas proliferated rapidly within the Islamic community, and its influence spread in the Gaza Strip and the West Bank. Such religious partisanship was a blow to the national unity of the Palestinians, and many Palestinian Christians recognized this. In fact, it caused not only an obstacle between Christians and Muslims, but it also brought about a split between "religious" and "progressive" Muslims. And, naturally, it contributed to feelings of fear and distrust in the Christian community. The rise of Hamas has made it easier for Israel to pit us against one another and control us.

In the Israeli daily newspaper *Ma'ariv*, journalist Ben Kaspit wrote, "I know that Israel was the one who helped Hamas emerge (the Shamir government with the support of the Minister of Defense Rabin in order to weaken Fatah[5]). And Israel supported the emergence of Hizballah (the government of Begin with the initiative and implementation of Sharon in order to drive out Arafat [from Lebanon])."[6] In other words, Kaspit claimed that Israel aided the emergence of Hamas in order to break the backbone of the PLO by using the power of religion, religious sentiment in its crudest and most emotional form. As Hamas developed, it became a thorn in the flesh of the PLO, but it also proved to be a spike in the spine of Israel. If, indeed, Israel contributed to the emergence of Hamas, then it would also reap the whirlwind. In the 2006 Palestinian parliamentary election, Hamas succeeded in defeating Fatah, the largest party in the PLO. Whereas the PLO was ready to make peace with Israel on the basis of UN resolutions 242 and 338, Hamas had more stringent demands.

THE BIRTH OF SABEEL

In many ways, the first stirrings of Sabeel, an ecumenical center that applies a theological approach and nonviolence to address the Palestinian/Israeli conflict, took place at St. George's Anglican Cathedral in Jerusalem several years before the name Sabeel was even adopted. As soon as the *intifada* started, I felt that my preaching had to become more relevant to our new political context. This small Anglican congregation in Jerusalem, like the rest of the Christian community on the West Bank and in the Gaza Strip, was in need of comfort and courage. It needed to hear the word of God addressing their particular situation of life. If the Bible had nothing to say to them in their pain and sorrow, in the midst of injustice and oppression, then the Bible had no relevance for their lives.

The themes of my weekly sermons became centered on justice and truth. When I turned to the Bible I found a preponderance of texts that emphasized justice and righteousness as well as mercy and love. Yet it was difficult to preach peace and reconciliation when injustice and oppression were the daily ration of the Palestinians. The only response had to be a prophetic response in the spirit of the great prophets of the Old Testament, on the one hand, and, on the other, in the spirit of Jesus and the New Testament.

At the same time, I felt that my sermons could not be complete without the direct response of the people in the Christian community that gathered there. So every Sunday after the church service most of the congregation that was present would pick up a cup of coffee and spend an additional hour in the small parish hall discussing the sermon. Without a doubt, it was then that the seeds of a Palestinian theology of liberation began to sprout and grow. The ideas I first articulated as a graduate student in Berkeley began to take form within this community of faith where the people of God wrestled with how they should apply the word of God to their daily lives. Every week they took the sermon, chewed it and digested it. They added their own illustrations from their own experience during the previous week and that of their relatives and neighbors. They talked about the people who had been killed or injured or imprisoned.

The sermon and the texts of scripture were brought to bear on all these experiences. People challenged each other, struggling with the demands of the gospel against the human tendency to respond with violence and exact revenge. They refused to dilute the gospel by lowering it to the level of hate and violence. Together we were able to hear Christ challenging us to love and not to hate. While the Israeli army was increasing its oppressive measures and Israeli soldiers were breaking the bones of Palestinian children for throwing stones, as well as humiliating and even killing them, the natural response was to give in to resentment and the desire for revenge and to be pulled down to the level of the subhuman. It was a constant challenge to our faith to resist this natural response, and to be pulled up by Christ to be the people God wants us to be. It was there that the Palestinian theology of liberation in its early stages began to be applied and tested.

The first conference on a Palestinian theology of liberation was held at Tantur, an ecumenical center in Jerusalem, in 1990--approximately a year after my first book *Justice, and Only Justice* was published. We were able to invite ten theologians from various parts of the world to Jerusalem. There, with approximately forty local Palestinian Christians, we were able to introduce a Palestinian theology of liberation that was relevant to the Palestinians, the indigenous people of the land. With the help of Rosemary Radford Ruether and Marc Ellis, we were able to publish the proceedings of that meeting.[7] The beginnings of this movement were now sprouting through workshops, small gatherings of people, and discussions inside and outside of St. George's Cathedral.

Fortunately, Hamam, the Movement of Christian Resistance intended to be a counterpart of Hamas to recruit Christians to counter the violence of the occupation with Palestinian violence, was dead. In its stead, a new movement was born within the Palestinian Christian community; it was founded in the spirit of Jesus, the spirit of love and nonviolence. It recognized the evil and the international illegality of the Israeli domination of the Palestinians and its occupation of their country. It recognized the necessity and the importance of resisting such an evil but it chose the path of nonviolent resistance. This is the way of Jesus. Those who claim to be his followers must walk in his footsteps.

The response of the grassroots Christian community in Jerusalem was encouraging. While some people were anxious to know more about this movement of Palestinian liberation theology, some people (including some clergy) were skeptical. Most people had never heard of liberation theology and were curious to find out more about it. Others had heard the name but responded negatively. They knew it had begun in Latin America, but they immediately connected it with Marxism and totally rejected it. Thus from the beginning we faced the quite formidable task of educating people about this contextual theology of liberation that is deeply biblical and has as its main objective making the gospel relevant to Palestinian Christians. Through God's grace we were able to overcome these obstacles and attract into this movement clergy and lay members from the various churches of the land, including Orthodox, Catholic, and Protestant. Toward the end of 1993, the name "Sabeel" was adopted. Sabeel is Arabic for "the way" and "the spring." We were convinced that we were and continue to be on a journey charting the way for justice, peace, and reconciliation (in that order).

Sabeel came into being as an ecumenical movement within the Palestinian Christian community of the Holy Land of Israel and Palestine. Sabeel is not a political organization and is not affiliated with any particular political party or denomination inside or outside of Israel-Palestine. Sabeel's theology, philosophy, and ideology are biblically based and founded on the life, teachings, and example of Jesus Christ. From the beginning it was important to be specific about its main objectives, which were based on the urgent needs of the Palestinian community.

First: A Theology of Liberation

The first primary objective of Sabeel is to articulate a Palestinian theology of liberation that can help Palestinian Christians and their friends and supporters address the conflict from within their faith. Although the conflict, in its origin, is political and rooted in European colonialist and imperialist ideologies, since then Zionists, both Christian and Jewish, have given Israeli expansion theological underpinnings supported by scriptural language. Since the war of 1967, the Zionist ideology that had started as a secular movement at the end of the nineteenth century gradually shifted until its most pronounced expressions became religious. Both Western Christian Zionists and Jewish religious Zionists used scripture to endorse Israeli claims over the entire land of Palestine and justify the oppressive actions of the Israeli government against the Palestinians. It is essential, therefore, to critique such a theology of militarism, domination, and injustice as a biblical aberration and emphasize instead that the authentic message of the Bible is a message of justice, mercy, and peace.

It is important that Christians see the fallacy of a Zionist approach to the Bible: the modern state of Israel cannot ignore the principles of morality and justice, and it cannot continue to defy the principles of international law that are based on morality and justice. At the same time, there is a great need to help ordinary Christians use the Bible as a tool for justice and peace. There is a need to critique violence and evil being done in the name of God and God's word but there is also an equal need to highlight the rich biblical tradition in both the Old and New Testaments that can help in the pursuit of peace and freedom.

Such a theology can be truly liberating for people living under an occupation and can, in turn, help them work for the liberation of others. One of the most powerful and effective tools among Palestinian Christians has been their way of perceiving Jesus Christ as the ultimate paradigm of liberation. Readers who are familiar with Middle Eastern Christianity know how theologically "loaded" the Eastern churches are with a Trinitarian faith. The divinity of Christ is strongly emphasized and continuously reiterated in the various liturgies. Such an emphasis reflects the theological controversies that faced the early church during the first five centuries. In fact, Christ's divinity is emphasized so much that it is easy for many people to forget Jesus' full humanity. In many ways, a Palestinian theology of liberation has reestablished the balance between Christ's two natures—his divinity and his humanity. Palestinian liberation theology focuses on the humanity of Jesus of Nazareth, who was also a Palestinian living under an occupation.[8] For many years, this fact was missed by Palestinian Christians. It simply escaped our attention, and we did not realize its potential impact. Perhaps because we had placed a large divine halo around Christ, we could not imagine him as a human being living at a time in history like any one of us. Once Palestinians rediscovered Jesus Christ's humanity, the relevancy of his human life became amazingly apparent; the experience of Palestinian Christians who live today in oppressive conditions under the Israeli occupation are quite similar to the experience of Jesus and his followers under the Roman occupation.

We then fleshed out the implications of such a comparison. Like many Palestinians today, Jesus was born under occupation and throughout his life knew only a life under occupation. All his travels, his eating and drinking, his teaching and healing ministry, his relationships with others—every aspect of his life—were carried out under the oppressive domination of the Romans. Finally, he was executed by the occupation forces in collusion with the religious leaders of first-century Jerusalem.

When we approach the Gospels through this lens, we discover a theology of liberation in a context that truly is relevant for Palestinian Christians who live their lives today under Israeli occupation.

Second: A Liberation of Theology

The Christian community of the Holy Land has lived there for the last two thousand years. It has not always been easy but with God's grace, it has survived. Due to many historical changes, its numbers have shrunk from a majority in Palestine by the end of the fourth century to a meager and vulnerable minority today. Palestinian Christians have always known that their savior and Lord Jesus Christ was not a violent person nor did he promote violence. In difficult and dangerous times, and in order to survive, their theology over time became a theology of resignation, isolation, and noninterference. Such a theology could be justified biblically: people are encouraged to "wait patiently on God" to come and rescue them. This theology was also impacted by Paul's teaching that "all authority is from God," so to resist the authority is to resist God (Rom. 13:1-2).

I believe these two examples, more than others, have caused members of the church to become submissive and passive. As a result, in some areas over the centuries the prophetic ministry of the church has suffered. As the church celebrated its liturgies and practiced its ceremonies and rituals, the prophetic word was silenced by a progression of oppressive governors with no qualms about crushing those who dared to raise their voices. In the Middle East, theologies tend to be imprisoned within liturgies, rites, and ceremonies that cry out for liberation. On the one hand, we give thanks that our liturgies go back to the early church fathers; however, there is a great need to express our faith in today's language. At one point in history these liturgies were relevant to their times; the same needs to be done today. Liturgy is what the people do and it cannot be fossilized. Liturgy should help people translate their faith into everyday life and practice rather than be an expression of the past.

There is always a need to look carefully at the theology of our churches and, if necessary, liberate them from biblical misinterpretation and misunderstanding. There are, however, other dimensions of our theologies that also need to be liberated, not least of which is the de-Zionization of the Bible, that is, learning to read the Bible as a story about a loving, just, inclusive God of all people rather than as a story of one particular nation or ethnic group. The Bible has been often used to justify the injustices that have been committed by the Zionist Jews and the state of Israel. It has been equally abused by millions of Christian Zionists who use it to support Israel's claim to the "Holy Land." This topic is addressed in chapter 6.

These two areas—a theology of liberation and the liberation of theology—must go hand in hand. Once we have a vision of the liberator Christ, we have to critique any theology that silences the people of God in the face of evil. We must critique those biblical passages that glorify violence and present God as a god of war. Indeed, it is important to keep articulating a theology that helps liberate our theologies and, at the same time, helps us understand what it means to walk with God and do God's work in the world today. Any theology that does not contribute to the liberation of the oppressed must be rejected as inadequate and irrelevant.

In fact, someone has suggested to me that we must begin with the liberation of theology before we can talk about a theology of liberation. She feels that so much of our theologies has shackled people instead of liberating them. One of the best examples of such an incarcerated theology is the silence of many church hierarchies in the face of the political powers that oppress and enslave people. Such silence is deadly. The Middle East has a long history of repressive regimes that have not allowed people to express their views on public policy. Any dissent has been harshly addressed. Consequently, people's views have been suppressed as they live under the mercy of governors. In such a climate, church leaders have tried their best to be on good terms with the people who hold power, and the price of that good relationship has been their silence. Yet some have dared to speak out, and many of those have lost their lives. Today, we need to be inspired again by the early Christians who dared to stand up and speak for the poor and oppressed of the world. This demands courage and the liberation of our theologies.

Liberation continues to be at the heart of the work of Sabeel. Yet Sabeel is much more than a theological think tank. The name itself expresses action and dynamism. It means "the path" and "the way" as well as a spring of fresh water, and this implies walking the way and drinking from the spring. It is an active word. Therefore, once Sabeel came into being it had to be translated into programs. The objective of these programs has been precisely to examine two major areas: to develop a theology of liberation as well as to liberate any stagnant and dormant theologies.

Sabeel's first conference, held in 1990, focused on introducing the concept of a distinctively Palestinian theology. For us at Sabeel it was also a time for discernment. By 1993, the name Sabeel was adopted and its work began to expand. In 1996, Sabeel reached out internationally to establish Friends of Sabeel (FOS) in other countries. Today, the ministry of Sabeel is both local and international through the commitment of supporters from various racial, ethnic, and cultural backgrounds. All are committed to justice, peace, and reconciliation for all the people of Israel and Palestine.

Sabeel emerged to make the gospel relevant to Palestinian Christians who live under Israeli occupation. As it developed, Sabeel has grown more aware of its multifaceted responsibilities and thus has devised a three-dimensional agenda. The first dimension addresses the accumulation of a two-thousand-year-old Christian tradition. It promotes ecumenical relations with all the Christians of the land, whether living within the state of Israel or in the occupied Palestinian territories. It aims to strengthen Christians' faith in Christ and their love of Christ, drawing them closer together so that they can transcend denominationalism while appreciating their own particular rich church tradition. There is a need to preserve the rich Christian mosaic in the Middle East while at the same time emphasizing the importance of working together ecumenically.

A second dimension of the work of Sabeel concerns Christian-Muslim relations. We cannot be faithful to God in our work if we do not address interfaith relations with our Muslim brothers and sisters. Although we belong to one Palestinian people, we are deeply affiliated with two religious faiths: Islam and Christianity. Throughout the vicissitudes of history, in good and bad times, we have lived together. Unfortunately, at present, due to the propensity of the oppressive Israeli occupation to drive wedges between our two faiths and the rise of religious fundamentalism and extremism, we have been experiencing certain difficulties that have been driving some of our people apart. This is distressing for many of us, Christian and Muslim alike. It has been very important, therefore, to work together for three essential interfaith objectives: greater understanding between the two faiths, respect for one another's faith traditions, and acceptance of the religious differences between us.

A third dimension is our work for justice and peace. In many ways, this is the most important dimension and it constitutes our priority. Once peace is achieved, even the ecumenical and interfaith ministries will be easier to promote. Sabeel's work in this area takes into consideration both the demands of international law and the U.N. resolutions on the one hand, and our strong faith in the God of justice and peace on the other. We maintain that no permanent peace is possible if it is not built on justice.

On this level of Sabeel's ministry we cooperate with many different individuals and groups, Christians, Muslims, and Jews, locally and internationally, people of faith or with no faith, provided they believe in the power of nonviolence and are willing to commit to work through nonviolent methods. As a Christian movement, Sabeel believes that, following in the footsteps of Jesus Christ, we cannot condone or practice violence. Therefore, we must persist in lifting a prophetic voice and taking a prophetic stand against any injustice and oppression and continue working for justice and witnessing for peace.

These three dimensions of ministry are interconnected and interrelated. Sabeel came into being to serve. Its objective is to be involved on all these levels and, with God's grace, to make a difference. Our motives and objectives must be pure and clear: we are working for a just peace that honors the God of justice and peace and respects all the people of the land whether they are Muslims, Jews, or Christians. It works to give them equally the benefits that justice and peace can provide.

The road ahead may be long and tortuous, but we are determined to tread it. Although there is an urgency to achieve change and progress on every one of the above levels, at this time Sabeel is giving priority to the achievement of a just peace between Palestinians and Israelis. A just peace must be the foundation for our future work, and, indeed, progress and change on all other fronts hinge on the establishment of peace and freedom for all the people of the land.

Chapter 2

The Generous Offer of the Palestinians

"Grant me justice."
—Luke 18:3b

THE DEMANDS FOR JUSTICE

Biblically speaking, the concern for justice has always been present in the Old Testament, the Hebrew Scriptures. We find it in the Torah: "The Rock, his work is perfect; and all his ways are just" (Deut. 32:4).[1] It also forms the basis for the Exodus narrative God liberated the ancient Israelites from slavery because God is a just God: "And if your neighbor cries out to me, I will listen, for I am compassionate" (Exod. 22:27).

As the Hebrew Scriptures continue, the theme of justice is vibrantly articulated in the Wisdom literature ("The LORD is a stronghold for the oppressed, a stronghold in times of trouble" [Ps. 9:9]), and we find its mature expressions uttered by the great prophets before and after the Exile.

> But the LORD of hosts is exalted by justice,
>   and the Holy God shows himself holy by righteousness.
>
> (Isa. 5:16)

> I am the LORD; I act with steadfast love, justice, and
>   righteousness in the earth, for in these things I delight,
> says the LORD. (Jer. 9:24b)

> But let justice roll down like waters,
>   and righteousness like an everflowing stream.
>
> (Amos 5:24)

In the Old Testament, God demands that justice be done. Those who know and fear God must do justice.

In the New Testament, with the exception of a few cases, the word "justice" is replaced by the word "righteousness." The righteousness of God is shown to us through the death and resurrection of Jesus Christ. The Hebrew words in the Old Testament that are usually translated justice are *tsedek* and *mishpat*.[2] The Greek term *dikaiosyne* in the New Testament captures the meaning of both justice and righteousness—of people being in right relationship. Righteousness expresses God's justice combined with God's mercy.

Justice remains foundational to faith not only for Judaism and Christianity, but equally in Islam. It is foundational for every religion because just relationships among people are the fruit of one's faith in God. Theologically speaking, no god is worthy of the name if justice is not emphasized as basic for that faith tradition.

We can easily trace the development of laws and regulations in the different societies and cultures. It stands to reason that legislators enacted laws to govern people's relationships with each other, and judges were appointed to administer the laws in society so that people could experience peace and security. Justice, therefore, has always been the most basic and fundamental cornerstone for life in one's community, nation, and the world. The most elementary understanding of justice includes an element of fairness for all people, especially the poor and the marginalized.

GIVE ME JUSTICE!

Since justice is so intrinsic to all human societies, this chapter acutely focuses on its significance from a biblical and a political perspective. The importance of justice is recognized in a short parable given by Jesus Christ and recorded in the Gospel of Luke.

> Then Jesus told them a parable about their need to pray always and not to lose heart. He said, "In a certain city there was a judge who neither feared God nor had respect for people. In that city there was a widow who kept coming to him and saying, 'Grant me justice against my opponent.' For a while he refused; but later he said to himself, 'Though I have no fear of God and no respect for anyone, yet because this widow keeps bothering me, I will grant her justice, so that she may not wear me out by continually coming.'" And the Lord said, "Listen to what the unjust judge says. And will not God grant justice to his chosen ones who cry to him day and night? Will he delay long in helping them? I tell you, he will quickly grant justice to them. And yet, when the Son of Man comes, will he find faith on earth?" (Luke 18:1-8)

Jesus was a skilled storyteller. His parables are very compact: within a few words, he incorporates rich and concentrated ideas. The writer of Luke's Gospel explicitly connects this parable with Jesus' teaching about the importance of persistence in prayer. Yet, it is also quite probable that on other occasions during his ministry Jesus used this parable to speak about the importance of standing for justice. Since it is such a significant theme in his teaching, another way of introducing this parable could be the following: "Then Jesus told them a parable about their need to do justice and not to lose heart. . . ."

THE CONTEXT OF OPPRESSION AND DESCRIPTION OF THE OPPRESSORS

In the second sentence of the parable above ("There was a judge who neither feared God nor had any respect for people"), Jesus sums up a reality of life that must have been tragic and miserable for the people in the judge's community. A person with authority and power who does not fear God or respect humans is the utmost in depravity. The judge was devoid of any morals. These words can describe many people of power who lost their humanity and became ruthless and calloused in their climb to the top. The nature of the judge aptly describes the context of injustice and oppression present in many parts of the world today: power is too often in the hands of people who are without morality or a system of ethics. A modern way to describe such an entity would be, "There was a government that neither feared God nor had any respect for international law."[3]

In this parable, Jesus, the ultimate liberation theologian, begins with a context of life that seems hopeless for the helpless people of the community. The judge, the person who represents law and order and who is expected to do justice, has become himself corrupt and hardened. In this context, it is important to remember that behind this judge stands the Roman Empire with its oppressive systems of laws. "What was a 'new world order' for those of power and privilege was experienced as a disruptive, disorienting, or even devastating new world disorder for many of the subject peoples. . . . Jesus and his movement were located in Roman imperial geopolitics."[4]

In our Palestinian context this one verse describes the reality of the injustice and oppression our people face. By virtue of its unjust actions, the government of Israel seems to demonstrate no fear of God or respect for people. It enacts laws that discriminate between Jews and Palestinians, and its judges enforce these laws. It created a legal system that allows the Israeli government and Jewish settlers to confiscate Palestinian land and build settlements on them. Although these settlements are illegal under international law, the Israeli legal system views them as legal. Israeli law gives automatic citizenship to any Jew from any part of the world while denying the same to Palestinians. It tortures Palestinian prisoners to extract information out of them, a practice that is rightly illegal under international law, but permitted by Israel. Israeli, Palestinian, and international human rights organizations have provided many documented accounts of daily violations, contraventions, and breaches of international and humanitarian law by the Israeli army. Behind the judges who enforce the laws lies an unjust and discriminatory racist system that reflects the moral bankruptcy of the people holding power in Israel. Israel's legal system forms a context of oppression in much the same way as the Roman Empire during the first century.

THE ACTION OF THE OPPRESSED

In the parable of the unjust judge from Luke, the word "widow" encapsulates a description of an oppressed person: "There was a widow who kept coming and saying, 'Grant me justice against my opponent'" (v. 3). By using this terminology, Jesus focuses attention on the most oppressed and vulnerable segment of society. At the time the Gospel was written, when a woman's husband died, she became dependent on the mercy of others. The husband was both the breadwinner and her protector. In his absence she was vulnerable: people could exploit her and take advantage of her. For this reason, special laws in the Old Testament were established to protect members of four vulnerable groups: the poor, widows, orphans, and strangers. With no one to protect them, God became their protector.

The judge has all the power and the widow has none. The contrast is immense. The judge does not need to openly oppress the widow; he can simply ignore her. When she asks for justice, he simply does not respond. Ignoring and disregarding the oppression of victims only compounds the injustice. Thomas Merton captures the essence of this insidious injustice:

> We also have to recognize that when oppressive power is thoroughly well-established, it does not always need to resort openly to the "method of beasts" because its laws are already powerful—perhaps also bestial— enough. In other words, when a system can, without resort to overt force, compel people to live in conditions of abjection, helplessness, and wretchedness that keeps them on the level of beasts rather than of men [and women], it is plainly violent. To make men [and women] live on a subhuman level against their will, to constrain them in such a way that they have no hope of escaping their condition, is an unjust exercise of force. Those who in some way or another concur in the oppression—and perhaps profit by it—are exercising violence even though they may be preaching pacifism. And their supposedly peaceful laws, which maintain this spurious kind of order, are in fact instruments of violence and oppression.[5]

It is possible to compare the Palestinians in their vulnerability with that of the widow. Israel, with its power and powerful allies, has been able to oppress, exploit, dominate, and suppress the Palestinians.

Do people of power realize that they are oppressing others? In the parable, the judge seemed to be aware of what he was doing: "For a while he refused; but later he said to himself, 'Though I have no fear of God and no respect for anyone, yet because this widow keeps bothering me, I will grant her justice, so that she may not wear me out by continually coming' " (Luke 18:4-5). Do the Bushes and Blairs of this world know what they are doing? Do the Saddams know? Do the Sharons know? Or do they actually convince themselves that they are doing what is best for the people as well as for themselves?

While many times people know what constitutes the doing of justice, they still refuse to do it, and then they justify and rationalize their injustice. A prime example of people knowing what is just but ignoring it is demonstrated in the statement of former Israeli Prime Minister Shimon Peres that going to Gaza was a mistake. Oppressors need to be forced to confront their own oppression.

The action of the widow is important. When an injustice occurs, the protest—the cry of "Grant me justice"—must be consistent and insistent. Only justice can bring peace to both the judge and the widow. The doing of justice, however, must not be the work of the widow (the oppressed) alone; it must be the work of all those who witness the injustice.

The demands for justice must never disappear from our world. Because oppressors are prone to prolong, to drag their feet hoping that people will forget the injustice, this prophetic cry must never be silent. Furthermore, oppressors generally hope the oppressed will get used to their situation, or at least will soften their demands and accept unjust compromises. Advocacy for justice means bothering people in power, exposing them, and dismantling their respectability in the community by calling into question their legitimacy. The goal of advocacy should be to liberate the judge (the oppressor) as well as the widow (the oppressed). It means reminding the oppressors continuously of their injustice and never giving up.

In the parable the judge says, "I will grant her justice, so that she may not wear me out by continually coming." Another translation reads, "so that she may not finally come and slap me in the face," or as some have suggested, "so that she may not come and give me a black eye." One wonders whether a widow could even get close enough to the judge to slap him or give him a black eye. Is it not the oppressors who usually initiate violence? Even when there are nonviolent demonstrations (like that of the widow who stands outside carrying her slogan), is it not the oppressors who send the army to break up the demonstrations, and often violently? The words of the judge are revealing of the psychology and mentality of oppressors.

Again, it is important to remember that the judge in the parable represents the Roman Empire. Judges are to implement the laws of the empire. To discredit the justice of the judge is to discredit the justice of the empire. At the roots of the injustice of this one juror is the unjust system on which the entire empire is built.

When Rosa Parks refused to sit in the back of the bus, she was resisting the discriminatory laws of the state of Alabama. When Mahatma Gandhi led massive demonstrations of civil disobedience by boycotting the salt tax in India, he was challenging the British colonial system. When Nelson Mandela fought against the system of total racist segregation in South Africa and was sentenced to life in prison, he was standing up against and eventually defeating the apartheid structure of his country. When Archbishop Oscar Romero became a leading voice for the voiceless in El Salvador, opposing the power structure that eventually assassinated him, he was faithfully following his Lord and savior in the path of justice.

This is what must happen in the struggle over Palestine because the oppressed are not totally powerless. They have the power of truth and justice. They must "wear the oppressors out" by crying out again and again, by demonstrating, and by standing up for their rights. The doing of justice in the face of oppression requires the concerted and persistent effort of the oppressed and all those who stand with them. As noted above, the framework of injustice is the framework of empire. Today Israel does not stand alone, but has an empire behind it that continuously supports and feeds it. Justice, which is the only foundation on which true peace can be built, usually remains apart from empire.

The parable comes to a close with the lines, "And the Lord said, 'Listen to what the unjust judge says. And will not God grant justice to his chosen ones who cry to him day and night? Will he delay long in helping them? I tell you, he will quickly grant justice to them'" (vv. 6-8a).

The Arabic translation of the first sentence is more precise: "Listen *carefully* to what the unjust judge says." Did Jesus say these words sarcastically? Do the unjust judges, legislators, and executives of this world act out of a sense of justice? Do the laws of empire easily change in order to take into consideration the needs of the oppressed?

These laws and their corrupt enforcers have to be forced to change in order to render justice and liberation to the oppressed. The oppressors act out of selfish interests and ambitions, and they change only when sufficient outside pressure mounts against them. Their consciences appear dead as they do not operate out of a sense of justice. When Jesus told the people to "listen carefully," he was speaking to ordinary people who could easily detect the hypocrisy and corruption of people of power. People need to open their eyes and ears to what the Saddams and the Sharons of the world are doing and saying.

THE OBSTRUCTERS OF JUSTICE IN OUR WORLD

Jesus was very clear: God is a just God who wills justice for all the oppressed of the world. Even in the superficiality of our faith, Palestinians, Christians, and Muslims alike appeal to God as our protector against the powers of empire. It is not God who obstructs justice but the oppressors. God wills justice, peace, and liberation while human beings stand in the way and frustrate the will and purposes of God. The God in whom we believe and hope is not a divine warrior who strikes down the oppressors and imposes justice through an iron rod of judgment. Our liberator is the God of Jesus Christ who suffered the shame of the cross. It is the God who did not create us as automatons, but human beings with free will to choose, even to choose to disobey and reject God.

Jesus and the prophets have established the principle that God will certainly grant justice, because God is just. There is no question about this. God has built this world on justice. The problem is whether humans are working and laboring with God, and whether the judges of this world are exercising justice.

The last sentence in the parable poses a question: "And yet, when the Son of Man comes, will he find faith on earth?" (v. 8b). At first glance, this verse seems to be out of place as it does not appear to relate in any way to the parable. However, on deeper reflection, it is precisely in the right place. Jesus is asking if, when he comes, there will be people who are adamantly committed to justice and are willing to risk their lives for it. This statement becomes the heart of the matter. It is an evangelical challenge for everyone: will we who care about the oppressed have the courage to take a stand and advocate for justice on their behalf? Will we be able to stand before the unjust powers of this world and insist that justice be done? Only true faith can produce such courage. And so the parable of the persistent widow and the unjust judge ends with a challenge to which each Christian generation must respond: when the Son of Man comes, will he find faith on earth?

This parable clearly is one of the strongest statements of Jesus' teachings about justice. It stimulates our hearts and minds, providing the needed inspiration to shed our apathy and reluctance as we become involved in the work of justice and peace.

On a number of occasions, I have been turned away from preaching in churches because they did not want to hear about justice. It was made clear to me that speaking about justice was tantamount to speaking about politics; these churches wanted to stay away from such themes. It is startling to see how many Christians fail to understand the Bible's concern for justice. When did justice become the monopoly of the political realm? Indeed, it is a tragedy that some clergy and churches have abandoned justice and left it for the politicians. But justice can never be divorced from faith and love. If justice is relegated to the domain of government, politics, and politicians, justice will then be defined in a way that satisfies the interests of one's nation, one's state, and even the personal interest of political leaders. Such travesties caused the great Old Testament prophets to lift their voices in outrage against the injustices of kings and religious leaders. Using some of his strongest recorded language, Jesus confronted the religious leaders of his day, pointing out to them the heart of true faith:

> "Woe to you, scribes and Pharisees, hypocrites! For you tithe mint, dill, and cummin, and have neglected the weightier matters of the law: justice and mercy and faith. It is these you ought to have practiced

without neglecting the others. You blind guides! You strain out a gnat
but swallow a camel!" (Matt. 23:25-26)

We must not dichotomize life into private and public spheres. Instead, we
must witness to God's love and justice in all areas of our existence. There
is no aspect of our life that stands outside the purview of faith. There is no
area of our life that is closed to our possibility to witness, especially when it
comes to issues of justice. In essence, justice is the other side of love.

The Christian faith considers love to be the greatest virtue of all. Justice
is simply the other side of the coin. When true love exists, so do justice and
fairness. Paul's great hymn of love in his first letter to the church in Corinth
reads, "Love is patient; love is kind; love is not envious or boastful or arrogant
or rude. It does not insist on its own way; it is not irritable or resentful; it
does not rejoice in wrongdoing, but rejoices in the truth." All these virtues
apply also to justice. Another translation reads, "[Love] does not rejoice in
injustice, but rejoices in the truth" (1 Cor. 13:4-6).

Most of our difficulties and problems, whether in personal or communal
relationships, stem from the feeling that we have been dealt with unjustly
and unfairly and lead to the breakdown of relationships. Justice and love
are so interconnected that when we are treated unjustly, we feel unloved.
When we teach people to love one another as they love themselves, we are
also teaching them to live justly.

The reality of the Israel-Palestine conflict is an injustice that reflects our
broken and selfish humanity; it is a reality that has expressed itself historically in the failure of Jews and Palestinians to love each other. This failure
has given birth to the conflict and is the source of its continuation. It is this
simple, and yet, in the way it has evolved, it has become terribly complicated.
Thus, we Christians have a faith mandate to untangle the knots and find a
solution that honors the Palestinians' need for justice and peace and Israel's
need for security and peace. God demands of us faithfulness in this work.
And the words of Jesus remind us that we are blessed when we do the work
of peace: "Blessed are the peacemakers for they shall be called children of
God" (Matt. 5:9).

JUSTICE AND THE PEACE PROCESS

Unfortunately, the peace process that has been undertaken between Palestinians and Israelis has not truly addressed the injustice at the root of the
conflict. In *Justice, and Only Justice*, I examined the history of Palestine
and Israel up to the first intifada, revealing the injustice wrought upon the
Palestinian people. But much has happened since then.

In the late 1980s and early 1990s, four factors that affected our region
led to the Oslo Peace process. The first, in 1987, was the eruption of the first
Palestinian intifada, which took the world by surprise and focused renewed

attention on the Palestinian/Israeli conflict. A second factor only two years later was the collapse of the Soviet Union in 1989. As the Cold War between two power structures in the world ended, one superpower, the United States of America, emerged. The United States was then free to act unilaterally without serious interference or competition. The third factor was the first Gulf War in 1991. Saddam Hussein invaded Kuwait, connecting his occupation of Kuwait with Israel's occupation of the Palestinian territories. He used the occupation to pressure the United States and the Western powers to force Israel to end its occupation of the Palestinian territories. The United States reacted strongly with military force and pushed Saddam's army out of Kuwait. The Gulf War led to the Madrid Peace Conference in October 1991, which in turn opened the way for the fourth significant factor: recognition of the Palestine Liberation Organization (PLO) as the representative of the Palestinian people.

The Oslo peace process, which resulted in the Oslo Accords of 1993, was welcomed by most Palestinians with great jubilation and hope that it would lead to a resolution of the conflict. Sadly, this did not happen. Instead of contributing to ending the occupation, it further consolidated the occupation of Palestinian land and entrenched the injustice. Israeli settlements expanded tremendously and many new ones came into being; the West Bank and the Gaza Strip were fragmented by hundreds of checkpoints; more Palestinian land was confiscated for the building of roads and highways to the settlements; and most significantly an elaborate system of laws and regulations were established by Israel to control and oppress the Palestinians.

The Palestinians are always startled about the shrewdness and cunning of the Israeli government in taking agreements, like the Oslo Accords—potentially leading to peace—and then twisting and manipulating them to not only render them ineffective but to turn them into additional instruments of injustice against the Palestinians. Palestinians feel this indicates clearly that the Israeli government is not serious about peace. Since the Madrid Peace Conference, the Palestinians have been vacillating continuously between hope for a peaceful solution and despair due to the worsening status quo.

Foundering Peace Initiatives

During the period between 1987 and 2006, no fewer than thirteen different meetings, agreements, and initiatives were undertaken, in one way or another, to move the peace process forward. Sooner or later all of them came to naught, and most of the time the blame fell on the Palestinians. The scenarios that weakened or ended these agreements are well known. The most common tactic has been that the Israeli Army or Air Force launches an attack on Palestinian areas, assassinating leaders, killing innocent men, women, and children, destroying Palestinian homes, and arresting and kidnapping Palestinians. This violence usually elicits an immediate reaction by Palestinian extremists and results in a suicide bombing in Israel or an attack on Jewish settlers. This reaction derails the talks or halts negotiations, practically cutting off any agreement that may have been reached. When ongoing talks appear to give some hope of moving forward, many Palestinians feel that Palestinian extremists are unconsciously or even consciously playing into the hands of the Israelis.

In struggling to understand the difficulty of arriving at peace, it is important to remember that there is no symmetry of power in the region. Israel holds the power militarily, politically, and economically, not only over the Palestinians, but in the entire Middle East. If Israel chooses, it is capable of moving the peace process forward, and it is capable of obstructing or stifling it altogether. Most of the time, the Palestinian Authority is simply reacting to Israeli actions, initiatives, tactics, and schemes against the Palestinians. At the same time, Palestinian extremists are reacting against Israeli state terror with their own violence, and the cycle of violence escalates as hopes for peace fade once again.

Official diplomats in Israel and Palestine report such events back to their home governments as well as to the United Nations, yet their reports have little if any effect on the daily lives of Palestinians. The occupation, with its repressive and oppressive policies, continues unabated in its ferocity and viciousness. One example is the presence of the Temporary International Presence in the City of Hebron (TIPH).[6] Established by U.N. Security Council Resolution 904, international TIPH personnel monitor the unruly behavior of the Jewish settlers against Palestinians in Hebron. They also report misconduct by Palestinians. Daily reports are sent to the U.N. headquarters, but their recommendations, which are not binding, are not even publicized, and the violence and viciousness of the Hebron settlers go unchecked.

Scenarios of domination are continuously at play in the occupied territories. Although Palestinians are usually blamed for atrocities, most often the real instigator is the Israeli army or the armed settlers. It is always easy to blame the weak and the powerless who do not have the strength to challenge the powerful. Their influence on the power brokers of the world is, at best, minimal.

Because the United States gives nearly blind support to Israel, the Israeli government is able to "interpret" the atrocities committed against Palestinians. As a result, it is usually the victims of injustice and oppression who are blamed. The interpretations of the Israeli government seem to be adopted wholeheartedly and without questioning by the American Congress and the administration. Moreover, Washington's position is generally followed by U.S. allies, especially the Western powers. Former President Jimmy Carter summarizes this situation in his book *Palestine: Peace Not Apartheid*:

> Two other interrelated factors have contributed to the perpetuation of violence and regional upheaval: condoning of illegal Israeli actions from a submissive White House and U.S. Congress during recent years, and the deference with which other international leaders permit this unof-

ficial U.S. policy in the Middle East to prevail. There are constant and vehement political and media debates in Israel concerning its policies in the West Bank, but because of powerful political, economic, and religious forces in the United States, Israeli government decisions are rarely questioned or condemned, voices from Jerusalem dominate in our media, and most American citizens are unaware of circumstances in the occupied territories.[7]

The exceptions are few, as are those who dare to question the Israeli government's stance. Fewer still have the courage, when they actually know the truth, to stand up and squarely face the injustice.

Palestinians' Outstretched Hands for Peace

It is quite revealing to view the thirteen different major initiatives since the first intifada in 1987. None has generated a lasting peace.

- Shultz Peace Plan (1988)
- Madrid Peace Conference (1990)
- Multilateral talks (1992)
- Declaration of Principles (1993)
- Oslo Peace Process (I) and Early Empowerment Agreement (1994)
- Oslo II (1995)
- Hebron Agreement (1997)
- Wye River Memorandum (1998)
- Sharm El-Sheikh Agreement (1999)
- Camp David II Summit (2000)
- Taba talks (2001)
- U.S. "Road Map" (2003)
- Geneva Accord (2003)

Why have these thirteen different peace initiatives, individually and cumulatively, failed? The government of Israel has successfully maintained in the United States and in most Western countries that it has been the fault of the Palestinians, but is this so? Without being negligent or blind to the blunders and the reactive violence of the Palestinians, and this cannot be totally disregarded, I wholeheartedly believe that we Palestinians are facing the Israeli government's unwillingness to implement international law and U.N. resolutions. Israel's avarice for more Palestinian land is a primary reason that prevents it from making peace with the Palestinians.

In fact, many Palestinians recall when, under the leadership of Arafat during the first stage of the Oslo Peace Process, Palestine had the rudimentary semblance of a state. Palestinians were moving forward in building their region and showing mature signs of bearing a responsibility for the nation. The government of Israel became uneasy since it had not reached its expansionist goals and Israel created conditions to halt and even reverse that trend.

Since the mid-1990s Israel has been taking more Palestinian land to expand its settlements. In many ways, Israel has been forced to curtail its original Zionist dream of controlling the vast territory of the Middle East. Nonetheless, there are major religious forces in Israel that believe that the entire land of Palestine as well as large areas of adjacent Arab land belong to Israel. This conviction is supported by Christian Zionists[8] all over the world who speak of Israel's biblical rights to the land stretching from "the Nile to the Euphrates" (Gen. 15:18). While I believe that the government of Israel has realistically abandoned that dream, some ministers and settlers have not abandoned their dream of taking over the entire West Bank and removing all Palestinian inhabitants (ethnic cleansing). Such a plan negates any desire or political will to work for peace.

Another scenario may also be at work. Since a "new Middle East" is still being shaped by the United States and Israel, neither can be serious about pursuing peace with the Palestinians until a "new" Middle East might begin to unfold. In the meantime, Israel must continue to increase its control of the Palestinians. It must force as many as possible out of the country and create a docile remnant that will simply accept its place as "hewers of wood and drawers of water" who serve their Israeli masters.

For its own public image in the world, Israel cannot openly say "no" to peace initiatives, especially when the United States is involved. Indeed, while it can immediately ignore or dismiss any initiatives that originate from Russia or Europe or the Arab countries, when the initiative comes from the United States, Israel complies, usually after sending its points of reservations (as it did with the Road Map). On the surface, Israel seems to be engaged in the negotiations. But, in reality, the Israeli government is unwilling to commit itself to any final resolutions so long as its long-term objectives remain unfulfilled, and so long as the Palestinians continue to insist on resolving the conflict based on international law and U.N. resolutions—the very things Israel is trying to dodge.

Furthermore, if Israel feels that in any way it is cornered or might be cornered, it uses its influence through AIPAC (the American Israel Public Affairs Committee) and other friends in the American Congress or the administration to stifle, freeze, or kill that initiative. Until Israel achieves its ultimate goal—ownership of all of Palestine—it will continue its strategy of delaying and frustrating any proposed plans for peace, even if it entails much suffering and agony for its own people, not to mention for the Palestinians.

Closer examination must be given to the connection between U.S. support of Israel and the failure of the "peace process" to bring lasting peace between Israelis and Palestinians. In 2006, John J. Mearsheimer, a professor of political science at the University of Chicago, and Stephen M. Walt, a professor of international relations at the Kennedy School of Government at Harvard University, authored a well-documented report on "The Israel Lobby and U.S. Foreign Policy."[9] The rather startling report clearly articulated the problems today in the Middle East. The conclusion was clear: due to the power and influence of the pro-Israel lobby, it has been difficult for the United States to play the role of an honest peace broker in the Israel-Palestine conflict.

"The Lobby" is a "loose coalition of individuals and organizations who actively work to steer U.S. foreign policy in a pro-Israel direction."[10] The lobby does not have a central leadership, nor is it a unified movement. Its core is made up of American Jews, but its membership also includes a significant number of American Christian neoconservatives who are staunch supporters of Israel.

In the U.S. Congress, Israel remains "virtually immune from criticism."[11] The lobby ensures that Israel is portrayed in a positive light "by repeating myths about [Israel's] founding and by promoting its point of view in policy debates. The goal is to prevent critical comments from getting a fair hearing in the political arena. Controlling the debate is essential to guaranteeing US support, because a candid discussion of US-Israel relations might lead Americans to favor a different policy."[12]

The influence of the lobby remains equally strong whether a Republican or Democrat president is in office. As an example, the document notes that during the Clinton (Democrat) and both Bush (Republican) administrations, the policy advisors on the Middle East were largely American Jews and neoconservative Christians who were staunchly pro-Israel, including people such as Martin Indyk, Dennis Ross, Aaron Miller, Elliot Abrams, John Bolton, Douglas Feith, I. Lewis (Scooter) Libby, Richard Perle, Paul Wolfowitz, and David Wurmser. Mearsheimer and Walt conclude that "these officials have consistently pushed for policies favored by Israel and backed by organizations in the Lobby."[13]

The lobby also includes a number of pro-Israel American Jewish organizations such as the Conference of Presidents of Major Jewish Organizations, the Anti-Defamation League, the American Jewish Committee, and others who have strong clout with the mainstream media. Many newspapers and television channels refrain from criticizing Israel's actions against the Palestinians. Mearsheimer and Walt quote journalist Eric Alterman, who "lists 61 'columnists and commentators who can be counted on to support Israel reflexively and without qualification.'"[14] In other words, the influence of the lobby is so comprehensive and effective that Israel is not only insulated against criticism in the seat of power in Washington, it is equally insulated by the American media.

As already mentioned, the lobby includes key members who are Christian Zionists. Two prominent groups of Christian Zionists exist within the United States, the first of which supports Israel on ideological and political grounds. It views Israel as a bastion of democracy in the Middle East that shares Western values with the United States and is strategically important to it. This group is represented by people like John Bolton (former secretary of education and former ambassador to the United Nations), William Bennett (former U.N. ambassador), and others. The second group, which appears to be larger, includes conservative Christian evangelicals who are biblical literalists and theologically conservative. They believe that Israel stands at the center of God's plan for history, that it was established in fulfillment of biblical prophecy, and that Israel has a central and crucial role to play in the events that would lead to the second coming of Christ and the consummation of the present world. Millions of Americans who belong to such fundamentalist churches are totally committed to the support of Israel so that it can fulfill the role that God has charted for it. Members of this group include the late Jerry Falwell, Gary Bauer, Pat Robertson, Ralph Reed, and many other influential religious leaders.

In 2006, a new group of evangelical Christian Zionists established a specifically Christian lobby to support Israel. Christians United for Israel (CUFI) was founded by John Hagee of Cornerstone Church in San Antonio, Texas, one of the most ardent Christian zealots today. An indication of the commitment of CUFI members came from Congressman Dick Armey, the former majority leader in the House of Representatives, in September 2002 when he said, "My No. 1 priority in foreign policy is to protect Israel."[15] It seems surprising that his "priority" in foreign policy was not to protect America but Israel. Christian Zionists provide unflinching support for Israel.

Although pro-Israel supporters come from other Western countries as well, they do not come close to matching the strength or effectiveness they enjoy in the United States. Furthermore, since nearly all decisions regarding war and peace are determined by the United States, it is difficult to foresee any positive movement toward peace in the Middle East so long as the pro-Israel lobby and religious neoconservatives wield such tremendous influence.

The political clout of the pro-Israel lobby within the political system in the United States has worked to the detriment of peace in the Middle East region because it has proven itself utterly biased and one-sided. It is important, however, to guard against generalizations. Not all American Jews belong to the lobby. The Jewish community, like most others, is diverse in its views and positions. In fact, a 2004 survey showed that approximately 36 percent of American Jews said they were not emotionally attached to Israel.[16] Furthermore, some of the most vociferous champions of justice for the Palestinians are themselves American Jews. People such as Rabbi Elmer Berger, Alfred Lilienthal, Noam Chomsky, Marc Ellis, Phyllis Bennis, Sara Roy, Norman Finkelstein, and Rabbi Michael Lerner, to name only a few, have been in the vanguard of the struggle against Israeli's illegal occupation of Palestine.

Today, many people in the world perceive the policy of the United States regarding Israel-Palestine as unjust and oppressive. By standing in the camp of the United Nations, the United States could contribute to the healing of the world because of its tremendous power and resources; instead, it has allowed itself to be a party to injustice and oppression. As a member of the United Nations, the United States could be serving as an arbitrator that champions justice and truth. Sadly, this has not happened. William Sloane Coffin, a prominent American theologian, wrote, "The United States doesn't have to lead the world; it has first to join it. Then, with greater humility, it can play a wiser leadership role."[17]

Many people feel that it is not only the West Bank and the Gaza Strip that are occupied by Israel, but also the United States. Its total identification with one side has stripped it of credibility as well as its ability to broker a peace longed for by millions of people throughout the Middle East. Many people within the United States, as well as outside of it, have long sensed the disproportionate influence of the Jewish lobby; however, the Mearsheimer and Walt report revealed in full its stark force and ugly tentacles.

What is tragic about such blind support for Israel is that it not only prevents peace from coming about in Palestine and Israel, but also encourages violence throughout the Middle East. One of the main causes of Muslim resentment against the United States is America's unnatural and illogical bias against justice for the Palestinians. President Carter has noted that the United States has used its U.N. veto power more than forty times in order to protect Israel against resolutions condemning it for its injustice. He concludes, "There is little doubt that the lack of a persistent effort to resolve the Palestinian issue is a major source of anti-American sentiment and terrorist activity throughout the Middle East and the Islamic world."[18]

Of the more than 200 million Arab Muslims and 14 million Arab Christians who live in the Middle East, the vast majority see the United States as the main obstacle to a just peace. From their perspective, the United States is being held hostage by Israel through the pro-Israel lobby. Israel's existence is not in jeopardy. Israel is one of the strongest military powers in the world today with a formidable nuclear capability.[19] What poses a grave danger to Israel, though, is the health of its soul: Israel appears to be devoid of any sense of justice or respect for human rights. And because of its close association with Israel, the United States is also tainted.

In December 2006, the Iraq Study Group Report was published. Due to the deteriorating situation in Iraq, the U.S. Congress appointed a bipartisan group of ten persons to take a good look at the war in Iraq and submit its findings and recommendations. The group was co-chaired by James A. Baker III, a former secretary of state and secretary of the treasury, and Lee H. Hamilton, longtime member of the U.S. House of Representatives. Although the mandate of the group focused on Iraq, the final report includes a number of references to the Israel-Palestine conflict. One of the clearest and boldest statements of the report reads as follows:

> The United States cannot achieve its goals in the Middle East unless it deals directly with the Arab-Israeli conflict and regional instability. There must be a renewed and sustained commitment by the United States to a comprehensive Arab-Israeli peace on all fronts: Lebanon, Syria, and President Bush's June 2002 commitment to a two-state solution for Israel and Palestine. This commitment must include direct talks with,

by, and between Israel, Lebanon, Palestinians (those who accept Israel's right to exist), and Syria.[20]

At different points, the report alludes to the conflict over Palestine and places it at center stage:

Iraq cannot be addressed effectively in isolation from other major regional issues, interests, and unresolved conflicts. To put it simply, all key issues in the Middle East—the Arab-Israeli conflict, Iraq, Iran, the need for political and economic reforms, and extremism and terrorism—are inextricably linked.[21]

The report recommends a negotiated peace between Israel and the Palestinians that would include the following points:

- Adherence to U.N. Security Council Resolutions 242 and 338 and to the principle of land for peace, which are the only bases for achieving peace.
- Strong support for Palestinian President Mahmoud Abbas and the Palestinian Authority to take the lead in preparing the way for negotiations with Israel.
- A major effort to move from the current hostilities by consolidating the ceasefire reached between the Palestinians and the Israelis in November 2006.
- Support for a Palestinian national unity government.
- Sustainable negotiations leading to a final peace settlement along the lines of President Bush's two-state solution, which would address the key issues of borders, settlement, Jerusalem, the right of return, and the end of conflict.[22]

It is very clear that the Iraq Study Group saw the centrality of the solution for Palestine to the situation in Iraq. Their sober and objective analysis recommended that any solution to the conflict in the Middle East must be based on U.N. resolutions, exactly what Palestinians and Arabs have been pleading for many years.

ISRAEL, AN UNWILLING PARTNER FOR PEACE

At this time Israel can achieve peace because the Palestinians and Arabs are seriously and genuinely ready for it. By doing so, a just solution for the Palestinians would aid in achieving peace and security for all of the Middle East. However, the Israeli government has chosen and still chooses not to accept peace. Israel chooses to live under the illusion that with more land it can create a greater ring of security for its people. As long as Israel remains in a state of war, it can use its military to address any threat. Once peace is achieved, Israel will have to face what it considers to be the greatest threat of all: demographics. In spite of Israel's oppression and ethnic cleansing of Palestinians, the Palestinian population is increasing in the West Bank and Gaza, as well as within Israel itself through its Arab minority.

Tragically, Israel has established a policy based on the exclusion of many of its neighbors, rather than on their inclusion. If Israel were willing to curtail its greed for Arab and Palestinian land and its lust for domination, Israel could have been living in peace with all its Arab neighbors. Indeed, the world is ready for peace even though the Israeli government seems content to keep peace at bay.

In the past, some Israeli protagonists have spread a myth that the Palestinians have never missed an opportunity to miss an opportunity for peace. This is not the truth, but many people believed it. For nearly half a century, it is the Israeli government that has continuously, persistently, and intentionally missed many opportunities that could have achieved peace with the Palestinians and resulted in a good measure of security and prosperity for Israelis as well as for its neighbors. In his book, President Carter reveals that Syria, as well as the Palestinians, were ready to make peace on the grounds of U.N. resolutions but Israel refused. Mr. Carter writes, "Israel put confiscation of Palestinian land ahead of peace. . . ."[23] He argues that Arafat was willing to arrive at a peaceful solution:

[I]n September 1993, Chairman Arafat sent a letter to Prime Minister Rabin in which he stated unequivocally that the PLO recognized the right of Israel to exist in peace and security, accepted U.N. Security Council Resolutions 242 and 338, committed itself to a peaceful resolution of the conflict, renounced the use of terrorism and other acts of violence. . . .[24]

Carter is the first U.S. president to place the responsibility on the leaders of the state of Israel who have consistently refused to implement U.N. resolutions and international law, and who have been the real obstacles to peace.

It is helpful to review the various initiatives that have been presented by the Palestinians and the Arabs since the first intifada that constitute Israel's missed opportunities for a real and genuine peace.

- In 1988, for the first time, the Palestinians produced their Declaration of Independence. In many ways the Arabic text of the declaration was a masterpiece in both content and eloquence. A significant point in the declaration is its implied acceptance of the 1967 boundaries. This step was significant for the Palestinians at the time. If Israel had been interested in peace, it would have immediately seized the moment and responded favorably; it did not.
- In 1991, at the Madrid Peace Conference, the Arab delegations made

clear their openness to peace on the basis of U.N. Resolutions 242 and 338. Israel was not interested.

- In 1993, the Declaration of Principles and the handshake on the lawn of the White House was an indication of the willingness of the Palestinians to move toward peace by way of the two-state solution (U.N. Resolutions 242 and 338).
- In 1998, the Palestinians officially changed their charter so as to "recognize the right of the State of Israel to exist in peace and security," thus expressing their willingness to enter into peaceful negotiations to resolve the conflict.[25]
- In 2002, the Saudi Peace Initiative was a clear commitment on the part of all the Arab states of their readiness to enter into peace agreements with Israel provided it withdrew from the occupied territories in accordance with the U.N. resolutions and international law.
- In 2003, the Road Map was proposed on the basis of U.N. resolutions and the Arab peace plan. This was endorsed by the Palestinians. Israel reluctantly accepted it after submitting fourteen reservations, and then later found ways to stifle the initiative.

Peace is achievable, but the Palestinians *and* the Israeli government must have the political will to bring it about.

THE PALESTINIAN OFFER FOR PEACE

I am often asked, "Why did the Palestinians refuse the generous offer of Israel's Prime Minister Ehud Barak?" "Did not Barak offer them 95 percent of the West Bank?" "Why did they reject it?" "Does that not show that it is really the Palestinians who do not want peace?" These questions reflect one of the latest myths that paint the Palestinians as the real culprits against peace. Although a comprehensive article by Jeff Halper of the Israeli Committee Against House Demolitions entitled "A Most Ungenerous Offer" responds quite clearly to these questions,[26] it is also important to review in some detail the true nature of Barak's "generous" offer.

At the Paris Peace Conference of 1919 after the end of World War I, the World Zionist Organization presented a map outlining the area of the Middle East where Zionists hoped to establish a Jewish state (Appendix A). The area proposed was not confined to Palestine: it also encompassed southern Lebanon, the Golan Heights of Syria, the central portion of modern-day Jordan, and all of what became British-mandated Palestine. The plan called for Jewish ownership of all the fertile land of the region, including the main water resources.[27]

The 1919 Peace Conference did not endorse the Zionist proposal but accepted the British "Balfour Declaration" (Appendix B) and approved the British Mandate over Palestine. The British appointed Herbert Samuel, a

British Jew, as the first high commissioner, signaling British intentions to fulfill its promise to the Zionists.[28]

By the end of World War I as the Zionist project became clear to the Palestinians, Arab resistance began to mount. By the mid-1940s, the situation had become intolerable in Palestine as Zionist Jews had swelled to almost 33 percent of the population. The Palestinians resisted the increasing power of the Zionists, and the British were caught in the crossfire.

After the end of World War II, the Zionists, due to the suffering of their fellow Jews under the Nazis, pushed for the immediate establishment of a Jewish state. When the newly formed United Nations considered the problem of Palestine, it seemed that the only way out was to partition the country into two states: Jewish and Arab. Research has shown that if not for pressure from Zionist leaders on the United States and Britain, the plan would never have been approved.[29] The Zionist Jews who were the new immigrants in Palestine and who actually owned less than 6 percent of the land were granted over 55 percent of it. The Palestinians, who have lived there for centuries, were given less than 45 percent. The Zionist Jews, who had no legal foothold in Palestine, immediately accepted the plan while the Palestinians rejected it as a gross injustice. Once the partition plan was approved by the United Nations, the Zionists began ethnically cleansing Palestinians from the areas designated for a Jewish state.[30]

When the Zionists experienced success in driving the Palestinians out of their towns and villages, they did not stop at their designated 55 percent, but kept pushing the Palestinians out of their own (Palestinian) areas. When the war of 1948 ended, the Zionists had taken approximately 78 percent of the land—an additional 22 percent over what had been granted to them. Due to the support of the Western powers to the Zionists, the United Nations failed to force Israel to go back to its allotted area, the designated 55 percent, nor was it able to compel Israel to allow Palestinian refugees to return to their land.

Today the Palestinians seek to build their own independent Palestinian state, not on the 45 percent of the land agreed to by the United Nations, but on the remaining 22 percent that Israel occupied in the war of 1967. Moreover, Israel refuses to withdraw and has continued to flout international law that considers the occupation illegal. Israel perceives itself not as an occupier of the land but rather a "claimant" to it.

Israel considers itself an heir to the land by virtue of history—religious Jews would say by virtue of divine right. International law, however, states that the acquisition of territory by force is illegal and that Israel's occupation must end. Tragically, millions of Western Christians, as well as many Christians in Africa and Asia, accept Israel's claim because of their (mis) interpretation of the Bible.

The Palestinian offer of peace to Israel is actually generous. Palestinians are willing to accept Israel as a state and to allow Israel to maintain 78 percent of the land instead of the 55 percent assigned to it by the United Nations.

Yet Israel continues to shun and reject this offer. For the sake of peace most Palestinians are ready to absorb a further injustice so they can live in security on only 22 percent of the area of Palestine (Appendix C).

In fact Prime Minister Barak never made a "generous" offer. This is a myth. President Carter affirms this: "The fact is that no such offers were ever made. Barak later said, 'It was plain to me that there was no chance of reaching a settlement at Taba.' "[31] Palestinians, on the other hand, did make a generous offer in their willingness to yield land to Israel for the sake of a genuine peace in which the two states of Israel and Palestine could live next to each other without fear.

A crucial point is that having failed to take the whole of Palestine or to win the sanction of the international community, Israel continues to force Palestinians to yield more land. This must end. The Palestinians need 22 percent of the land to form a viable state.

The latest unjust mechanism exercised by Israel is the building of the monstrous wall, pictured on the cover of this book, most of which snakes through Palestinian land (see the map, Appendix D), in the face of international protests. But Israel has always lived by a philosophy of fait accompli. At opportune times during these last decades, it has seized more Palestinian land to expand its territory. Israel seems to believe that the Palestinians will eventually accept its demands and yield more concessions: the more land it takes, the less it will have to give back. Israel believes that the international community will ultimately condone its annexation of additional land.

There also seems to be a belief that if Israel increases its pressure on the Palestinians, it will succeed in driving them to despair so they will leave. There is also the belief that if Israel continues its violence, the Palestinians will react violently, giving Israel an excuse to justify killing them. This can serve as an excuse to terminate or interrupt any peace process, blame the Palestinians, and sustain the occupation. We have now come full circle, returning to the story of the widow and the unjust judge.

Justice remains essential. The cry of the widow is the cry of the Palestinians before the unjust judges of the government of Israel: "Give us justice!" There is no offer more generous than the offer of a genuine peace. The greatest development possible is looking each other in the eye and saying, "Let us share the land and live together in peace as neighbors." The Palestinian offer seems to be more generous than fair, and yet it is refused, and the tragedy continues. Israel's greater military power has made it haughty and arrogant; it acts as though it has all the rights to the land while the Palestinians have none. It is this arrogance that perpetuates the injustice and continues to breed violence in Palestine and Israel.

Chapter 3

The Breeding of Violence

I have often thought that the most important issue of our time is not racial prejudice or color prejudice or anything else. It is this question of how we overcome evil without becoming another form of evil in the process.
—Laurens van der Post[1]

It was a hot summer day in Beisan (now called Beth Shean), and I was about nine years old. I was playing outside in front of our home, which was on the main street. Sitting under the shade of a big tree, I dangled my feet in the small canal of water that came through the side of our home. Beisan was famous for these types of streams. Two boys were fighting across the street, not far from where I was playing. One of the boys got away, and the other was chasing him and tossing stones at him. Then something tragic happened: as the boy tried to avoid one of the stones, he jumped into the road just as a big truck was passing. The truck hit the boy and killed him instantly.

Due to the heat of the day, hardly anyone was on the road at the time. It did not take long, however, before dozens of people with pitchforks and clubs gathered who wanted to kill the driver. The driver managed to escape to the nearest refuge, which was our house. He asked my father for protection so my father hid him inside. The men outside demanded that my father turn over the man so they could kill him. My father replied in the spirit of Arab culture and tradition, "This stranger has come into my house and asked me to protect him. If you want to kill him, you have to kill me first." A few minutes later, the police arrived at the scene, dispersed the crowd, and took the driver into custody. As the police left our house, one officer asked, "Did anyone see what actually happened?" When I instantly replied, "I did," the police wrote down my name.

A few weeks later, I was asked to go to the courthouse in Beisan to give my testimony. I remember my father taking me to the courthouse. He left me there and went to his shop that was not too far away. Before he left, my father said to me, "Naim, just speak the truth. Tell the judge what you saw. Don't be afraid. God is with you."

I sat down outside the courtroom to wait for my turn. Several men went in before me to witness and later came out. I was the last witness. My young mind wondered about the identity and testimony of the other people, because I was sure that no one else had been on the street but me. When I entered the room, I saluted the judge as my father taught me. Then the judge looked me in the eye and said, "Tell me what happened. What did you see?" I told the judge that the accident happened at noon and that there was no one around. The boy tried to avoid the stone by jumping into the street as the truck was passing and the accident happened. The judge then thanked me, and I left the courthouse for my father's shop.

A few days later, my mother told me that the truck driver came by our house and kissed her hands, saying, "Thank you. Your son saved me."

This incident is imprinted in my memory, and I have passed it to my children. The truth, simply told, has power. I will always remember my father telling me, "Naim, just speak the truth. Tell the judge what you saw. Don't be afraid. God is with you." I realize now that in most cases standing for truth and justice does not bring the quick and simple resolution of that day long ago, yet we must never abandon the truth or give up on justice.

SPEAKING THE TRUTH ABOUT VIOLENCE IN PALESTINE

The history of Palestine, both ancient and modern, indicates that Palestinians were not more or less violent by nature and temperament than other people in the Middle East. Palestine has always been a hodgepodge of ethnic and racial groups. For most of its existence, Palestine was occupied by another power because of its strategic geographical location. Before the emergence of the great ancient empires, the different Canaanite tribes, including the ancient Israelites and Philistines who were living on the land, survived through local alliances with other tribes. That was how they defended themselves from the onslaughts of their rival neighbors. The Old Testament chronicles many of these tribal wars (see especially Judg. 1-3; 6-7; 20).

With the emergence of larger regional powers and empires, the circle of strategic alliances expanded to include some of those empires. Without these alliances the smaller countries would have been crushed by greater powers to the north or south. Palestine is a relatively narrow strip of fertile land that armies used to cross from south to north and vice versa. Because it was an important buffer zone for the ancient empires, many wars were fought on its soil. Egypt has always been the greatest power to the south, and to the north, there were a number of successive empires, including Assyria (modern-day northern Iraq), Babylon (southern Iraq), Persia (Iran), and Greece, and eventually Rome in the west. The kingdoms of Israel (northern Palestine) and Judah (southern Palestine) could survive only through alliances that made them subservient to one of these great empires. In spite of these agreements, the kingdom of Israel was destroyed by the Assyrian Empire in 722 BCE and the Babylonian Empire crushed Judah in 587 BCE.

The accession and eventual overthrow of these empires always left its mark on the people living in the Palestinian region. Some of the invading conquerors, of various ethnic and racial backgrounds themselves, intermixed and intermarried with the local population and eventually remained in the country. Thus, today many different ethnic and racial features are visible in Palestinians.

In modern times, the circle of alliances has broadened even further, but the dynamic has remained the same. As some Arab states entered into alliances with the former Soviet Union in order to protect themselves, others forged alliances with the United States. The greatest example has been the relationship between Israel and the United States. In fact, many people in the Middle East view this alliance as an empire that seeks to spread its control over the whole region. Many perceive Israel as a strategic ally of the United States but also as an extension of the American Empire. At times it seems that little has changed from ancient times. Countries, nations, and states forge alliances, whether military or economic, in order to protect themselves from the onslaught of their enemies and thus to survive and prosper.

Tragically, from ancient times empires have been built on violence and war. In his book, *War Is a Force That Gives Us Meaning*, journalist Chris Hedges quotes Simone Weil: "Force is as pitiless to the man who possesses it, or thinks he does, as it is to its victims; the second it crushes, the first it intoxicates."[2] To prevent people's struggles for liberation and freedom, empires resort to brutal repressive methods. The use of force aligns with the old Athenian proverb, "The strong do what they can; the weak suffer what they must." At the basis of this growing and expanding violence are human greed and selfishness, pride and arrogance, lust for power and vengeance, as well as many other evils of which human beings are capable.

While some people thought we might be able to enter into this new millennium seeking peace and finding justice for the oppressed, we discover instead that empires are their old unconverted selves, full of avarice and lust for domination and control. The new century started with a profusion of violence and bloodshed in Iraq, Afghanistan, Palestine, Israel, and Lebanon. If this trend continues, the twenty-first century will be worse than its predecessor (now on record as the bloodiest century) in the number of deaths and destruction it generates.

THE EVOLUTION OF VIOLENCE IN PALESTINE

Although Palestinians are not by nature more violent than other peoples, the term "Palestinian" has become coterminous with the word "terrorist" in the minds of many people in the West. How did this come to be?

Elementary Strife and Communal Relationships

At the beginning of the twentieth century, Palestine was composed predominantly of adherents of the three Abrahamic faiths. According to a 1921 census, Palestine was largely populated by Muslims (590,000), and marginally by Christians (89,000) and Jews (84,000).[3] All were called "Palestinians," and all lived together. In some places, people tended to congregate around their religious groupings, yet oftentimes they lived as neighbors within the same neighborhoods. As far as we know, the level of violence varied, but most of it centered on interpersonal matters, interfamily feuds, or interreligious issues. Most of the time, the feuds were dealt with through communal intermediaries who at least brought about uneasy peace between the antagonists or even succeeded in bringing reconciliation among adversaries.

One cannot deny that religion played an important role in the lives of people and was at times the cause of tension, yet most people were nominal in their religious affiliation. History also shows that at times certain prejudices and discrimination surfaced that resulted in attacks against others. When blood was shed, the family of the perpetrator had to leave town. Minor strife was resolved through the wise services of the *mukhtar* (village chief) and elders of the town.

Before the rise of the Zionist movement at the end of the nineteenth century—along with the growing awareness of its future goals for Palestine—the small Palestinian Jewish community shared the fortunes and predicaments of all Palestinians, the joys and sorrows of a generally depressed community living under the occupation of the Ottoman Turkish Empire.

Marginalizing the Palestinians

Palestinians became aware of the gradually rising number of Zionists coming into the country, but the full impact of the Zionist project was not felt until the end of World War I. The victory of the British and their allies over Germany and Turkey, the collapse of the Ottoman Empire, and the establishment of the British Mandate over Palestine set in motion the implementation of the Balfour Declaration (Appendix B). This was the spark that ignited violence in Palestine.

In other words, the responsibility for the flames of violence fell on the shoulders of two groups: the British government that wanted to implement the Balfour Declaration, and the Zionist leadership that insisted on its immediate execution. In many ways, these two sides share responsibility for the original crime against the indigenous people of Palestine. The spirit behind the British action was colonialism and imperialism. Since they had the power, they could colonize, exploit, and do as they wished. They did not have to consult the people of the land; the people were irrelevant.

Furthermore, some of the British leaders, such as Lord Balfour, the foreign secretary, and Prime Minister Lloyd George, were biblically predisposed to the return of Jews to Palestine in "fulfillment" of biblical prophecy. Lord Balfour saw himself in the role of Persian King Cyrus, who in 538 BCE issued an edict for the return of around fifty thousand Jews to Jerusalem, thereby ending their Babylonian captivity.[4] These predispositions from influential British Zionists coincided well with the political interests of the British Empire. The interests, influence, and pressure of the Arabs—though nominally considered—were ultimately irrelevant and cast aside. And the Palestinians simply did not count. They were not even mentioned by name in the text of the Balfour Declaration.[5]

Before the British government accepted the declaration, President Wilson was consulted. Wilson was reluctant to endorse it. When Chaim Weizmann, the most prominent Zionist in Britain, heard of Wilson's ambivalence, he cabled the text to U.S. Supreme Court Justice Louis Brandeis, the preeminent Zionist leader in America at the time, asking him to pressure President Wilson to change his mind. Weizmann then contacted other influential American Zionists, and intense pressure was placed on the president. Within two weeks Wilson changed his mind and sent his approval to the British. Some scholars contend that Wilson would not have approved had it not been for prominent Zionist pressure; and, of course, Britain would not have adopted the declaration without the approval of the American president.[6]

It is important to remember this part of the history of Palestine. The violence unleashed in this land had its origins in the minds and hearts of many people outside the boundaries of Palestine. Today we can trace the varied forces that coalesced to bring about the tragedy of Palestine and ignite the original spark of the violence back to colonialism and imperialism, to poor and misguided biblical scholarship, to a Christian Europe that made Jews unwanted and carried out massacres and pogroms against them, to a Zionist movement that capitalized on the spirit of colonialism for its own advantage, and to some influential Protestant evangelicals who used scripture to support Zionist objectives while ignoring issues of justice and self determination for the indigenous people of Palestine who had been living there for millennia. In retrospect, it was a conspiracy to displace innocent people from their land and to replace them with another people. Is it surprising then that violence ensued?

THE ROLE OF TERROR LEADING TO THE STATE OF ISRAEL

It became clear from the beginning that the British were committed to implementing the terms of the Balfour Declaration. In fact, as mentioned in the previous chapter, even before the mandate officially began, in 1919 the World Zionist Organization submitted a map of Palestine showing the area proposed by the Zionists for the future Jewish state (Appendix A) to the Paris Peace Conference. This map included large areas of land that belonged to Lebanon, Syria, and Jordan. It was a huge colonial project that totally ignored the indigenous people who lived there.

The Zionist Invasion of Palestine

A Polish Jew who visited Palestine in the 1920s is reported to have said, "The bride is beautiful, but she has a bridegroom." To which Golda Meir, a future prime minister of Israel, is said to have quipped in return that the bridegroom is weak and the bride can be taken from him. The Zionists anticipated that the powerless groom—the Palestinian people—would stay powerless forever.

The increase of Jewish immigration into Palestine, both legally and illegally, brought an increase in violence. The violence of the Zionists was met with the reactionary violence of the Palestinians as they defended their rights to their land and country from the onslaught of the recent arrivals. Palestinians saw this as double colonialism. They had already endured the British colonial system, and now a more sinister and devious colonialism was in the making. The former would eventually end, but the latter intended to stay.

It was also clear that the Zionists were better organized and equipped, militarily and economically, than the Palestinians, and the Zionists enjoyed strong outside support. In spite of the fears of the indigenous Palestinian community—concerns about the land and their poor and inadequate resources—Palestinians were determined to resist the British colonial system and the Zionists.

Through the 1930s and 1940s, the rapidly escalating violence was beginning to get out of hand. There was the violence of the British mandatory power as it tried to maintain law and order, and there was the violence of the two conflicting sides—the Zionists and the Arab Palestinians—who fought each other on the one hand, and the British on the other. The indigenous Palestinians cried out for the independence of Palestine in line with President Wilson's policy of self-determination,[7] while the Zionists called for the establishment of a Jewish state in Palestine. In addition, some Zionist organizations were fighting the British as fiercely as they were fighting the Palestinians. In fact, in the lingua franca of the British in those days, some of the Zionist leaders were deemed "wanted terrorists."[8]

According to Israeli historian Ilan Pappé, the Zionist movement itself was surprised by the relative lack of violent response from the Palestinians:

> The first meetings [of Zionist leader David Ben-Gurion's Consultancy] in December [of 1947] were devoted to assessing the Palestinian mood and intention. The "experts" reported that, despite the early trickling of volunteers into the Palestinian villages and towns, the people themselves seemed eager to continue life as normal. This craving for normality remained typical of the Palestinians inside Palestine in the years to come, even in their worst crises and at the nadir of their struggle; and normality is what they have been denied since 1948.[9]

Pappé goes on to argue that the leadership of the Zionist movement often went to great lengths to instigate a violent response from the Palestinians in order to create a pretense for expelling them. In one meeting of the Consultancy, a small group of Zionist leaders, a prominent leader "called for a more aggressive policy—despite the fact that there were no offensive initiatives or tendencies on the Palestinian side."[10]

There are many examples of the violence of the Zionists at that time. The Palmach (short for *Plugot Machats*, meaning crushing battalions), a core group of Zionist fighters from Hagana (the main Jewish underground militia), sank three British patrol boats on the lookout for illegal Jewish immigrants in October 1945. Moreover, the Palmach destroyed fifty different segments of the Palestine railroad and damaged Haifa's railroad shops.[11]

In 1946, Hagana blew up nine bridges, leaving only one bridge linking Palestine with its neighbors. As a result of these terrorist activities, in June the British sealed off the Jewish agency's offices in Jerusalem and searched the buildings in an attempt to arrest Zionist leaders. On July 22, 1946, Menahem Begin's "Irgun Leumi Z'vai" Zionist fighters, with the help of Hagana, blew up part of the King David Hotel in Jerusalem, killing almost a hundred British, Jews, and Palestinians in the process. Although the British arrested 787 persons, they did not catch the bombers.

Pappé records a variety of terror tactics employed by various Zionist groups, including so-called violent reconnaissance, which was the term given to an operation in which Zionist troops would "enter a defenseless village close to midnight, stay there for a few hours, shoot at anyone who dared leave his or her house, and then depart."[12] There were also sniper attacks, bombs thrown into Arab crowds, and a host of other "methods of intimidation":

> The Jewish troops [in Haifa] rolled barrels full of explosives, and huge steel balls, down into the Arab residential areas, and poured oil mixed with fuel down the roads, which they then ignited. The moment panic-stricken Palestinian residents came running out of their homes to try to extinguish these rivers of fire, they were sprayed by machinegun fire.[13]

While it is not my intention to dwell on the past, it is important to point out that even before the establishment of the state of Israel, Zionists were using violence and terrorism unashamedly to achieve their goals. Many people in the world today, especially in the West, speak of Palestinian violence as if the entire Palestinian people are terrorists by nature. Yet when the Zionists sought to create a state for themselves, they used violence—brutally, viciously, and relentlessly. History shows that all the different Zionist factions at the time were active through violence and terrorism: "[The] Hagana attacked British naval vessels and radar stations, Irgun attacked army equipment, Stern Gang attacked British personnel."[14] Among the many Jewish terrorists on the wanted lists of the British government were Menahem Begin and Yitzhak Shamir; they headed these organizations and later became leaders of the state of Israel.[15]

Whether we like it or not, violence and terrorism are part and parcel of the legacy of the Zionist Jewish resistance movement, before and after the establishment of the state of Israel. They used terror in order to achieve their goals. Although pro-Israeli Jews and non-Jews may have forgotten this part of their history, or do not wish to recall it, in no way were the Zionists morally superior to Palestinian extremists who today use violence and terror to achieve the liberation of their country. In fact, as has been noted earlier, the violence and terrorism in Palestine were initiated by the Zionists as part of their plan to expel Palestinians from the land. Be that as it may, all human beings have the propensity for evil and violence, as has been noted even about the ancient Greeks: "The Athenians were not interested in 'right' or 'wrong'; for them, morality was secondary to the interests of power."[16]

1948 to Present

After the creation of the state of Israel in 1948, approximately 150,000 Palestinians remained inside the Palestinian territory that became Israel. Most of them did not practice any form of violence. They remained in shock at what had happened, at the ease with which they had lost their country.[17] Most of these Palestinians were engaged in self-recrimination, especially against their own ineffective leadership, and were infuriated at the weakness and disorganization of the Arab states. At the same time, many saw a Western conspiracy against them, particularly in the Partition Plan of 1947 led by Britain and the United States: "The truth is that there never could have been a partition of Palestine by ethically acceptable means. Israel was created through terror and it needs terror to cover up its core immorality."[18]

It was not difficult for the fledgling state of Israel to control its Palestinian citizens. Indeed, when some Palestinians who were forced out or fled from their villages and towns tried to cross the armistice line to return to their homes, Israeli soldiers repelled them by fire and many were killed. Documents show that many Palestinians who remained in Israel, as well as many of those who became refugees, were not soldiers and most barely knew how to use a gun. Ilan Pappé records the meetings of the Zionist leadership in early 1948, in which advisors to Ben-Gurion told him that the "Palestinians showed no inclination to fight" and that "rural Palestine showed no desire to fight or attack, and was defenseless."[19] After all, the Palestinians had emerged from four hundred years of repressive Turkish rule and thirty years of a British Mandate that kept them under its control. They were hoping that the British would recognize their rights for self-determination and independence. It did not happen.

There were some Palestinians who wanted revenge for the killing of one of their relatives or the loss of their village and country, and there were also small groups of resisters who carried out raids against Israel. It is no surprise that eventually several Palestinian organizations, both political and military, were established. And Israel continued to carry out its own offensives. Once Israel had established itself as a state, it began to announce that "Israel has the right to defend itself." Although it was the aggressor, it was able, on the vast majority of occasions, to justify its violence even in the form of preemptive strikes. Pappé argues that the Zionists used a strategy of violence in order to prevent a peace from being reached that would threaten their overall goals:

> In a way, the hesitations in the global community about the way things were going [in early 1948] and the highly limited nature of the pan-Arab military activity could have restored calm to Palestine and opened the way for a renewed attempt to solve the problem. However, the new Zionist policy of an aggressive offensive that the Consultancy hastened to adopt blocked all possible moves towards a more reconciliatory reality.[20]

The level of violence of Israeli retaliation was always much more severe and deadly than that of the Palestinians. Right-wing Israelis lived by a philosophy of violence that was expressed by the adage "ten eyes for an eye." This mind-set can be illustrated by Israel's army attacks and massacre in Gaza in 1955; the massacres in Qalqilya (seventy dead, including women, children, and the elderly), Kufr Qassem (forty-nine dead, including children), and Khan Yunis (over five hundred dead) in 1956. In 1966, Israel attacked As-Samu village near Hebron and left the hilltop town in rubble.[21]

According to research by Ian Lustick, a professor of political science at the University of Pennsylvania, Israel employed three methods of control against its Arab Palestinian citizens: segmentation, cooptation, and dependence. To a great extent, Israel successfully controlled its Palestinian citizens without too much pain. This system of control was obviously not unique to Israel. In one form or another, it has been practiced by people of power throughout history.[22]

Since the 1967 War, it has been quite easy for Israel to use its methods of cooptation and dependence on the Palestinians in the West Bank and Gaza Strip, Israel's newly acquired subjects. In the early years, the Palestinians in the occupied territories proved relatively docile, showing relatively minimal resistance against the Israeli army. Under Jordan's rule of the West Bank, the Palestinians were not permitted to have guns. Therefore, once the Jordanian army retreated in the 1967 War, there was little resistance from the Palestinians who were not trained in warfare and did not possess any military equipment or arms. In fact, in the beginning Israel did not even have to resort to segmentation. Palestinians from the occupied territories were free to move around and travel within Israel. Similarly, Israeli citizens—Arabs (Palestinians) and Jews—traveled in ease and comfort, without fear, in the occupied territories. This reality was an indication that in spite of the injustice, the Palestinians did not respond to the 1967 war with hatred and violence. On the contrary, now that Israel had taken control of all of geographic Palestine, Palestinians resumed their normal lives with the hope of arriving at a resolution of the conflict.

It was only after the first intifada in 1987 that the government of Israel started actively to enforce a policy of segmentation. By then the occupation of the Palestinian territories had been in existence for twenty-two years. However, when Israel realized that the Palestinians were not going to give up their right to self-determination and were not willing to legitimize the illegal occupation of their country, it began actively to pursue the segmentation of Palestine and enforce harsh measures of control.

By the time the second intifada erupted in 2000, the policy had been fully implemented with over six hundred checkpoints to segment and control Palestinian movement. Most of these checkpoints were not placed on the green line to guard and protect the Israeli borders from Palestinian infiltrators; instead, they were mounted inside the West Bank and Gaza in what seemed to be an effort to torment Palestinians and disrupt their lives. In addition, a network of roads and highways was built to isolate Palestinians by closing off their towns and villages. The confiscation of Palestinian land and the expansion of settlements has continued unhindered.[23]

Today, in many places Israeli settlers rule supreme. They harass Palestinian farmers and, with the help of the army, prevent them from reaching their land. Furthermore, as already noted, Israel has constructed a wall around the West Bank. Although Israel calls it a "security fence," the wall is built not on the boundary between Israel and the West Bank but deep inside the Palestinian areas where it devours huge areas of Palestinian land. The Palestinians accurately call it an "apartheid wall."[24]

Violence against Palestinians

For many of us who witnessed these events it became clear that Israel was able to push the Palestinians into further bloodshed in order to justify its own violence and oppression. However, in spite of the escalation of Israeli violence, the Palestinians continued to show resilience and determination not to give up their struggle for freedom. Israel's resulting frustration has caused it to move from a system of control to a system of suppression. The Israeli army had been using elements of suppression before, but now a policy of subjugation and suppression was unquestionably being practiced to crush Palestinian resistance.

This policy of suppression shows no regard for human rights. Its aim is to frustrate the Palestinians into despair by increasing their humiliation and dehumanization. The objective is to make life so miserable that the Palestinians will either give up and leave the country or become totally docile and passive, accepting whatever the government of Israel wishes to do. The message of such a policy is clear: if Palestinians want to stay, they have to be totally submissive and acquiescent to Israel. If they dare to raise their heads, they will be crushed.

Oren Ben-Dor, a lecturer at the University of Southampton in Britain who grew up in Israel, wrote an article in July 2006 at the height of Israel's war with Lebanon entitled, "Who Are the Real Terrorists in the Middle East?" Here is how he describes the occupation:

> The very creation of Israel required an act of terror. In 1948, most of the non-Jewish indigenous people were ethnically cleansed from the part of Palestine which became Israel. This action was carefully planned. Without it, no state with a Jewish majority and character would have been possible. Since 1948, the "Israeli Arabs," those Palestinians who avoided expulsion, have suffered continuous discrimination. Indeed, many have been internally displaced, ostensibly for "security reasons," but really to acquire their lands for Jews.
>
> Surely Holocaust memory and Jewish longing for *Eretz Israel* would not be sufficient to justify ethnic cleansing and ethnocracy? To avoid the destabilisation that would result from ethical inquiry, the Israeli state must hide the core problem, by nourishing a victim mentality among Israeli Jews.
>
> To sustain that mentality and to preserve an impression of victimhood among outsiders, *Israel must breed conditions for violence*. Whenever prospects of violence against it subside, Israel must do its utmost to regenerate them: the myth that it is a peace-seeking victim which has "no partner for peace" is a key panel in the screen with which Israel hides its primordial and continuing immorality. . . . Whenever there is a glimmer of stability, the state orders a targeted assassination, such as that in Sidon which preceded the current Lebanon crisis, knowing well that this brings not security but more violence. Israel's unilateralism and the cycle of violence nourish one another.
>
> Amidst the violence and despite the conventional discourse which hides the root of this violence, actuality calls upon us to think. The more we silence its voice, the more violently actuality is sure to speak. . . . Silence about the immoral core of Israeli statehood makes us all complicit in breeding the terrorism that threatens a catastrophe which could tear the world apart.[25]

With the increase of Israeli state violence, how does Israel escape world condemnation? It is able to do so only by putting the blame on the Palestinians themselves. Israel has been successful in using the Western media to demonize the Palestinians: imputing all violence to them, blaming them for being the obstacle to peace, and coercing other Westerners to *perceive* Israel as the only democracy in the Middle East, as a peace-loving people with the right to defend its people and land from Palestinian violence. It all has to do with perception, not reality, but Israel has succeeded. Today, Israel basically acts with impunity, in large part because many people and countries have become conditioned to automatically blame the Palestinians.

Tragically, some Palestinian extremists have made matters much worse by collaborating with Israel, either consciously or unconsciously, providing

Israel with justification for its actions. Instead of recognizing Israel's ability to manipulate, they have fallen into its trap. Palestine's grievous slide into the morass of suicide bombings represents a tragic deterioration of the Palestinian community. At the same time Israeli propaganda is so strong that some people actually believe that the only obstacle to peace is the suicide bombings. The foolishness, ugliness, and atrocity of suicide bombings has brought immediate condemnation of the Palestinians, while it distracts attention from the root causes of the violence.[26]

It is interesting to compare modern warfare and suicide bombings. Due to sophisticated technology, war has become "impersonal." Bombs are fired from long distances. While reeking devastation and killing hundreds of people, distant soldiers do not see the enemy nor do they observe the wreckage. Chris Hedges has described "the impersonal slaughter of modern industrial warfare."[27] Viewers do not generally see the atrocities of warfare on television, but they do see the devastation wrought by a suicide bombing. How can they condemn the latter and not the former? How can people not be repulsed by the destruction of a helicopter gunship or an F-16 fighter jet, which kill many more people than a suicide bomber ever could? Our wars have become more vicious because they have become more impersonal. Suicide bombing, on the other hand, is a very personal thing, which makes it more revolting to people. B'Tselem, an Israeli peace organization, reported that in 2006 Palestinians killed 17 Israeli civilians (including 1 minor) and 6 Israeli soldiers; in the same period, Israeli forces killed 660 Palestinians, half of whom were not taking part in hostilities, and the number included 141 minors.[28]

The movement from control to suppression was accomplished through the use of excessive force and through the humiliation of people with no regard to age or gender. Vengeance, insult, and disgrace have stripped people of their human worth.

Israel has lost its soul: "The soldiers who harden their hearts at roadblocks, the pilots who loose bombs in the middle of cities, the attorneys who whitewash and the spokesmen who lie are not people who lack moral values. Most are merely victims of the situation created by the occupation."[29] President Jimmy Carter concluded that the Israeli government gives greater importance to holding onto land than to working for peace when he wrote, "Israel put confiscation of Palestinian land ahead of peace. . . ."[30] With the support of the United States, Israel can afford to enact laws that suppress the Palestinians, even if they violate international law.

Israel has developed one of the most comprehensive and lethal systems of control and suppression the world has ever seen. When American forces had difficulty controlling the Iraqis, they called on the Israeli Defense Force to teach them the "art" of control and security. Israel's strong allies in Washington cover up Israel's violations and heap blame on the Palestinians.

Israel has been successful in using propaganda against the Palestinians. It paints the Palestinians as violent and savage in order to justify its actions against them. Yet, as noted above, the Palestinians are not more violent than the Israelis. The Jewish Israeli Zionist extremists in Israel and their pro-Israel Zionist allies abroad spend millions of dollars on propaganda that keeps Westerners hostage. Although many people today perceive the Palestinians as violent and calloused killers, the fact is that no one is born a terrorist. We are all born human beings. However, as Mark Braverman has pointed out, "Violence is the outcome of unbearable stress. . . . Anyone can become violent when the relevant conditions are provided."[31]

Psychologist Robert Fein wrote, "Violence is a process, as well as an act. Violent behavior does not occur in a vacuum. Careful analysis of violent incidents shows that violent acts often are the culmination of long-developing, identifiable trails of problems, conflicts, disputes and failures."[32] The Palestinians watched in agony and helplessness the increasingly oppressive measures of the Israeli army and the daily injustice and humiliation to which they were subjected. Their constant cry went unheard, as it seems unheard today. So long as the United States protects Israel through its veto in the U.N. Security Council, no one dares to stand against Israel or has the power to stop its injustice. The Palestinian intifada of 1987 was a nonviolent attempt to impress on the world the need to come to its aid and lift the violent occupation. The world did not respond.

> No human can stand the perpetually numbing experience of his own powerlessness. . . . It is precisely when [people] feel powerless that some people begin to be at risk for violent or threatening behavior. To understand why this is, we must remember that violence is related to an overwhelming sense of desperation and isolation and a growing sense that nothing the person can do seems to help or change his situation.[33]

The crime against Palestinians was birthed in the minds and hearts of those Zionists who saw the Palestinians as dispensable beings. According to the journal of the French Lubavitch, an ultra-Orthodox Jewish group, "In the eyes of the Creator there is as much difference between Jews and non-Jews as between non-Jews and animals."[34] This belief that Palestinians are worth less than Jews, hidden in the hearts of some Zionists, began to be put into practice over time. It has been a slow and creeping genocide. For many years, Israel refused to use trained dogs against the Palestinians because it brought to mind the Nazis. Now Israel uses dogs to attack Palestinians.[35]

The psychological warfare against the Palestinians has been unyielding in its intensity. It is clear in the humiliation that Palestinians experience at the many checkpoints and even at Ben Gurion Airport in Tel Aviv. There, security personnel can tell from the identification number on an Israeli passport whether or not the individual is Jewish. Many times Israeli Arabs are subjected to overtly humiliating racial profiling security checks.[36] This protocol has nothing to do with actual security, because every passenger has to go through sophisticated electronic machines that detect the presence of any dangerous object; no, it is about humiliation. It has its roots in the Israeli psychological need to be in control and to humiliate its Arab citizens. Such actions breed resentment, hatred, and even violence. Many Israeli Arabs who carry Israeli passports and travel all around the world experience more respect from security officials of other nations than they do in their own country. If Israel treats its own citizens in this fashion, one can imagine how they treat the Palestinians in the West Bank and Gaza Strip.

Some experimental psychologists who study aggressive and violent behavior report: "The consensus that has emerged from this work is that the most potent stimulus of aggression and violence . . . [is] insult and humiliation. In other words, the most effective way, and often the only way, to provoke someone to become violent is to insult him."[37] Dr. Sonia Nimr, a professor at Birzeit University, mentions how an Israeli soldier put his boot on the neck of her husband as their young son was watching. Such incidents of insult and humiliation, whether physical or verbal, are common at checkpoints.[38] The insult and the humiliation that take place provoke anger and hate. As psychiatrist Herbert E. Thomas says, "In order to understand the violence around us . . . we must confront the pain we cause each other."[39]

Dr. Thomas has described the steps leading up to an act of violence. "[It begins] with a rejection, which elicits intensely painful feelings of shame, to which the person responds with anger, which he then expresses or acts out with an act of violence."[40] In the case of the Palestinians, it goes beyond personal rejection to the rejection of one's national identity, the denial of political rights, and the negation of human worth. Fortunately not all Palestinians and not all oppressed people in the world behave in violent ways. Many people are able to channel their anger through nonviolent means instead of resorting to violence.

What Israel has successfully done since 1967 is to paint the Palestinians as inherently violent. It projects itself as peace-loving while the Palestinians are the violent terrorists. The Israeli government has also successfully created the perception that whenever it attacks, kills, and destroys the Palestinians and their property, it is doing so in self-defense. Yet as the brief review of the history of the conflict above makes clear, from its inception in the rise of the Zionist movement to the latest incidents of violence in Palestine today, the government of Israel has intentionally cultivated, fed, and nourished violence within the Palestinian community.

By exposing this truth, I am in no way justifying Palestinian violence. I am merely trying to explain its source. All violence is wrong, and violence can never contribute to peace. Even though some glorify violence or piously disguise it, it must always be exposed and repudiated. However, the truth remains: the clearest expression of violence today is the occupation by Israel of the Palestinian territories. For the violence to stop, the illegal occupation itself must end.

PART II

PALESTINIAN LIBERATION THEOLOGY IN THE SERVICE OF NONVIOLENCE AND PEACE

Chapter 4

The Bible and the Land

Everyone knows that justice is relevant only among those who are equal in power: while the strong take whatever they can, and the weak concede whatever they must.
  —Paraphrase of an Athenian principle[1]

A number of biblical themes are clearly relevant to the Israel-Palestine conflict. Viewed both biblically and theologically through the eyes of Palestinian liberation theology, these themes, on the one hand, warn the reader against exclusive, nationalist, or violent interpretations and, on the other hand, promote an inclusive, universal, and nonviolent understanding that can lend itself to the achievement of justice, peace, and reconciliation for all the people of Israel-Palestine.

EXCLUSIVE THEOLOGIES OF THE LAND

Probably the most important form of exclusive theology for both Palestinians and Christians focuses on the land. At its roots, this conflict in the Middle East is really about control of the land. Palestinian Christians often feel trapped between two different forms of exclusivity, a Jewish form and a Muslim form.

At the beginning, it is important to point out that not every Jewish or Muslim believer holds these theologies. Many Jews and Muslims are secular and are not interested in such religious arguments. Nonetheless, it is important to understand these different theologies of the land to determine an appropriate faith response for Christians.

Many people do not realize that Muslims have a theology of the land. The Qur'an and the Muslim tradition, however, give much importance to the Holy Land, especially to the Al-Aqsa Mosque in Jerusalem. Dr. Mustafa Abu Sway of Al-Quds University describes two different ways that Muslims view the Holy Land as unique. In the first place, Muslims, as those who submit to God, are given the inheritance of the land after the children of Israel "were forbidden to enter the Land . . . as a result of their disobedience."[2] Abu Sway argues that some scholars interpret this in an inclusive sense, while others interpret it exclusively. He notes that in the Qur'an it is important that "genetic or biological descent is never sufficient in itself to merit such inheritance."[3] Some interpret this to mean that those who truly submit to the will of God—in other words, Muslims—enjoy exclusive right to the land. Others would interpret this to mean that the land belongs to those who are righteous.

A second important connection between Islam and the land is the importance given to Jerusalem and particularly to the Al-Aqsa Mosque. Abu Sway writes that "since the miraculous Night Journey of the Prophet Muhammad (Peace be upon him), *al-Isra' wa al Mi'raj*, took place more than fourteen centuries ago, Muslims have established a sublime and perpetual relationship with Al-Aqsa Mosque."[4] This relationship means that Jerusalem is of central importance in Islam, and the Al-Aqsa Mosque is the third holiest site for the faith (after the mosques in Mecca and Medina).

Although Islam has always placed great importance on Jerusalem and the Holy Land, it is worth noting that an exclusive theology of the land is not inherent in Islam. In a May 2003 document, the Church of Scotland published a document stating, "There is no place in Islamic theology for any particular people to be special to the Land—to the abandonment of others. . . . The only prerequisite is righteousness."[5] However, according to Colin Chapman, as the land was threatened by outside invasion, whether by the crusaders or by the Zionist movement, an exclusive theology of the land developed in response: "In recent years it has been Jewish/Zionist intrusion into the land that has stimulated Islamic thinking about the land once again and encouraged it to develop a theology of the land which has strong similarities to Jewish theologies about the land."[6] Thus, although the theological importance of the land has always existed in Islam, its exclusive form is a relatively new development. When land is threatened, its theological importance is combined with its economic importance:

> For Islam a basic premise is that of trusteeship: Muslims believe that the land belongs to Allah, and their job is to look after it, and not to damage it. Within the general Palestinian culture, the Islamic understanding of the trusteeship of land is highly important. Land is never just a neutral economic asset. To sell one's family land is counted a disgrace, and to have it taken from one inflicts a deep wound to one's honour. The way in which land is tied up with honour can become a potent force when the political and religious dimensions are added.[7]

Palestinian Christians oppose any exclusive theology of the land. However, it can be more difficult to escape the exclusive theology of the land in Judaism, because this theology comes from scriptures that we also consider sacred. When Zionists and Israeli Jewish settlers quote from their scriptures to justify taking Palestinian land, they are also quoting from our Christian scriptures. It is important for Christians to understand the use of an exclusive theology of the land in the Old Testament *and* how the New Testament renders such an exclusive reading unacceptable.

READING THE BIBLE AS A PALESTINIAN CHRISTIAN

In the last chapter of *Theology of the Old Testament*, scripture scholar Walter Brueggemann discusses what he terms "Some Pervasive Issues." One of these topics is Old Testament theology in relation to the New Testament and to the church.[8] He writes that "Old Testament theology has been characteristically a Christian enterprise," with its primary focus toward the New Testament. In Brueggemann's view, this has led Christians into a notorious supersessionism, "whereby Jewish religious claims are overridden in the triumph of Christian claims."[9]

Brueggemann does not accept the position of Brevard Childs that the two testaments "bear witness to Jesus Christ."[10] Brueggemann adds that "Such a way of presenting the Old Testament proceeds as if the community of Judaism was only an interim community, which existed until the New Testament and then withered into nonexistence and insignificance."[11] Although he believes that the "imaginative construal of the Old Testament toward Jesus is a credible act and one that I fully affirm," he argues that this reading is not appropriate for Old Testament scholarship:

> For purposes of Old Testament theology, however, it is important, theologically as well as historically, to insist that the connections between the two Testaments are made, as surely they must be, from the side of the New Testament and not from the side of the Old Testament. Thus it is completely appropriate to say in an act of bold, imaginative construal, as the New Testament frequently does, "The scriptures were fulfilled." Such an affirmation can be made only from the side of the fulfillment, not from the side of the Old Testament.[12]

Brueggemann holds that the Old Testament is polyphonic in its testimony and that it is a misinterpretation to present only "one single, and exclusivist construal, namely, the New Testament christological construal, thereby violating the quality of generative openness that marks the Old Testament text."[13]

Brueggemann's words are provocative and allow for a stimulating discussion. In response, however, I maintain that as a Palestinian Christian I read the Old Testament through the lens of my Christian faith. It is a part of my religious heritage and my holy scriptures. It is integrally connected with the witness of the early church of the New Testament. What renders the Old Testament important for me is the presence of the New Testament. The Old Testament alone, without the incarnation and redemption, without its fulfillment in Jesus Christ, would be interesting reading about the history and heritage of the Jewish people but would lack personal religious significance for me.

It is true that the Old Testament, as Brueggemann writes, is polyphonic and allows for different interpretations. As a Christian I must interpret it in a way that makes sense with my own faith tradition. The Hebrew Scriptures are cherished and studied because they form the backdrop to our faith. The initial interpreters of the text were themselves Jewish and the ancestors of our faith.

It is important to note that the Old Testament is the foundation of two religious movements: Christianity and Rabbinic Judaism. Both interpret the Old Testament for their own religious community and within their own faith's understanding of it. It is also important to note that the Old Testament does not stand on its own for Judaism or for Christianity. Jews have found its fulfillment and use in the Mishna and the Talmud, and Christians have found its fulfillment in the New Testament. Incidentally, Christianity preceded the emergence of Rabbinic Judaism, but both religions are indebted to the Old Testament as their foundational text.

Today most Christians are "gentiles," while in the earliest years of the church, the original apostles and followers of Christ were Jewish. They were knowledgeable about the contents of the books that eventually became the Old Testament. They are the ones who saw that in Jesus Christ "the scriptures were fulfilled." The significance of the early Jewish Christian community is found in its ability, in spite of initial resistance, to understand that God's purposes for history, as guided by Jesus Christ, were much broader than one group of people. Obviously, Paul deserves much credit in this endeavor. From its inception, the Christian faith opened the door to include both Jews and gentiles. At the time members of both groups discovered that God's original purpose has always been to have one humanity in Christ, and thus they found themselves together as equal members in the one community.[14]

To read the Old Testament through Christian eyes—or human eyes or Palestinian eyes—does not preclude its reading through Jewish eyes or even secular eyes. One cannot deny or negate the Old Testament's polyphonic character, yet, for me, the text makes most sense when read primarily through the lens of Jesus Christ. In reading it with my Palestinian eyes, I see its meaning and its relevance for my social and political context.

When I read and study the Old Testament, it is with an eye toward those narratives that reflect the inclusive and nonviolent message of Christ. From this perspective I see the author of the book of Jonah as an archetypal Palestinian liberation theologian. Although the book is seemingly less significant than the works of the major prophets, it possesses some attributes that enable it to surpass, theologically speaking, prophets like Isaiah and Jeremiah. While I discuss the inclusive theology of the book of Jonah in greater detail in the next chapter, it is sufficient here to note that while the greater prophets fluctuate between an exclusive and inclusive view of God, people, and the land, and vacillate between a nationalist and a universal view, the author of Jonah is very consistent in his inclusive and universal message. He critiques much of the theology around him and maintains that any religion that reflects a tribal and xenophobic god cannot be genuine. It is possible that Jonah might have built on the universalism of Second Isaiah, but he used a simple narrative for his theology instead of the language of poetry. In my understanding, the inclusive text of Jonah is a standard against which Old Testament theology must be measured.

When the author of Jonah portrays God as forgiving the worst enemies of Israel, he questions exclusive claims to the land. Obsession with the land proved disastrous for both Israel and Judah and did not bring them rest or peace; the land became a liability more than a blessing. The revolutionary theology expressed in the book of Jonah regarding the land was apparently not shared or accepted by most Jews, who still entertained a narrow and exclusive understanding of land. The promise of the land to Abraham reiterated over and over again to Isaac and Jacob had a greater impact on people than did the movement toward a more universal understanding of God, the nations, and land.

Even the greater prophets used racist utterances, as demonstrated in a text from Second Isaiah. This beautiful poem that is often used by Christian preachers has quite disturbing racist implications:

> But now thus says the LORD,
> He who created you, O Jacob,
> He who formed you, O Israel:
> Do not fear, for I have redeemed you;
> I have called you by name, you are mine.
> When you pass through the water, I will be with you;
> And through the rivers, they shall not overwhelm you;
> When you walk through fire you shall not be burned,
> And the flame shall not consume you.
> For I am the LORD your God,
> The Holy One of Israel, your Savior.
> I give Egypt as your ransom,
> Ethiopia and Seba in exchange for you.
> Because you are precious in my sight,
> And honored, and I love you,
> I give people in return for you,
> Nations in exchange for your life. (Isa. 43:1-4)

How do Egyptians feel about being a ransom for Israel, or Ethiopians and Nubians who would be given in exchange for Israel? According to Second Isaiah, entire nations are to be given away so that Israel can be saved. There is a great need to "de-Zionize" these texts.

Second Isaiah provides another example, a text that includes the famous words that Jesus himself quoted in his sermon in Nazareth (as recorded in

Luke 4). In the latter part of this poem, Isaiah again uses language that today we would consider narrow and racist:

> Strangers shall stand and feed your flocks,
> Foreigners shall till your land and dress your vines;
> But you shall be called priests of the LORD,
> You shall be named ministers of our God;
> You shall enjoy the wealth of the nations;
> And in their riches you shall glory. (Isa. 61:5-6)

In the *Good News Bible*, the last two stanzas are translated as, "You will enjoy the wealth of the nations, and be proud that it is yours." This exclusivist text is unacceptable today, whether it has to do with God or people or land. It must be de-Zionized as well.

THE LAND ISSUE AT THE HEART OF THE CONFLICT

Justice, and Only Justice: A Palestinian Theology of Liberation, my previous book, provides a scant account of a theology of land; it was the very beginning of my journey on this important theme. The issue of the land is, undoubtedly, the heart of the conflict in the Middle East. The sole objective of Zionists (Christians and Jews alike) has been the acquisition of the land of Palestine for the Jewish people. Because the Zionists wanted the land without the people who inhabited it, the major policies and laws of the state of Israel were designed to strip Palestinians of their land. It is possible to identify four pretexts or rationalizations that were used verbally or nonverbally by the state of Israel to do this.

Because of virulent antisemitism and the Holocaust, Jews received sympathy from many people, especially Westerners. In addition, the genuine suffering of Jews during the Holocaust has led many Israeli Jews to feel that their "special" suffering gives them the "right" to do as they choose. The feeling that the world owes them for the injustice done against them has added to a cycle of injustice. By playing on feelings of guilt about the Holocaust, Zionists have been able to make this attitude dominate in public discourse. It has been used to justify all the wrongs and injustices committed by Israel. Under the guise of the injustice and suffering wrought upon the Jewish people, Israel confiscated Palestinian land while the world looked on, unwilling to act against a new injustice.

After the 1967 war, Israel began to confiscate Palestinian land in the West Bank, including East Jerusalem, and the Gaza Strip. The main justification for this was religious, based on Old Testament texts. Religious Jews and Western Christian Zionists were both supportive as the land was stripped from the Palestinians under the pretext of the Bible and God. Religion was used not to critique unethical and immoral behavior, but to support and encourage robbery. Religion became a servant of the state, and God was and is being used to legitimize and sanction crime.

The Oslo Peace Process (1991-2000) resulted in a loss of more Palestinian land. While Israeli and Palestinian leaders were negotiating peace, Israel continued to expropriate more land and expand its colonies or settlements on the West Bank. The process continues today. Since the beginning of the second intifada (September 2000), huge strips of land have been confiscated by Israel under the pretext of security. The last expression of this "need" has been the building of the separation wall. However, as many people have observed, it was not built along the "Green Line," the boundary line that existed between Israel and the West Bank before 1967. Instead, the wall devours huge pieces of land inside Palestine. It is a political wall of *hafrada* (separation) intended, under the guise of security, to strip away more Palestinian land.

Looking back at actions of the Israeli government, it seems clear that the primary objective is to confiscate the land of Palestine itself. Israeli hopes are that the wall will force Palestinian farmers to leave the West Bank because they cannot get to their land or because they must watch as their crops wither and die and their fruit trees (including the olive groves) are uprooted and bulldozed. To Israel's shock, the Palestinians are not leaving. On the contrary, the Palestinian population is actually increasing, and some statistics have shown that by 2020, there will be more Palestinians than Jews on the land.[15]

Since the conflict in this part of the Middle East revolves around the issue of the land—and since God and the Bible have been used to justify the theft of the land—it is important to continue to study the Bible to discover if God and the Bible are indeed a party to such injustice. Frankly, if the passages used to create and support injustice compose the heart of the biblical message regarding the land, most Palestinian Christians (and many others) would not want to have anything to do with such a Bible or god.

Before looking at specific biblical texts about land, a few observations should be noted.

- For many years biblical scholars did not pay much attention to a theology of land.
- Since the 1970s we notice greater attention given to the question of land. Books on the topic opened the way for more studies.[16] The Palestinian issue, it is believed, has encouraged such study.
- The study of land in the Bible carries within it great stimulation and benefits to biblical students and ministers because it opens a number of doors of study that have to do with God and God's relationship with people and land.
- Discovering the inclusive biblical theology of land helps many people become advocates for a just peace in Palestine and equips them to counteract a false biblical theology of land.
- It is important to study the theology of land in both the Old and the New Testaments. Although the political problem lies largely in the

Old Testament, it is important for Christians to be grounded in a New Testament theology of land.

The basic questions for us Christians are: Can we justify biblically any exclusive claim by Jews over the land? From a New Testament perspective, can we conclude that Jews have a legitimate exclusive claim?

NEW TESTAMENT PASSAGES

If we are true to the witness of the New Testament, we cannot surmise that there is a religious exclusive right given by God to Israel or the Jews. Unfortunately, many Christians have been so influenced by a narrow Old Testament theology of land that they cannot accept the new perspective created by the New Testament.

As Christians it is appropriate for us in the study of the issue of land (as well as other issues) to begin with the New Testament, the point of fulfillment, although adherents of Judaism may naturally begin with the texts of Genesis. The advent of Jesus Christ causes all the New Testament writers to see the land in a totally new light. Whereas the Old Testament vacillates between exclusivity and inclusiveness, the thrust of the New Testament is much more inclusive. In fact, many students of the Old Testament have found the seeds of inclusiveness within its more generally exclusive texts, and even within the Torah itself. Christopher J. H. Wright, while affirming the importance of the land within the Old Testament, writes of the "loosening" of exclusive theology in the prophets:

> [In] the eschatological visions of the prophets we can discern a loosening of, almost a dispensing with, the ancient land-kinship basis of the covenant. . . . In other words, the theological themes of security, inclusion, sharing and responsibility, which were once linked to the land, remain valid; but they are loosened from their literal, territorial moorings, as the scope of salvation is widened to include non-Israelites.[17]

For me, the New Testament constitutes the final draft of a theological dissertation that has undergone many stages of development through hundreds of years of history. While it is quite informative and interesting to study the previous drafts, ultimately the most binding for a Christian is the final draft, verified by the witness of Jesus Christ. Unless Old Testament references correspond to a view held by Christ, they form a rough or previous draft and cannot be considered binding. It is extremely important as a Christian and as a Palestinian to study the way the writers of the Gospels and other New Testament texts have recorded their thoughts on the important topic of land. Here are a few examples.

Matthew 5:8—Blessed are the meek for they shall inherit the earth. The meek are those willing to live with full knowledge that they are not permanent residents. In other words, they recognize the land does not belong to them, that it belongs to God. They are but mere tenants, strangers, aliens, and sojourners; the real owner is God. This is well expressed in Leviticus 25:23b: "the land is mine; with me you are but aliens and tenants." In Psalm 37, the phrase, "the meek will inherit the land" (v. 11), is repeated several times. The context for each is a comparison of evildoers and those who are meek. Meekness is viewed as the antithesis of evil. The meek are those who hope in God (v. 9) and are blessed by God (v. 22); they are the righteous (v. 29), the ones who wait on the Lord and keep to his way (v. 34). The meek are summarized in these words: "Trust in the Lord, and do good; so you will live in the land, and enjoy security" (Ps. 37:3).

The meek are not weak; they are strong yet not aggressive or harsh. They are gentle and kind. The meek are the truly human who live in obedience to God. Similarly, the land is not for those who conquer and exploit it, but for those who take care of it for their own good and the good of others. The land is for those who live under God's rule and sovereignty. It is for use by those who are merciful and compassionate toward their neighbors. A clear expression of the fate of those obsessed with ownership of the land would be the flip side of Jesus' pronouncement in the beatitudes: "Woe to those who are obsessed with the land and are not willing to share it for they will lose it."

The text in Matthew 5:8 is one of the few references in which Jesus mentions the land. It is important to note, however, that he is talking about membership in God's kingdom. The earth is meant to be a significant part of God's kingdom: anywhere God's reign of justice and love is in effect, there is God's kingdom. People who live anywhere who acknowledge God as supreme and sovereign in their life and acknowledge God as father, lord, savior, sustainer, and liberator are living within God's kingdom. These are the meek who, according to God, will inherit the earth. The kingdom is not for those who cling to the land in an exclusive and aggressive way, denying others their God-given right to live on the land and share the blessings of life. In the end, the land does not belong to people of power who occupy it, rule it, exploit its resources, and oppress others; they are the fools of history, a history that will ultimately condemn them.

Although Jesus quotes Psalm 37 about the land, he articulates a new understanding of the land that applies not only to one land but to the entire earth. The small land of Palestine becomes a prototype or a model for the earth. God has created the earth as a dwelling place for the meek. Jesus critiques false nationalism and patriotism that ties one's heart to the land. Perhaps he had in mind the Zealots and Sicarii, the revolutionaries of his day who used violence and terror. They were not the meek, but rather had an obsession with the land and contributed to its devastation.

Although we do not experience the reality of this beatitude in our daily lives, it remains a statement of faith that we must promulgate. We must proclaim it as God's intention for a fully lived life under God. We must live as meek people.

John 1:43-51—And he said to him, "Very truly, I tell you, you will see heaven opened and the angels of God ascending and descending upon the Son of Man." At the end of the first chapter of the Gospel of John, Jesus tells Nathaniel, a newfound disciple, that he saw him under a fig tree. Nathaniel, impressed, tells Jesus that he is the king of Israel. Jesus replies with the words above. On the surface, the exchange seems innocuous, but upon deeper reflection, one can see it points to a very important truth about the land.

The words of Nathaniel reflected the popular understanding at that time of the coming of the messiah. The expression "king of Israel" implies a nationalist understanding. A king controls a kingdom of land and an army. The focus is on patriotic zeal, similar to recruiting a band of nationalists to initiate a movement of rebellion against the Roman occupier. This was a reality in first-century Palestine.

When Jesus replied with the words, "You will see heaven opened and the angels of God ascending and descending upon the Son of Man," he made a very subtle reference to an Old Testament story, to which Nathaniel could immediately relate. When Jacob was fleeing from his brother Esau, he stopped on the way at Bethel to spend the night in the open air. In his sleep, he had a dream: "There was a ladder set up on the earth, the top of it reaching to heaven; and the angels of God were ascending and descending on it. And the LORD stood beside him and said, 'I am the LORD, the God of Abraham your father and the God of Isaac; the land on which you lie I will give to you and to your offspring'" (Gen. 28:12-14). The promise that had been given to Abraham and Isaac was now reiterated to Jacob. In his dream and in the words that the Lord spoke to Jacob, the emphasis is clearly on the land. Jacob's offspring, the twelve tribes of Israel, saw in the repeated reiteration of the promise further proof that the land of Canaan was a gift granted to them by God.

Jesus conveys a very important point in this passage when he announces that the angels of God were ascending and descending not on the land, but on the Son of Man. In other words, it is no longer the land that is significant, but Jesus Christ. The land is no longer the vehicle through which God expresses his faithfulness to people. Belonging to the kingdom of God, not the inheritance of a particular land, is what is important. From a Christian perspective, the land no longer has any covenantal importance. The new covenant with God is based on the person of Jesus Christ. In essence, Jesus attempted to shift Nathaniel's attention from a messiah who would establish an earthly kingdom to a messiah who transcends the land under God's reign.

Although the gift of the land was supposed to give Abraham's descendants peace and security, it did not. It was a source of constant strife and conflict with neighbors and also among the twelve tribes. The coming of Christ fulfilled the true intention of God's gift of land. Peace and security would be achieved through trust in God's gracious goodness in Jesus Christ. Ultimately, God's fidelity is not to a particular land, and God does not designate a particular segment of humanity to live in sovereignty over the land. Instead, God's fidelity is to people who live in faith wherever they may be.

Romans 4:13—"For the promise that he would inherit the world did not come to Abraham or to his descendants through the law but the righteousness of faith." In this passage Paul reinterprets the promises given to Abraham through Christ. According to the promise given to Abraham in Genesis, his prodigy would inherit the land of Canaan. The promise was reiterated to Isaac and Jacob, and it became the cornerstone of the ancient Israelite theology of land. It also forms the basis for today's Jewish religious theology for the acquisition of Palestinian land. From a Zionist religious perspective, all the land confiscations in the occupied territories and the building of the settlements have hinged on these Genesis promises and other texts in the Torah. What is truly significant is that Paul, after coming to know Jesus Christ, began to interpret God's promises and the covenant itself in light of Jesus Christ. In this text from Romans, Paul expresses his new understanding in a truly revolutionary way: the promise given by God to Abraham was to inherit not the land of Canaan, but the world (the cosmos).

Nowhere in the Old Testament is a promise given to Abraham that his descendants will inherit the world, but this is precisely Paul's argument. This interpretation can only mean that Paul saw the fulfillment of the promise to Abraham realized in Christ, not by the ancient Israelites. In Galatians, Paul writes:

> Brothers and sisters, I give an example from daily life: once a person's will has been ratified, no one adds to it or annuls it. Now the promises were made to Abraham and to his offspring. It does not say, "And to offsprings," as of many; but it says, "And to your offspring," that is, to one person, who is Christ. My point is this: the law, which came four hundred thirty years later, does not annul a covenant previously ratified by God, so as to nullify the promise. For if the inheritance comes from the law, it no longer comes from the promise; but God granted it to Abraham through the promise. (Gal. 3:15-18)

For Paul, the promise takes precedence over the law. If God through Jesus Christ was going to bring to fruition God's ultimate and eternal purposes for the redemption of the world and all of creation, then the real and authentic promise to Abraham was fulfilled in Christ in whom the redemption of the world would be carried out. In other words, the way Isaac or Jacob and the tribes understood it and acted on it was really at best a misunderstanding of the real purposes of God or, if given the benefit of the doubt, only a stage that awaited the intended fulfillment. The promise to inherit the world was truly achieved with the coming of Christ who is the true heir or "offspring" of Abraham.

The promise to Abraham could not be annulled by the law, but had to await Christ for fulfillment. Thus Christians need not interpret the ancient texts about the land in the same way as the ancient Israelites. God was not talking about a small strip of land that was being promised or given to a few tribes forever. Abraham, a man of faith who walked with God, was promised that all of humanity would be brought to God through another person, Jesus Christ. Although Abraham failed to engender peace and harmony in his two sons, Ishmael and Isaac, through Christ, God will bring peace and liberation to all of God's creation. The promise about inheriting a physical land becomes irrelevant. While Jews are free to interpret their scriptures according to their own faith tradition, given the presence of Christ, Christians cannot accept or sanction such an interpretation. On this note, N. T. Wright has written:

> The Land, like the Torah, was a temporary stage in the long purpose of the God of Abraham. It was not a bad thing now done away with, but a good and necessary thing now fulfilled in Christ and the Spirit. It is as though, in fact, the Land were a great advance metaphor for the design of God that his people should eventually bring the whole world into submission to his healing reign. God's whole purpose now goes beyond Jerusalem and the Land to the whole world.[18]

Ephesians 2:19-20—So then you are no longer strangers and aliens, but you are citizens with the saints and also members of the household of God, built upon the foundation of the apostles and prophets, with Christ Jesus himself as the cornerstone.

Viewing history from the vantage point of its fulfillment in Christ, we need to consider God's original purpose for humanity. In this sense, the letter to the Ephesians is an exemplary expression of New Testament theology, comparable to Jonah in the Old Testament.[19] According to Ephesians, God's purpose for creation goes back to eternity. From the foundation of the world God's purpose for history was to create one humanity in Christ. "With all wisdom and insight he has made known to us the mystery of his will, according to his good pleasure that he set forth in Christ, as a plan for the fullness of time, to gather up all things in him, things in heaven and things on earth" (Eph. 1:8b-10). In addition, God wanted "to make everyone see what is the plan of the mystery hidden for ages in God who created all things" (Eph. 3:9). What is this mystery? "In former generations this mystery was not made known to humankind, as it has now been revealed to his holy apostles and prophets by the Spirit: that is, the Gentiles have become fellow heirs, members of the same body, and sharers in the promise in Christ Jesus through the gospel" (Eph. 3:5-6). The writer adds, "This was in accordance with the eternal purpose that he has carried out in Christ Jesus our Lord . . ." (Eph. 3:11; see also Col. 1:26).

After all, the first few chapters of Genesis deal with one human family, reflecting God's initial or original purpose in creation. It took thousands of

The Bible and the Land 63

years, however, before some people began to comprehend the purposes of God for the world. Jonah's theology, though unheeded, was one attempt to reveal God's larger purpose for humanity—one God, one humanity, one world. Although the coming of Jesus Christ and the emergence of the church made this fully known, it is a goal difficult to achieve.

The historical development of people and religion in the Middle East indicates that three important factors were linked together in these ancient societies: the tribe/s, its god/s, and the geographical area of land where the tribe lived and moved. Most people lived in henotheistic societies, in which a tribe or group of tribes believed that their god or gods were supreme. This perspective is illustrated in Psalm 95, where the psalmist says, "For the LORD is a great God, and a great King above all gods" (Ps. 95:3). In some societies, the land was part of a covenant between the god(s) and the tribe(s): it belonged to the god/gods, and the king or the people were entrusted with it.

There was, however, a slowly developing movement within the Old Testament toward a more universal understanding of one God and God's relationship with all people rather than with one tribal group. Beginning with Amos, we find a theology that vacillated between nationalism and universalism, between bigotry and openness, exclusivity and inclusiveness. And although some learned during the exile that there is one creator God who is concerned about others (as expressed by some of the prophets), many held on to a narrow theology of God and a chosen people. Unfortunately, such a theology is the source of the conflict over Palestine today.

Alluding to an Old Testament reference to people and land, the Letter to the Ephesians makes another significant point.

> So then you are no longer strangers and aliens, but you are citizens with the saints and also members of the household of God, built upon the foundation of the apostles and prophets, with Christ Jesus himself as the cornerstone. In him the whole structure is joined together and grows into a holy temple in the Lord; in whom you also are built together spiritually into a dwelling place for God. (Eph. 2:19-22)

This passage is pregnant with Old Testament references to the land that become redundant in Christ. The first is the reference to "strangers and aliens," or those non-Israelites who had no right to the land, yet were supposed to be treated kindly and justly because God was their protector. After the exile, according to Ezekiel, the aliens were supposed to receive the same inheritance to the land by order of God.

> So you shall divide this land among you according to the tribes of Israel. You shall allot it as an inheritance for yourselves and for the aliens who reside among you and have begotten children among you. They shall be to you as citizens of Israel; with you they shall be allotted an inheritance among the tribes of Israel. In whatever tribe aliens

reside, there you shall assign them their inheritance, says the LORD God. (Ezek. 47:21-23)

This is one of the rare moments in the development of Old Testament theology where a new theology breaks in, a theology that includes non-Israelites and gives strangers and aliens the same inheritance of the land. Undoubtedly, the exile had a great impact on the Israelites and stretched their concept of God. These words of Ezekiel must have seemed a great contradiction of the many injunctions in the Torah against even making peace with the indigenous people of Canaan. The Torah leaves only two options in dealing with the indigenous people of the land: expulsion or annihilation. Ezekiel (whose theology can also be quite narrow) has radically changed course by writing that God demands an equal inheritance for all the residents in the land, regardless of their ethnic or racial background.

The writer of Ephesians goes a step beyond Ezekiel in revealing God's purpose when he says that in Christ there are no longer aliens or strangers because all have become members of the family of God. This is echoed by Paul in his letter to the Galatians, "[F]or in Christ Jesus you are all children of God through faith. . . . There is no longer Jew or Greek, there is no longer slave or free, there is no longer male and female; for all of you are one in Christ Jesus" (Gal. 3:26, 28). The coming of Jesus the Christ does not allow Christians to revert to a narrow theology of the land.

Acts 7:48—Yet the Most High does not dwell in houses made by human hands. Stephen's long speech before the council of elders in Acts is another New Testament expression of a new and revolutionary theology regarding the land. Stephen stresses that God's purpose is not centered on the land or a building. In fact, the ancient Israelites were closer to God when they wandered in the wilderness before they entered the "promised" land and before they worshiped in the temple. It is impossible to contain God in a temple or a land. God is universal and cannot be the private property of one nation.

What is the essence of these passages that relate to a theology of the land and the current state of the Palestinian/Israeli conflict? For Christians, a biblical theology of land must be grounded in the New Testament, and not in the Torah. The Torah, as well as the rest of the Old Testament, provides a background or a history and not a binding theology. Any Christian who looks primarily to the Old Testament for a theology of land (or any other theology) may be misled about God's purpose unless she or he looks to the New Testament for its fulfillment. Although the Old Testament indicates the development of an inclusive theology of God and land, its evolving movement toward inclusion is incomplete and at times vacillating. While it finds clear expression in the message of Jonah, it still continues to be largely overshadowed by a narrow and exclusive understanding.

Although some Jews might use the Hebrew scriptures to claim the land of Palestine as an eternal inheritance for them, Christians cannot accept this claim theologically. Anyone who accepts such a claim succumbs to a theology that reflects an incomplete development in the understanding of God and God's relationship with the world.

The conflict between Palestinians and Israelis is not due to a biblical promise or covenant that the Palestinians have not accepted. Instead it has to do with human greed for the land and the refusal to share the land with others. It has to do with the violation of human and political rights and with the flouting of international law and U.N. resolutions. There is no basis for granting divine legitimacy to the state of Israel. It is wrong to use the Bible, or parts of it, or God to justify the theft of land. A chasm exists between a Christian reading of the Old Testament regarding the land and a Zionist reading of it. As Christians, we must not succumb to Zionism, but stand firm and with boldness and courage read texts from our own faith tradition.

The message of the land in the New Testament is a message that has matured through many centuries and is fully expressed in the coming of Jesus Christ. It is a message about God, the loving creator of the whole world. There were ancient Israelites who recognized that the land where they were living belonged to God and that they were mere tenants and strangers on it (Lev. 25:23), but their understanding faded from view over time. In Christ we have received the full revelation of God: the whole world belongs to God. Therefore, we must acknowledge God's sovereignty and live as good stewards of the earth that God has graciously given to all people as an inheritance.

We also believe that through the incarnation when God's promise took on human flesh, the whole world has been sanctified. Therefore, we must strive to make it a better world for all the people who live on it, and especially for our brothers and sisters who are the poor and oppressed. We must work for just solutions to conflict, and we must strive to do so through nonviolent means. We must commit ourselves to the ministry of reconciliation because this is the mandate that we have received from God.

In Palestine, we must continue to stand for what is just and against all injustice that dehumanizes people. In our struggle for peace and reconciliation, we have found that the primary and paramount stage in the development of a just solution is the ending of the illegal occupation by Israel of the West Bank and the Gaza Strip. Yet, as Palestinian Christians, we are conscious that our supreme allegiance is to God. Indeed, God has placed us in the land of Palestine from time immemorial. Our ancestors have been members of that great cloud of witnesses who were among the early followers of Jesus Christ. Christ's call to us today is as fresh as it was then. We must follow faithfully in his footsteps and in the footsteps of forefathers and foremothers. Although we do not have an exclusive claim to it, we love this land. As Christopher Wright points out, "Paul might have seen no reason why Jews and Jewish Christians should not continue to feel an emotional and cultural bond with the land of their ancestors. But their *faith*, their *hope*, and their *worship* must no longer be localized there, but on Christ alone."[20] This is God's world and we stand firm in our witness. We strive to see God's kingdom, the reign of God, spread everywhere to engulf and fill the whole earth.

Finally, we must not despair as we see the immensity of evil, injustice, and oppression around us. We believe that ultimately God will triumph. We must continue to labor with God in establishing God's kingdom here on earth. We must continue in our study, interpretation, and application of biblical texts in our own context. As Jesus said, "Therefore, every scribe who has been trained for the kingdom of heaven is like the master of a household who brings out of his treasure what is new and what is old" (Matt. 15:32). There will always be things that are old that we cannot use and things that are new that are crucial to our everyday life. We must pray that in Christ we remain open to new understandings.

Blessed Lord, who caused all holy Scriptures to be written for our learning: Grant us so to hear them, read, mark, learn, and inwardly digest them, that we may embrace and ever hold fast the blessed hope of everlasting life, which you have given us in our Savior Jesus Christ; who lives and reigns with you and the Holy Spirit, one God, for ever and ever. Amen.[21]

Chapter 5

Jonah, the First Palestinian Liberation Theologian

Because I began reading the Bible as a boy long before I went to seminary to study theology, I was already grounded in knowledge of the Bible. My father trained me to read through the entire Old Testament once every year and the New Testament twice, as he used to do. He said it was central to my faith.

The book of Genesis and parts of Exodus were fun. Leviticus and Deuteronomy were boring, but part of the book of Numbers contained stories I enjoyed. The stories in the books of Joshua and Judges were interesting, but when I got to the prophets I had to plow through page after page of material that I did not enjoy and could not understand. In the midst of what appeared to me to be a barren land, I arrived at the oasis of Jonah, which I found refreshing. The book of Jonah comprises four short chapters. It is a beautiful story that is simple enough for children. On the surface, it did not seem as profound as Isaiah or Jeremiah, but I felt it was a story I could understand, a light narrative placed in the midst of a string of prophetic books that were wordy and often dull. My young imagination ran wild as I thought of Jonah in the middle of the storm at sea and in the belly of a whale.

As I grew older, the most difficult part of the story was the big fish. Was the story historically true? I was brought up to believe that if it is written in the Bible, it must be true and literally so. God is able to do anything, after all. I remember discussing this story with my friends. If any doubted the historicity of the story I would jump to the defense of the Bible. I felt this was my duty as a Christian. I still remember once reading a story in the newspaper that intimated that a person could actually survive in the belly of a whale. I clipped it and showed it to my friends to prove the credibility of the Bible. Many similar stories have circulated throughout history, especially among maritime people, of whales and sea monsters swallowing people and throwing them out alive; some people have seen those stories as evidence for the historicity of Jonah.

JONAH AND THE BOOK

Before turning to the heart of the message of Jonah, three points are crucial:

1. First, the gospels include two references to Jonah. In Matthew 12:38-41, Jesus uses the experience of Jonah in the belly of the big fish as a sign of his death and resurrection: "For just as Jonah was three days and three nights in the belly of the sea monster, so for three days and three nights the Son of Man will be in the heart of the earth." Then in Luke 11:29-32, Jesus refers to Jonah as leading the people of Nineveh to repentance: "For just as Jonah became a sign to the people of Nineveh, so the Son of Man will be to this generation. . . . The people of Nineveh will rise up at the judgment with this generation and condemn it, because they repented at the proclamation of Jonah." Apparently, the text of Jonah must have been popular at that time. As very few prophets are mentioned by name in the New Testament, it is significant that Jonah, a minor prophet, is among them.

2. Approximately three miles north of the city of Nazareth in Galilee is a small village called Al-mashhad; traditionally known as Gath-hepher, it is the home village of Jonah. In this Muslim village, villagers point to the tomb of the prophet Jonah who is known to them as Yunes or Nabi (prophet) Yunes. The village mosque is built over the tomb of Jonah.

It is fascinating to speculate why Jonah is then overlooked in the Gospel of John as a prophet from Galilee. When the chief priests and the Pharisees sent their men to apprehend Jesus (John 7:45-52) and they returned without him, the leaders were upset and asked, "Why did you not arrest him?" When a discussion ensued about the pros and cons of arresting Jesus, Nicodemus, one of the elders, pointed to the importance of interrogating Jesus before pronouncing any sentence against him. The Pharisees and the chief priests then replied, "Surely you are not also from Galilee, are you? Search and you will see that no prophet is to arise from Galilee" (John 7:52).

Although one ancient manuscript reads "*the* prophet will not come" from Galilee, greater textual evidence suggests that the passage should instead read "no prophet ever comes" from Galilee.[1] If this is the case and the text is referring to any prophet and not the messiah in particular, then one wonders if the Pharisees had forgotten that Jonah was also from Galilee. Or was Jonah so insignificant that even the chief priests and the Pharisees in Jerusalem had forgotten his origins?

3. Besides the book of Jonah, the only other mention in the Old Testament of the prophet Jonah is in 2 Kings.

In the fifteenth year of King Amaziah son of Joash of Judah, King Jeroboam son of Joash of Israel began to reign in Samaria; he reigned forty-one years. He did what was evil in the sight of the LORD; he did not depart from all the sins of Jeroboam son of Nebat, which he caused Israel to sin. He restored the border of Israel from Lebohamath as far as the Sea of the Arabah, according to the word of the LORD, the God of Israel, which he spoke by his servant Jonah son of Amittai, the prophet, who was from Gath-hepher. (14:23-25)

In other words, Jonah prophesied that Israel (the northern kingdom) would reconquer all of the territory that it had lost from the north down to the Dead Sea. When one combines this text with the book of Jonah, it is possible to surmise, as some scholars have, that the man Jonah must have been remembered as a patriotic prophet who represented a narrow Israelite jingoism.[2]

To drive his lesson home in an ingenious way, the writer of the book of Jonah chose a prophet with a nationalist streak as a main character and chose as a setting the nation of Assyria, which was remembered as the deadliest enemy of Israel. In 722 BCE it was Assyria that destroyed the northern kingdom of Israel where Jonah presumably lived. It is easy, therefore, to understand why a patriotic prophet like Jonah would refuse to go to any place in Assyria, let alone Nineveh, its capital, in order to preach a message of repentance that carried within it the possibility of God's mercy.

The writer shows how Jonah, an ardent nationalist who harbored deep contempt for the Assyrians, wished for their total destruction. As an Israelite nationalist, Jonah's deepest feelings against the Assyrians could be described by the words of the prophet Nahum; Nahum's entire book celebrates the fall and destruction of Nineveh and the Assyrian Empire around the end of the seventh century BCE. Nahum viewed the destruction of Nineveh as God's judgment against Israel's most oppressive enemy.[3] Instead of eagerly hoping for the repentance of the Ninevites, Jonah wished to celebrate its destruction. Jonah would have echoed the words of Nahum:

> Doomed is the lying and murderous city,
>   Full of wealth to be looted and plundered!
> Listen! The crack of the whip,
>   the rattle of wheels,
>   the gallop of horses,
>   the jolting of chariots!
> Horsemen charge,
>   swords flash, spears gleam!
> Corpses are piled high,
>   dead bodies without number—
>   Men stumble over them!
> Nineveh the whore is being punished.
> Attractive and full of deadly charms,
>   She enchanted nations and enslaved them.
> The LORD Almighty says,
> "I will punish you, Nineveh!
>   I will strip you naked and let the nations see you,
>   See you in all your shame.
> I will treat you with contempt
>   and cover you with filth.
>   People will stare at you in horror.

All who see you will shrink back.
>   They will say, 'Nineveh lies in ruins!
>   Who has any sympathy for her?
>   Who will want to comfort her?'" (Nahum 3:1-7,
>   Today's English Version)

THE STORY

The story begins with God asking Jonah to go to the city of Nineveh in order to preach against the evil ways of its people and to call them to repentance. Instead of going east toward Nineveh (in present-day Iraq), Jonah went west to Jaffa, the main seaport of Palestine, where he boarded a ship sailing to Spain. At sea a great storm raged, threatening everyone on board. The sailors tried to lighten the load by throwing things overboard, and everyone prayed to the gods but to no avail. Finally, the sailors cast lots to determine whose fault it was, and the lot fell on Jonah. He confessed that he had disobeyed his God and that the only way to survive the storm was to throw him into the sea. After deliberating, they did just that and the sea became calm.

God prepared a big fish to swallow Jonah. For three days, Jonah remained in the belly of the fish while praying for mercy and affirming his faith in God. At the end of that time, the fish spit Jonah up on the beach. God asked him once more to go to Nineveh and preach repentance. This time Jonah made the journey to Nineveh and proclaimed that unless the people repented in forty days God would destroy their city. The story reports that all people of Nineveh repented, from the king to the lowliest. They put on sackcloth, fasted, prayed, and turned away from their evil ways. God accepted their repentance, had mercy on them, and did not destroy the city.

When Jonah saw this, he was very angry and asked God to end his life. He said, "I knew that you are a patient and merciful God and you will change your mind and not punish those who repent, that is why I fled from your face and did not want to go to Nineveh." Angrily Jonah went to the outskirts of the city and sat there waiting to see what would happen.

God made a castor bean plant or a gourd to grow quickly to shade Jonah from the hot sun. Jonah was pleased with the shadow of the plant. Then the next day God sent a worm that ate the roots of the plant and it immediately withered away and died. When the hot sun struck Jonah's head he became very angry and again wished he were dead. Then God asked Jonah, "What right do you have to be angry about the plant?" Jonah replied, "I have every right to be angry—angry enough to die." God replied, "This plant grew up in one night and disappeared the next; you didn't make it grow—yet you feel sorry for it! How much more, then, should I have pity on Nineveh, that great city? After all, it has more than 120,000 innocent children in it, as well as many animals!" And then the story ends abruptly, leaving the reader and hearer to draw out its meaning.

The traditional interpretation of the book usually centers on Jonah's God-assigned mission to preach repentance to the people of Nineveh and the way in which Jonah disobeyed God and fled from God's face. But, as the psalmist says, it is impossible to hide from God:

> "Where can I go from your spirit?
>   Or where can I flee from your presence?
> If I ascend to heaven, you are there;
>   if I make my bed in Sheol, you are there.
> If I take the wings of the morning
>   and settle at the farthest limits of the sea,
> even there your hand shall lead me,
>   and your right hand shall hold me fast." (Ps. 139:7-10)

God had to teach Jonah the great lesson of obedience. After Jonah's experience in the belly of the whale, he obeyed God, journeyed to Nineveh, and successfully completed his mission. When the people of Nineveh repented, the Lord was merciful and spared the city from destruction. God is indeed merciful and loving toward all. God has "no pleasure in the death of anyone," and "if the wicked turn away from all their sins that they have committed and keep all [God's] statutes and do what is lawful and right, they shall surely live; they shall not die" (Ezek. 18:32, 21). The book of Jonah has served as a powerful resource for foreign missions, which is one way church tradition has regarded this story.

Modern biblical scholarship interprets the book of Jonah as an allegory, similar to the parables of Jesus in the New Testament. Its deeper meaning emphasizes God's care and concern for Jews, but equally for non-Jews—in other words, the inclusive nature of God. I interpreted the story of Jonah in this light in my first book.[4] Since then, after much more reflection, I understand the text in a more radical and revolutionary way. My experience has been like that of the blind man who cried out after being healed by Jesus—"I was blind but now I can see"—or, even more poignantly, the blind man whom Jesus healed in Bethsaida, a village on the northern shore of the Sea of Galilee. Jesus put saliva on his eyes, laid his hands on him, and then asked, "Can you see anything?" The blind man answered, "I can see people, but they look like trees, walking." When Jesus again put his hands on his eyes his full sight was restored and he was able to see everything clearly. I felt this same excitement and delight in sensing the power of the story of Jonah in the context of Old Testament theology and its relevance to the Palestine/Israel conflict today.

The story of Jonah can be a significant resource for peacemaking and for arriving at a solution to today's Middle East conflict. It also addresses basic theological problems that still face us today. For me, the writer of Jonah appears to be the first Palestinian liberation theologian, someone who has written the greatest book in the Old Testament. While Jonah truly reflects the genius and climax of Old Testament theology, its theology also approaches most closely that of the New Testament.

To the credit of the Hebrew religion the book was retained and included in the canon. With its deep critique of the narrow nationalism of the day, how did this book survive? Did Jews really understand the revolutionary nature of its message? Or was it a story that was so attractive that the tradition could not dispose of it?

Scholars tell us that the story was most likely not written in the eighth century BCE when the historical Jonah, the prophet of Gath-hepher, presumably lived. Due to its literary style and the extensive use of Aramaic words, many scholars suggest that the book was most likely written much later, probably toward the end of the fourth century BCE.[5] If that is the case, then it is probably one of the last, if not the last, books of the Old Testament to be written. If that is so, then it would not be unreasonable to think that it best articulates, in parable form, the theology that stands as the zenith of Old Testament theology.

Years ago I read G. Ernest Wright's book, *The Old Testament against Its Environment.*[6] Wright concludes that the Old Testament came to an end without a definite solution to the question of salvation (110-12). While that still holds, I believe that Jonah provides a theological climax that points where authentic theology should be going.

THE THEOLOGICAL MESSAGE OF JONAH

The gifted writer of Jonah begins with his life context, as a liberation theologian might do. He assesses the religious situation of his day (the signs of the times), and concludes that it has become desperate. If the author were writing between 400 and 200 BCE, he was in a position to assess the dramatic historical changes that affected his country,[7] starting with the devastation of the northern kingdom of Israel by the Assyrians (722 BCE) and followed by the destruction of the southern kingdom of Judah by the Babylonians (586 BCE). In both cases, most of the people who formed the elite were taken into exile. In fact, Jeremiah described those who were taken to exile as a basket of good figs and those who remained in the land as a basket of bad figs (Jer. 24).

Later, when the Persians came to power, the Jews could return to Palestine. Although some did so sporadically, many stayed. Those who returned found that Palestine had undergone significant demographic changes during their years of exile. There was a greater ethnic and racial mix of people living in the country. The work to rebuild the walls and restore the temple in Jerusalem did not proceed as smoothly as they had hoped as they encountered resistance. They tried to protect their community by turning inward. Nehemiah and Ezra emphasized the purity of Jewish blood, which led to conflicts with some people in the land, especially the Samaritans. Some leaders and prophets of the time began to use narrow, exclusive language. Instead of exercising greater tolerance, they became more legalistic and narrow-minded. On one hand, some voices did advocate universalism and a greater acceptance of diversity. On the other hand, competing voices expressed bigotry and a narrow nationalism. Prophesies of the judgment and subjugation of the nations competed with prophesies of a peaceful and voluntary pilgrimage of the nations to the mountain of Zion to learn God's word.

In essence, the writer of Jonah seems aware that some positive theological developments gained during the exile, including important expressions of universalism expressed by Second Isaiah and others, were being replaced by a narrow xenophobia within the community. Instead of a more universalistic view of openness to others, the propensity was for bigotry and racism.

In order to address this critical situation, Jonah's author chose as his main character the prophet Jonah, a believer in ethnic nationalism. The choice of a narrative, a story, seems a literary convenience for the author; it was a vehicle for addressing the people of his day with a revolutionary theology that critiqued their narrowness and called them to a genuine and authentic faith in God. The writer focused on three areas: a theology of God, a theology of the people of God, and a theology of land.

A Theology of God

In the book of Jonah, God is the one God, the creator of the world and the Lord of history: "the God of heaven, who made land and sea" (1:9). God is sovereign over and above all. God is not limited to one country or to any one place but everywhere; no one can hide from God. When God asked Jonah to go eastward to Mesopotamia, Jonah headed westward instead, thinking he could flee. But no matter where he might go, there was no place in the universe where Jonah could escape the presence of God. Jonah discovered that God was in the depths of the sea. Indeed, the sea and all that is in it as well as all of nature obey God, its creator and ruler. For Jonah, God is a "gracious God and merciful, slow to anger, and abounding in steadfast love" (4:2). God is a liberator and a savior of oppressed and sinful people, and a God of justice who demands just living from all people.

Some time ago, a Jewish woman settler was interviewed on Israeli television. She was asked, "Doesn't it bother you to be living on somebody else's land?" She answered simply in a straightforward manner, "If it doesn't bother God, why should it bother me?" The basic flaw in such an attitude is its limited conception of God. The settler's answer reduced God to a prejudiced and unfair god who is the prisoner of a particular group. However, when God takes the initiative to act in the world, God calls all people who do wrong and commit evil to repentance and seeks their salvation and liberation. God shows no partiality to any culture or nation or race or ethnic group. God's love encompasses all of humanity, not just the people of Jonah. God listens to anyone who turns to him in earnest prayer. In the story of Jonah, even the heathen sailors turned to God in prayer (1:16). The story of Jonah is a description of God that critiques any narrow or nationalist understanding.

A Theology of the People of God

The essence of the story of Jonah is that God's people are not restricted to Israel. Those who speak of God's chosen people and limit the chosen to Israel have an inadequate theology of the people of God. It is not sufficient to believe that God cares about and shows compassion for other "decent" people: God's love, care, and compassion extend even to the Assyrians, the deadliest enemies of Israel. It is important to recall that the destruction of the northern kingdom of Israel took place in 722 BCE at the hands of the Assyrians. From their power base in Nineveh, the capital, the Assyrians destroyed Israel and then captured the elite and scattered them throughout their empire. Samaria was completely devastated. The story of Jonah announces provocatively that even the ugly, savage, and brutal beasts called the Assyrians fall within the care and embrace of a God who shows concern for their well-being.

The author of Jonah tackled one of the most difficult issues that faced the community. In many ways his message intended to liberate God from the narrow theology of the day and liberate his people, the Israelites, from a tribal mentality that produced arrogance, haughtiness, and presumptuousness. They needed to wake up to the fact that God is the God of all and that they constitute but one small part of the people of God. God cannot be boxed in by such a closed and narrow theology.

A Theology of the Land

The theology of the land presented in the book of Jonah is as revolutionary as the book's theology of God and God's people. God's activity and presence are not limited to one land. God could not be confined or contained within the boundaries of the little land of Israel. Indeed, the exile stretched many people's concepts of the land. The psalmist notes that the exiles cried out, "How can we sing the LORD's song in a foreign land?" (Ps. 137:4). The prophet Jeremiah's response was that they should build homes in Babylon, get married, have children, and pray to God. He even commanded the exiles to pray for the leaders of Babylon so that all could live in peace (Jer. 29). God could no longer be perceived as a tribal god contained within a small geographic location. The psalmist celebrated God, the creator of the entire world: "The earth is the LORD's and all that is in it, the world, and those who live in it" (24:1). No matter where one lives, one is still in the presence of God. Some postexilic prophets did express such a universal view, and even before the exile the prophet Amos expressed God's concern for other lands and other people.

Are you not like the Ethiopians to me,
  O people of Israel? says the LORD.
Did I not bring Israel up from the land of Egypt,
  and the Philistines from Caphtor and the Arameans from
  Kir? (Amos 9:7)

In the contemporary conflict over the land, people must understand that a comprehensive biblical theology of land is inclusive rather than exclusive. The message of the two testaments together moves clearly toward a greater inclusiveness. Those who still hold to an exclusive view must be prodded forward. When appeals are made to international law or U.N. resolutions on behalf of the human and political rights of the Palestinians and the answer is that "We are interested in divine rights and not human rights," the reference is to an exclusive interpretation of the Bible that gives the Jewish people a higher and prior claim. Such a theology does not lend itself to peace and must be rejected on both exegetical and theological grounds.

WHAT IS THE RELEVANCE OF JONAH TO THE ISRAELI-PALESTINIAN CONFLICT?

The theological message of the book of Jonah is so profound that many people miss its impact due to the simplicity of the narrative. It seems so mundane and humorous at times that many might miss its radical implications. Its impact is similar to Jesus' use of parables: as Jesus reminded his disciples, "To you has been given the secret of the kingdom of God, but for those outside, everything comes in parables; in order that 'they may indeed look, but not perceive, and may indeed listen, but not understand; so that they may not turn again and be forgiven'" (Mark 4:11-12). The cynical ending of this quotation from Isaiah describes the apathy and the hardness of heart of people who have no interest in the challenge to repent and turn to God.

The story of Jonah is read each year on the day of Yom Kippur, the Day of Atonement, in Jewish synagogues throughout the world. Apparently, Jews perceive it as the only story in the Hebrew Bible in which God extends forgiveness to an entire community. Do Jews today understand the revolutionary nature of the story or its implications for modern-day Israel and its relationship with Palestinians? How do they understand and respond to its message today? Furthermore, how do Christian Zionists, most of whom are fundamentalists who surely know the story of Jonah, interpret and understand the story of Jonah? How can they read the text and still maintain a narrow theology of God, of the people of God and of the land?

The message of Jonah has great relevance for those of us who live in Israel-Palestine as it addresses the core religious and theological issues underlying the conflict. Many religious Jews continue to see themselves in a special relationship with God: they are God's chosen people, God belongs to them alone, and the entire land of Palestine is their eternal patrimony from God. They are unwilling to even entertain the idea of sharing the land with the Palestinians. In essence, what the author of the book of Jonah was battling against at the end of the fourth century BCE still constitutes the main theological problems we Palestinians face in the conflict today. In the name of an antiquated tribal theology that still insists on a special Jewish god, on the privileges of a special people of God, and on a unique Jewish right to the whole land of Palestine, the Palestinians are oppressed and dehumanized, and their claim to the land on which many families have lived for centuries is negated.

Christian Zionists who have placed the Jewish people at the center of God's plan for history have been complicit. Instead of seeing Christ at the center of God's purpose for history, they see Israel. Although secular Zionism brought about the founding of the state of Israel in 1948, a gradual shift began to take place after the 1967 war as the more conservative religious Jews grew in power. Ten years after the war they won the national election and assumed political leadership in Israel through the right-wing Likud party. This shift was the beginning of a new and special relationship between the government of Israel and fundamentalist Christians in the United States.

Today a strong alliance in the United States brings together Christian and Jewish Zionists with right-wing political conservatives in Washington. Together they dictate American foreign policy in the Middle East and lobby for the military, political, and financial supremacy of Israel. Some Christian fundamentalists ultimately have an anti-Jewish theological agenda in that they believe that at the end of history two-thirds of the Jews will be massacred and the remainder will be converted to the Christian faith. Obviously, Jews do not like this scenario, but they tolerate it in the face of a higher objective: they need the wholehearted support of these millions of fundamentalist Christians committed to the welfare of the state of Israel and the Jewish people, come what may.

Jewish religious extremists and Christian Zionists both advocate the expulsion and transfer of Palestinians from Palestine into Jordan. This form of ethnic cleansing through annihilation or expulsion of the indigenous people of the land is actually suggested in the Hebrew scriptures, as in the book of Numbers when God gives Moses instructions to pass along to the Israelites: "When you cross over the Jordan into the Land of Canaan, you shall drive out all the inhabitants of the land from before you, destroy all their figured stones, destroy all their cast images, and demolish all of their high places. You shall take possession of the land and settle in it, for I have given you the land to possess" (33:51-53).[8] As is amply clear, the theological underpinnings of such a position are exactly what the author of Jonah condemned centuries before. The message of Jonah is as relevant today as it was then.

For Christians, the theological message of Jonah can serve as a bridge that links the Old Testament with the New. The New Testament actually intensifies the basic message of Jonah. At every turn Jesus tried to shatter any exclusive and narrow concepts of God, the people of God, and the land. God is a God who loves and cares for all, a God who has sanctified the whole world through creation, incarnation, and redemption. It is wrong to restrict God's love. The beliefs of Christian and Jewish Zionists betray the nature, character, and knowledge of God.

The book of Jonah refutes and condemns all narrow, restrictive, or exclusive theologies. Although written over two thousand years ago, it is as relevant in its message today as it was then. Jonah's actual message is exciting and liberating and provides a fitting climax for Old Testament theology. Could it have possibly been written by a woman liberation theologian who cut across every religious taboo?[9] For us Palestinian Christians, it is our spiritual and theological life line. Thank God for Jonah!

Chapter 6

The Theology and Politics of Christian Zionism

I am certain the world will judge the Jewish state by how it will treat the Arabs [Palestinians].
  —Chaim Weizmann, first president of the state of Israel (1949-1952), quoted by President Carter[1]

Although we have seen how the Old and New Testaments together move toward a more inclusive understanding of God, the Bible continues to be used as the basis for exclusive theology. One of the most disturbing abuses of the Bible comes from the phenomenon of Christian Zionism. As mentioned in the previous chapter, Christian Zionism is an exclusive form of theology that constitutes a biblical and political menace to justice and peace for Palestinians and Israelis.

Such misuses and abuses are not new in the Christian church. In fact, throughout the last two thousand years, people and movements have twisted, manipulated, and misused a long list of topics found in the Bible. The Bible consists of many separate books, and by selectively picking different parts of text and tying them together, it is possible to prove almost anything.

Christians have justified wars and killing by using certain parts of the Old Testament, and passages from the New Testament have been used to silence women. We have also used the Bible to justify slavery, negating the humanity of many of our brothers and sisters. In the name of the Bible, we have killed, silenced, enslaved, and tortured. When people lack a theology of God whose very nature is love and liberation, it is easy to justify such acts. Some words of Jesus in the Gospel of John provide a good definition of a religious extremist: "Indeed, an hour is coming when those who kill you will think that by doing so they are offering worship to God" (John 16:2). By clinging to the literal meaning of any "holy" book instead of its spirit, it is relatively easy to become an extremist. As Paul said, "The letter kills, but the spirit gives life" (2 Cor. 3:6). Yet in many cases this is just what we have done: we have adhered to the letter (the surface) of scripture and missed the deeper meaning of the text. We have emphasized doctrine and dogma and ignored love. In the name of God we have condemned and persecuted our fellow human beings, even our fellow Christians. Again the words of Paul ring true, "If I have all faith, so as to remove mountains, but do not have love, I am nothing" (1 Cor. 13:2).

Christian Zionism is one of these tragic abuses that we must confront. It represents a primary challenge to an inclusive theology of love and justice. But Zionism must be confronted and challenged in a spirit of love so that we who challenge it do not become guilty of what we criticize. Although I believe that Christian Zionism is a modern-day heresy, care must be shown in challenging it. On the one hand, we must condemn the heresy as we have condemned the heresies of slavery or war, but at the same time we must reach out to Christian Zionists in a spirit of love. Many Christian Zionists may be simply unaware of the implications of their exclusive theology.

One principle is clear: any religion that does not promote justice, truth, peace, love, forgiveness, and reconciliation among people has lost its rudder and is undeserving of respect. At the same time, within every religion there are and always will be some who use their religion and its teachings as a destructive rather than a liberating force in the world. I would place Christian Zionists in this group.

In 2004, Sabeel conducted its Fifth International Conference in Jerusalem on the topic of "Challenging Christian Zionism." We had been considering addressing this topic for a number of years, but due to a lack of sufficient research we kept postponing it. It had not been taken seriously by the mainline churches and was regarded as theologically unsophisticated, biblically simplistic, and politically naive. It was dismissed as nonsensical, the province of extreme evangelical groups who did not have disciplined theological training.

Fortunately over the last few years a few Protestant scholars from different countries started to pay attention to this aberration known as Christian Zionism and to research its abuse of biblical texts and its potential threat to world peace. Included are Don Wagner, Gary Burge, and Timothy Weber from the United States; Goran Gunner of Sweden; Stephen Sizer and Colin Chapman from England, and a few others. In 2005 the Sabeel conference published the proceedings under the title of *Challenging Christian Zionism: Theology, Politics and the Israel-Palestine Conflict*[2]—to my knowledge, the first compendium on this topic.

Some people view the term "Christian Zionism" as a misnomer or a contradiction. They find a combination of these two words inconceivable. How can one be a Christian and a Zionist at the same time? How can one believe in Jesus Christ and his message of peace and nonviolence and at the same time believe in a Zionist ideology based on violence and terrorism that robs the Palestinians of their land and negates their political rights? Yet, whether we like it or not, millions of people in the world today see no contradiction between being a Christian and a Zionist.

Don Wagner has provided a very straightforward definition of this phenomenon: "Briefly stated, Christian Zionism is a movement within Protestant fundamentalism that understands the modern state of Israel as the fulfillment of Biblical prophecy and thus deserving of political, financial, and religious support."[3] Grace Halsell defines Christian Zionists as those who believe that "every act taken by Israel is orchestrated by God, and should be condoned, supported, and even praised by the rest of us."[4] Gary Burge describes Christian Zionism as a theology having six basic tenets:

1. The modern state of Israel as the fulfillment of God's covenant made with biblical Israel.
2. The "intrinsic link" between this covenant and Jewish ownership of the land of Israel.
3. The interpretation of prophetic books as predictors of modern events leading to the restoration of Israel and to Armageddon.
4. The importance of "blessing Israel" by defending its "theological or historical legitimacy."
5. A "two covenant" system in which the church is subordinate to the eventual restoration of Israel.
6. The restoration of Israel, as interpreted from Romans 9-11.[5]

Stephen Sizer's definition of Christian Zionism identifies seven basic tenets:

1. An ultraliteralist biblical hermeneutic especially in regard to Israel and Armageddon.
2. The Jews as God's chosen people, separate even from those "Gentiles" within the church.
3. The restoration to and occupation of Eretz Israel.
4. Jerusalem as the eternal, undivided, exclusively Jewish capital.
5. The rebuilding of the Jewish temple.
6. Antipathy toward Arabs and Palestinians.
7. A focus on premillennial Armageddon-oriented eschatology.[6]

Sizer adds another emphasis: "Christian Zionism is an exclusive theology that focuses on the Jews in the land rather than an inclusive theology that focuses on Jesus Christ, the Saviour of the world."[7]

The expression "Christian Zionists," therefore, refers to Christians who, due to a particular understanding and interpretation of the Bible, support the ingathering of Jews in Palestine. They believe that God has given the whole land of Palestine exclusively to the Jewish people. (Some Christian Zionists believe that Israel's land area should extend from the Nile to the Euphrates, according to Genesis 15:18.) The Jews must possess it all, govern it, and rebuild their temple in fulfillment of all the biblical prophecies. Such a fulfillment, they believe, will usher in the second coming of Christ, the defeat of evil, the end of history, and the establishment of God's righteous kingdom.

Historically Christian Zionism (though not known by this name originally) started with a theology based on a literal and uncritical study of the Bible. This was then translated into a political agenda that is now being implemented diligently and fervently in the land of Palestine. Christian Zionists believe that by standing with and supporting Israel, they are being faithful to God and are carrying out God's will for this world.

It is important to note that the term "Christian Zionism" can be misleading. Many terms have been used to describe these Christians but none has been totally satisfactory. Some call them "evangelicals," but not all evangelicals are Zionists.[8] In fact, many evangelical Christians oppose the doctrines and beliefs of Christian Zionism and resist it quite vociferously. Some use the term "conservative Christians" or "fundamentalist Christians" or "right-wing Christians," but again these terms are not precise because there are Christians who use these terms to describe themselves and yet they do not condone Israel's injustice against the Palestinians.

In addition, there are no exact numbers of Christian Zionists in the world. The United States alone has approximately 100 million evangelicals. Among those are a few million to approximately 30 million Christian Zionists. At the same time, the term "Christian Zionists" is used generally to describe millions of Christians in various countries who, as a result of their reading of the Bible, believe that they must support Israel even if it means hurting the Palestinians.

Finally, it is wrong to assume that Christian Zionism developed after the establishment of the state of Israel in 1948. In fact, Christian Zionism preceded the state of Israel by more than a century and actually antedated Jewish political Zionism by more than seventy years. In other words, Christian Zionists were active long before the establishment of the Zionist movement by Theodor Herzl in 1897, although they were not known by that name.

THE BASIC THEOLOGICAL QUESTION

Once the Bible became accessible in print to ordinary people after the sixteenth century, many Christians, mainly Protestants, both individuals and groups, began to study it. Many Bible readers began to ask a major question: when would the second coming of Christ take place so that the present evil world would end and the kingdom of God would be established? This biblical quest was enhanced in the nineteenth century by fiery evangelists and revivalists like D. L. Moody and others.

These Protestant and evangelical readers were earnest and sincere in their faith. They sought an answer to the question of the two white-robed men who appeared to the disciples after Christ's ascension: "Men of Galilee, why do you stand looking up toward heaven? This Jesus, who has been taken up from you into heaven, will come in the same way as you saw him go into heaven" (Acts 1:11). When is Jesus coming back, and what are the signs of his coming? Jesus had warned against such speculation:

But about that day or hour no one knows, neither the angels in heaven, nor the Son, but only the Father. Beware, keep alert, for you do not know when the time will come. It is like a man going on a journey, when he leaves home and puts his slaves in charge, each with his work, and commands the doorkeeper to be on the watch. Therefore, keep awake—for you do not know when the master of the house will come, in the evening, or at midnight, or at cockcrow, or at dawn or else he may find you asleep when he comes suddenly. And what I say to you I say to all: keep awake. (Mark 13:32-37)[9]

Such verses, however, did not prevent people from searching in the Bible for signs of Christ's coming. Many were convinced that they were living in the end times. The more they reflected on the words of the New Testament, the more they were sure that signs were ripe for the second coming of Christ.

During the last two hundred years a great body of material has been published by Christian Zionist leaders to explain their interpretation and reinterpretation of the Bible. They have treated the Bible as a jigsaw puzzle, moving pieces about continuously to fit their interpretation and the political changes endemic in the Israel-Palestine conflict.

Although there are variations in details and the order of historical events among the different groups of Christian Zionists, the following tenets represent some of their basic beliefs:

1. Christian Zionists cling to a literal belief in an inerrant and infallible Bible.
2. All biblical prophecies must be fulfilled literally.
3. The Jewish people are God's chosen people.
4. The land of Palestine is Eretz Yisrael (the land of Israel) and has been given by God to Jews exclusively as an eternal inheritance.
5. Jews must return to Palestine in fulfillment of biblical prophecies and establish their state (their kingdom).
6. Jerusalem belongs exclusively to the Jewish people.
7. The Jewish temple must be rebuilt in order to usher in the second coming of Christ.
8. The Rapture will remove Christian believers from the earth so they will avoid and escape the Great Tribulation.
9. The great battle of Armageddon will take place at the end of history when two-thirds of the Jewish people will be killed and the last third will accept Jesus as the true messiah.
10. Jesus will return to earth and reign for a thousand years. Then the forces of evil will rise up again and will be totally exterminated by Christ. A new heaven and a new earth will come into being and God's kingdom of righteousness will be established forever. The Jews will reign in their kingdom on earth and Christians will reign in their kingdom in heaven.

THE EARLY MAJOR PLAYERS

The beginnings of Christian Zionism were generally confined within groups of Protestant and evangelical Christians studying the Bible. However, from the outset such reflections and interpretations contained political implications. The development of this phenomenon is clear in the role played by three early Zionists.

John Nelson Darby (1800-1882)

Darby was an Irish Anglican priest who is considered by many to be the father of Christian Zionism. During an illness that left him bedridden for a long time, he spent his time studying the Bible, seeing a new and innovative way of interpreting its texts. As a result he recanted his ordination vows and began a new career of spreading his ideas that became known as "dispensationalism." He believed that the Bible presents seven historical dispensations, or periods of time, between the creation of the world and the end times. He believed that as the end of history is quickly approaching, the key and most essential players are the Jewish people. In order for God's plan for history to be accomplished, the Jewish people must return to Palestine and set up their kingdom. Such an event would set in motion the final scenarios that would lead to the end of the world with the second coming of Christ, the great battle of Armageddon, and the defeat of evil. Darby's dispensationalist theory continued to be refined, developed, and revised by his disciples. Darby propagated his ideas through eight trips to the United States, and his teachings, which became popular among evangelical and Protestant churches, influenced the beliefs of thousands of people.

Lord Shaftesbury (1801-1885)

Anthony Ashley Cooper, known as Lord Shaftesbury, was one of the first English politicians to translate religious or biblical convictions about the return of Jews to Palestine into political action. He believed that the return of Jews to Palestine was not only predicted in the Bible, but was important for the strategic interests of the British Empire.[10] In the 1840s, he lobbied Lord Palmerston, the British foreign secretary, to be God's instrument in carrying out the return of Jews to Palestine. On November 4, 1840, he put an ad in the London *Times* in which he wrote, "A memorandum has been addressed to the Protestant monarchs of Europe on the subject of the restoration of the Jewish people to the land of Palestine which secures that land to the descendants of Abraham."[11] Shaftesbury was the first to coin the phrase "A country without a nation for a nation without a country," which the Zionists later transposed to "A land of no people for a people with no land." This was more than fifty years before the rise of the Zionist movement.

William Blackstone (1841-1935)

William Blackstone was an evangelist from Chicago who was influenced by Darby's teachings on dispensationalism. In 1878, he published *Jesus Is Coming*, a book that became a best-seller and was translated into more than forty languages, including Arabic. Blackstone, like Shaftesbury, turned his biblical interpretations into a political campaign. In 1891, six years before the Zionist movement formed, he lobbied President Harrison to send American Jews to Palestine. Several years later, when Blackstone heard that Theodor Herzl was considering the possibility of setting up the Jewish state in countries of the world other than Palestine, he sent him a Bible, marking in red all the references that emphasized Palestine as the only venue to be considered because of its Jewish roots.

By the establishment of the Zionist movement in 1897, it was clear that Christian Zionist teachings were spreading among Protestants and evangelicals, especially in the United States, and that its doctrines were being widely disseminated. A great contributor to its spread was the Scofield Reference Bible that appeared in 1909. Through its footnotes and commentary, it promoted dispensationalism and indoctrinated thousands of people in Christian Zionism.

When the Zionist movement came into being, the three major Jewish religious organizations—the Orthodox, the Conservatives, and the Reform—rejected it as a heresy. While Jews at the time rejected it, Christian Zionists welcomed and embraced it.

IMPORTANT MILESTONES IN ZIONISM

Three important events in the history of the Zionist project confirmed for Christian Zionists that history was moving rapidly toward end times, toward the fulfillment of God's purpose.

The Balfour Declaration of 1917

Theodor Herzl, trying to find a European power to sponsor the Zionist project, approached the heads of Russia, Germany, Italy, and Turkey, as well as the pope, but to no avail. In 1917, twenty years after the establishment of the Zionist movement, the British government promised its sponsorship in the form of the Balfour Declaration. The first draft was submitted to the British government by the Zionist Organization in July 1917. It was then revised by the government into its final form and endorsed on November 2, 1917. Both Lloyd George, the prime minister, and Arthur James Balfour, the foreign secretary, had been brought up in evangelical homes and influenced by dispensationalism. Balfour wrote, "Zionism, be it right or wrong, good or bad, is rooted in age-long traditions, in present needs, in future hopes, of far profounder import than the desires or prejudices of the 700,000 Arabs who now inhabit that ancient land."[12] Balfour committed himself to the Zionist project at least in part because of his theological convictions. He had also written, "[History is] an instrument for carrying out the Divine purpose." Given the boost to the Zionists of the Balfour Declaration, the movement of history seemed to be on their side. After the end of World War I, Britain assumed the mandate over Palestine and proceeded to fulfill its promise to the Zionists.

The Establishment of the State of Israel in 1948

Christian Zionists were jubilant over the establishment of Israel as a state. They believed that a number of Old Testament prophecies had been fulfilled, especially Ezekiel 37. The events of 1948 reinvigorated their faith in "God's faithfulness" to the Jewish people. For many, the fulfillment of the purposes of God in history through the establishment of the Jewish state was more important than doing justice to the Palestinian people: the Palestinians became refugees as their towns and villages were destroyed by the Zionists.

The Occupation of the West Bank, East Jerusalem, and the Gaza Strip in June 1967

The occupation of East Jerusalem and the West Bank was final proof of the approaching end of history. Now that Jerusalem was under Israeli-Jewish rule, the Christian Zionist political agenda demanded the destruction of the Dome of the Rock on what Jews refer to as the Temple Mount, and the rebuilding of the temple in order to prepare for the second coming of Christ. When that did not happen, in 1969 an Australian Christian Zionist tried to enhance the process by setting Al-Aqsa Mosque ablaze.

Up to that point, contact between Christian Zionists and the government of Israel was relatively limited. After Likud, the right-wing party, won the Israeli elections in 1977 and Menahem Begin became prime minister, the relationship between the two became more concrete. Begin and Jerry Falwell, a prominent American Christian Zionist leader, enjoyed a special friendship. From then on, American Christian Zionists were always ready to support Israel politically in the U.S. Congress, economically through large financial support (including the building of settlements), and even militarily through the purchase of arms. Christian Zionists became a formidable ally of Israel, largely due to their biblical and theological understanding of the place of Israel in God's plan for history.

During their upbringing, U.S. presidents Jimmy Carter, Ronald Reagan, and Bill Clinton were also influenced by one form or another of Christian Zionism. In 1978, Jimmy Carter wrote, "The establishment of the nation of Israel is the fulfillment of biblical prophecy and the very essence of its fulfillment." Ronald Reagan said in 1984, "I turn back to the ancient prophets of the Old Testament. . . . I see signs foretelling Armageddon and I find myself wondering if we're the generation that is going to see that come about." In one of his speeches while still in office, President Clinton mentioned a conversation between him and his pastor in which his pastor told him, "Bill, if you abandon Israel, God will never forgive you." Such attitudes made these leaders sympathetic and sensitive to Israel's needs. Through the work of Christian Zionists in the Congress as well as that of AIPAC, the pro-Israel lobby, American foreign policy in the Middle East became increasingly pro-Israel.

CHRISTIAN AND JEWISH ZIONISTS UNITE

Since September 11, 2001, Jewish and Christian Zionists in the United States have begun to work much more closely together in spite of theological differences. The scenario of the end times that Christian Zionists espouse— that is, the massacre of two-thirds of the Jewish people in the battle of Armageddon and the conversion of the last third to the Christian faith—contains antisemitic and genocidal images with which one would expect Jewish people to be extremely uncomfortable. However, because of the Christian Zionists' unflinching love and support of Israel on the one hand, and their anti-Arab and anti-Islamic feelings on the other, some Jewish Zionists were willing to work together with them for the sake of the supremacy and domination of Israel.

A number of years ago, the Chicago branch of the Zionist Organization of America decided to honor Pat Robertson for his pro-Israeli broadcasts. A prominent American Jewish Zionist said, "I want their support now, and I don't care what their theology says down the line."[13]

Over the years some Jews have been concerned about the missionary activity of evangelicals in Israel, but because the evangelical support for Israel is so great and unflinching, they are willing to forget the few who are involved in proselytizing. Rabbi Daniel Lapin, president of the Jewish organization Toward Tradition, wrote at the beginning of July 2002 in a New York Jewish weekly that Jews owe a moral debt to the Christian religious right, and must hold back their criticism of antisemitic statements because they are all "devotedly pro-Israel."[14]

Besides the people who have been already mentioned, many Christian Zionist leaders especially in the United States are active in support of the state of Israel and in the demonization of Islam. They are active religiously and politically. Through regular TV programs as well as publications they propagate their religious and political bias. Some of them have produced books that have become best-sellers and have been read by millions of people. Some of the most well-known Christian Zionist names include the late Jerry Falwell, Pat Robertson, Hal Lindsay, Tim LaHaye, Ed McAteer, Tom Delay, Gary Bauer, and Franklin Graham.

Gary Bauer has a daily e-mail newsletter that goes out to 100,000 people.

After President Bush gave his speech on the Middle East in 2002 in which he mentioned the importance of the establishment of a Palestinian state, the Christian Right flooded the White House with e-mail messages. Bauer's message to the President was simple and direct: "Mr. President, we pray for you every day, I believe God wanted you to be president. If you abandon Israel, you will never get my vote again."[15]

A few years ago, Yigal Schleifer wrote an important article in the *Jerusalem Report* entitled "Newfound Friends."[16] He mentioned William Sutter, the executive director of Friends of Israel. The original name of this organization was Friends of Israel Gospel Ministries, but sometime later, the last two words were dropped off from the name. It has a 250,000-member mailing list that is kept abreast of what is going on in Israel. Sutter says, "Right now a prime motivation in our work as Zionists is to let Christians know the truth about what is happening in Israel."[17] Sutter was frank in saying that until recently, they had very little contact with Jewish groups, but now Jews are approaching them as never before. There are increasing ties that are embraced by the Jewish community. In fact, according to Esther Levens, the Jewish founder and president of the Kansas City–based National Unity Coalition for Israel, which partners some two hundred Christian organizations with projects in Israel, "There is certainly a much greater acceptance (in the Jewish community) of the Christian role in supporting Israel, a greater awareness of how important it is politically."[18]

To consolidate Christian Zionist support for Israel, Yehiel Eckstein, an Orthodox American rabbi who is president of the International Fellowship of Christians and Jews, started a Stand with Israel program. He has been successful in collecting millions of dollars from the evangelical community in the United States to assist in Jewish immigration and settlement building.

After September 11, 2001, there is a real sense among Christian Zionists that Western civilization—understood primarily as a heritage of Judeo-Christian values—is being challenged. In their view, the United States and Israel share this heritage and thus must stand together against that challenge. As an example, "The International Fellowship of Christians and Jews announced the launching of a Christian-led project called 'Stand for Israel' which hopes to mobilize some 100,000 churches to create an evangelical version of AIPAC. . . ."[19]

Janet Parshall, an evangelical radio host whose syndicated show reaches some 3.5 million Americans, gave a speech in April 2002 in a large pro-Israel rally in Washington. Her speech was more hawkish than what many Jewish Zionists would say: "We will not give up the Golan, we will never divide Jerusalem." She told the *Jerusalem Report* that "the number-one issue is where do you stand on Israel. You get that one right and we can start talking about where you stand on other issues." For Parshall any politician who believes in a land for peace formula would not pass her test.[20] Colin Chapman was right when he observed, "It is hard to think of another situation anywhere in the world where politics have come to be so closely bound up with religion, and where scriptures have such a profound effect on political action."[21]

It is important to emphasize the shift that has taken place in the United States. In the past, pro-Israel Jewish groups in the United States looked to liberal Democrats to support Israel. Today they are looking to conservative Republicans and the Christian right.

In 2006, John Hagee, an American Christian Zionist from San Antonio, Texas, started a new movement in the United States. His objective is to mobilize American support for Israel. The name of his new organization is Christians United for Israel (CUFI). It is equivalent to AIPAC and is rooted in American politics. An article in *Ha'aretz* entitled "The Gospel According to John" is a good summary of the politics of Christian Zionism in general and John Hagee in particular.[22] Hagee is clear in his intentions. He offers "support without any restriction, conditions, qualifications or apologies." John Hagee claims that he is acting out God's will. He would like to see the United States join Israel in destroying Iran's nuclear facility and the overthrow of the present Iranian regime. When he was asked about his view of Hamas, his response was very biblical. He opened his Bible and read from the King James Version, Deuteronomy 20:10-14:

> When thou comest nigh unto a city to fight against it, then proclaim peace unto it. And it shall be, if it make thee answer of peace, and open unto thee, then it shall be, that all the people that is found therein shall be tributaries unto thee, and they shall serve thee. And if it will make no peace with thee, but will make war against thee, then thou shalt besiege it: And when the LORD thy God hath delivered it into thine hands, thou shalt smite every male thereof with the edge of the sword: But the women, and the little ones, and the cattle, and all that is in the city, even all the spoil thereof, shalt thou take unto thyself; and thou shalt eat the spoil of thine enemies, which the LORD thy God hath given thee.

One can understand that in its historical context such passages reflect the ethics of war of many ancient people. The tragedy, however, is when people in the twenty-first century, like John Hagee, attribute these words to God and believe that they can be applied today. This is a very repulsive, dangerous, and heretical theology. It is a theology that is antithetical to the spirit and love of Christ and the New Testament.

CHALLENGING CHRISTIAN ZIONISM

This chapter has served as an introduction to the development and the problematic aspects of Christian Zionism. In concluding this brief introduction, I would like to leave the reader with the following points:[23]

1. Christian Zionism is a modern-day heresy that is based on misinterpre-

tation of the Bible. The dangers of Christian Zionism have not been taken seriously by the mainline churches all over the world. It has been perceived largely as the view of fundamentalist groups of Christians who are simplistic in their biblical interpretation and theologically naïve and unsophisticated. They have been seen as fringe groups who reject the scholarly approach to the Bible and cling to a literal interpretation, thus missing the essence of the biblical message. Therefore, there is a great need to help people understand who Christian Zionists are, what they believe, and how they impact the question of war and peace, especially in the Middle East today.

2. Many of us have assumed that Christian Zionism exists in fundamentalist and evangelical churches only. Upon closer observation, we have discovered that in reality Christian Zionism has permeated Christians within the mainline churches as well as among Catholics and Orthodox in various levels and forms. Christian Zionism often provides an unconscious framework for interpreting the Bible, especially when combined with a superficial reading. Our problem is not only with extremist evangelicals, it is with many goodhearted but badly informed Christians who need to be informed and educated.

3. Before the 1967 war, secular Zionism was the most dominant and influential expression of Jewish political Zionism in Israel. After the war a gradual shift took place from secular to religious political Zionism. By 1977, the right-wing coalition of political parties called Likud came to power with Menahem Begin as prime minister. Begin began to forge closer links between the right-wing government of Israel and the Christian right in the United States. Most of the Christians who belong to these groups are considered Christian Zionists. This collusion between right-wing Jews and the Christian religious right has served both sides. Although Jews do not believe in the Christian Zionist scenario of the end times, the close bond between them has brought advantages to Israel. Christian Zionists provide important financial, political, military, and moral support to Israel. In fact, they are perceived as the best friends Israel has. They give blind and uncritical support to Israel. They do not question Israel's unjust policies toward the Palestinians. From their faith perspective, they believe that, in order to be faithful to God, they must stand with Israel at all times.

4. It is important to differentiate between Jewish and Christian Zionism in this regard. Whether we agree or disagree with it, the goal of Jewish Zionism has been to bring Jews from their diaspora into Israel so that they might find a safe haven and live in security and peace. Yet frankly speaking, the goal of Christian Zionism, according to their scenario of the end times, is to bring the Jewish people to Israel in order to be annihilated or converted to the Christian faith. They believe that this would fulfill God's purposes in history and usher the second coming of Christ. The relationship between Jewish and Christian Zionists, therefore, reflects a tragic hypocrisy. Everyone is using the other for its own purposes. Perceived in this light, Christian Zionism is the worst antisemitism one can imagine.

5. For a number of years, it has been clear that Christian Zionists are close

to people in power in Washington, D.C. Because they represent a sizable voting power, they wield great influence. When one combines their influence with that of the neoconservatives and the pro-Israel lobby, AIPAC, their impact becomes formidable. In the political arena, they have been influencing American foreign policy in the Middle East, not for a just peace that takes into consideration the rights and well-being of both peoples—Israelis and Palestinians—but for whatever is in Israel's favor. In other words, they have sought to guarantee the continuation of Israel's domination and oppression of the Palestinian people.

6. Instead of interpreting the Bible theologically and within its own historical context, Christian Zionists manipulate the text to make it agree with their own political and religious presuppositions. Their interpretation seems to be "forcing God's hand" to do what they want rather than submitting themselves to understanding the deeper message of the Bible.[24] Christ has called us to be peacemakers (Matt. 5:9) and has entrusted us with the ministry of reconciliation (2 Cor. 5:18-20). This is the mandate that Christ has given us. We must be busy doing this rather than being engrossed in speculation about the end of the world. It is tragic to watch Christian Zionists show more interest in the end times rather than in the work of justice, peace, reconciliation, and healing between Palestinians and Israelis.

7. Christian Zionism promotes a violent theology of the end. They base this on selected passages from the Bible that are not in line with the authentic message and spirit of the scriptures. Indeed, many passages in the Bible talk about war and violence. But the biblical message is about peace, not war. It is about love, liberation, and forgiveness, not about violence, domination, and hate. A theology of Armageddon with its emphasis on a violent end of the world and the massacre of millions of people does not harmonize with God's nature as revealed to us in Christ. It is, therefore, a false and untenable theology of God that negates God's love for all people. That is why many of us see Christian Zionism as a biblical and theological aberration and fallacy and totally reject it. It does not take seriously God's love as shown to us in the suffering, death, and resurrection of Christ.

8. An integral part of Christian theology is to lift up the banner of justice and peace. It is a theology that calls people to act for truth and justice and to work for peace and reconciliation. It is a theology that resists empire and the forces of domination and calls people to a life of peace and service. God cannot be pleased when the forces of empire deny God's children their basic God-given rights to life and freedom. Faithfulness to God forces us to act on behalf of our fellow human beings who are oppressed and dehumanized.

9. It is worth noting that although Christian Zionists love and support Israel, one would have thought that their Christian compassion would compel them to equally support their Palestinian Christian brothers and sisters and be, at least, committed to alleviating their suffering and their struggle for human rights. This has never happened. Indeed, Christian Zionists do not relate to Palestinian Christians at all. Thousands of Christian Zionists visit Israel

every year. They do not go into the West Bank or visit people there. They do not even regard them as Christian. They see them as archaic, traditional, unconverted, and nominal Christians, an unwelcomed residue of the past.

10. Finally, in contrast to the position of Christian Zionists, most of the Catholic, Orthodox, mainline Anglican/Episcopal, Protestant, and a number of evangelical churches in the United States and outside of it have been very supportive of Arab Christians generally and Palestinian Christians particularly. Many churches and church-related organizations and institutions in the West have entered into close partnerships with Middle Eastern Christians and have supported them not only through various social, educational, medical, and religious projects but equally in the work of advocacy. For many years, these churches have taken a strong stand with the Palestinian people in their struggle against Israeli injustice and oppression. They have been consistent in calling for the end of Israel's illegal occupation of the West Bank including East Jerusalem and the Gaza Strip and the establishment of a Palestinian state.

Indeed, we have a great responsibility to inform and educate people around us on the dangers of Christian Zionism. Readers are encouraged to challenge their Christian Zionist neighbors with the truth and facts of what is happening in Palestine and how Christian Zionists are using the Bible as an instrument of oppression rather than as an instrument of liberation. Clergy are encouraged to study the phenomenon of Christian Zionism and to address it through their preaching and teaching. All of us must double our endeavors to seek and work for a just peace in Israel-Palestine.

The God whom we have come to know in Jesus Christ is not the god of Armageddon but the God of Golgotha—the God who loves us unconditionally and who is present with us in our pains and sorrows. This is the God who continues to call us to a loving service of our fellow human beings. Ultimately, it is only by the grace of God and the toil of dedicated people throughout the world that we can address not only the heretical teachings of Christian Zionism but all the evils and myths that are preventing us from achieving a just peace in Israel-Palestine so that Palestinians and Israelis can live as neighbors in peace and security and share the same land under God.

Chapter 7

Son of David or Suffering Servant?

Christian Zionism does not represent the first time that Christians have chosen a theology of violence and exclusion over one of justice, love, and inclusion. Ever since the Roman emperor Constantine issued the Edict of Milan in 313, the Christian community has made "un-Christian" choices. In the fourth century, although many people saw the advantages of reconciling church and empire, others saw the dangers. Christians began to deviate from the *sabeel* (or way) of Christ when we began to glorify military power, when we made peace with empire and became a part of it. We justified war and baptized it. We became merciless with our enemies and started to kill people in the name of God. We used the Bible to justify the actions of the empire and the church, reluctantly or not blessing the wars of the empire. Church fathers such as Augustine and Ambrose were instrumental in promoting this theology, and walking hand in hand empire and Christianity marched through history together.

As time went on, we placed war memorials in our churches and increased our military forces, spending enormous amounts of money developing the weapons of war and destruction. Our military power, which along with funding has increased exponentially, is devastating, and more people are killed in our wars as a result.[1] Instead of using our resources to eradicate poverty and in the service of education, health, and the well-being of people, we are using it for their destruction. Have we become mad?

Biblically and theologically we have abandoned the way of Christ. As we have justified our actions with the most violent texts of the Bible, especially those from the Old Testament, we have forgotten the spirit of the New Testament. We have destroyed the tree of life. There is no tree of life that will emerge from the war on Iraq, or the injustice in Palestine. Injustice and oppression have the upper hand because we refuse to implement the demands of justice and international law. We need to repent and turn to God and commit ourselves to the ministry with which we have been entrusted, that of reconciliation.

BIBLICAL CONTEXT

In the first century Jesus was born under the Roman occupation of his home country of Palestine. In fact, he lived all his life under the Roman

Empire and was killed in the end by the occupying forces. As a young man, Jesus, as well as many others of his generation, was attracted by different movements and groups within his society. Each had a basic philosophy about life and God, and each movement had its advocates and proponents as well as its adversaries and opponents.

For many centuries people in Palestine lived their entire lives under the Roman Empire. It was not a benevolent occupation. Any occupation is by nature oppressive because it refuses to grant people freedom and liberation. To a large extent, the options and choices that Jesus faced are still present in our different societies. While other comparisons are equally valid, our focus here compares the groups of Jesus' time with their counterparts in Palestine today.[2]

These groups arise from our basic nature as human beings and our propensity to relate to people of power, especially in situations when people live under foreign occupation. This was as true for the people of Jesus' time who lived under Roman occupation as it is for Palestinians today who live under Israeli occupation.

The Zealots

Without doubt, the group most attractive to many young people in Jesus' day was the Zealots.[3] They were the revolutionaries who believed that the only way to relate to the occupation of their country by the Romans was through armed struggle. The model of violent struggle was not foreign to them; there was a strong tradition for such action. The most recent paradigm was that of the Maccabees who had risen up against the Greek occupation of their country and won their independence. In Jesus' time, in their struggle against the Romans who had usurped control of their country, the Zealots used the tools of revolutionary violence, countering violence with violence. They believed that their god would fight with them in their righteous struggle.

There were some more extreme factions within the Zealot movement. The Sicarii not only killed their Roman enemies but were ready to assassinate any fellow Jews suspected of collaboration with the Romans. And all of this was done in the name of God.

Scholars tell us that it is likely that a number of the disciples of Jesus were Zealot revolutionaries.[4] They saw in him a leader who could command a great following and contribute to the liberation of the country. There are references in the Gospels that indicate such a temptation. John 6:15 offers an example: "When Jesus realized that they were about to come and take him by force to make him king, he withdrew again to the mountain by himself." Yet Jesus consistently rejected such temptations throughout his ministry, from the temptations of the devil's offer of the kingdoms of the world (Matt. 4:8-10; Luke 4:5-8) to the cries of the crowd to make Jesus king when he entered Jerusalem near the end of his life (John 12:12-19). The political language of these passages indicates that Jesus could have seized several opportunities to incite a mass insurrection against the Romans, which surely would have involved armed resistance.

The temptation to join the Zealots would have been very real because they shared many of the same goals as Jesus and his disciples. Jesus shared their concern for the poor and their passion for justice. They were both very committed to the cause, even to the point of death. Roman suspicion that Jesus was a Zealot certainly played a major role in his death.

Today in Palestine the equivalent to the Zealots are groups like Hamas and Al-jihad Al-Islami. They believe in revolutionary violence as the means to counteract Israeli state violence and force the Israeli army to end its occupation. They, too, are disciplined and committed to the cause of justice for their fellow Palestinians and have been very compassionate toward the poor and needy in their communities.

The Essenes

This group, disenchanted with the religious system of Jerusalem, left their towns and villages and withdrew into the desert. In the desert, they established communities, busied themselves in copying different texts of the Old Testament scriptures, and developed rules for the daily life of their communities. They avoided involvement with what went on outside.

The Essenes represented an escape from the reality of life, an escape that is still attractive to many people today. This option was open to Jesus: "He could have withdrawn from the tensions and conflicts of the urban center where government and commerce constantly polluted even the most well-intentioned sons and daughters of the law; he could have sought out a place where he could be pure and perfectly faithful."[5] Such an approach of escape or isolation can take various forms. People do not have to be enclosed within a monastery to live this way, although some do. Some people emigrate from the area of conflict, leaving everything behind. Others escape by totally withdrawing even within their community, living in isolation from the daily affairs of life.

The Herodians and Sadducees

These were the pragmatists and realists. The Herodians supported King Herod, believing it was better to give allegiance to the king who was closer to kin than the alien Romans. The wealthy and conservative Sadducees controlled the temple in Jerusalem and benefited immensely from it. They stayed on good terms with the people of power to expedite and facilitate daily solutions to contentious problems. They accepted the political situation in Palestine and to a large extent collaborated with it. They believed that since they could not change the occupation of their country, they might as well not only live with it but make the best of it. They made sure that worship in the temple was conducted properly and that nothing should disturb it.

In the conflict over Palestine, many Palestinians have arrived at such realism, accepting the Israeli occupation of their country. In order to advance their business activities or for reasons of prestige, they have allowed themselves to get close to the powers and cooperated with the occupation. In some cases this pragmatism has taken on a more sinister aspect, becoming blatant collaboration.

The Pharisees

These were religious fanatics who adhered to the letter of the law. Although the word "pharisee" means separatist, they lived among the people in the village and urban centers of the land, yet separated themselves from anything that in their opinion would defile them. They prided themselves on keeping the purity of the law in meticulous detail as regards eating and drinking, keeping the Sabbath, and many other aspects of daily life. Jesus criticized them for paying attention to the minute details of the law yet forgetting the more important issues of life such as justice, faith, and mercy (see Matt. 23).

The Pharisees comprise a sizable segment of our communities; regardless of the political environment, they continue to practice the rituals and ceremonies of their religion while ignoring the "weightier matters" of justice and love (Matt. 23:23; Luke 11:42). Many cling to the observance of the laws and regulations of religion because they have defined religion in terms of strict adherence to the teachings of the church, mosque, or synagogue regarding worship, fasting, feast days, and so on.

THE NEW WAY OF JESUS

These four options that confronted Jesus confront us today. People are attracted to one or another of them. Many societies offer similar options or philosophies of life that appeal to our human nature. We are always challenged by the "righteous" violence of revolutions, or by escapism and isolationism, or by pragmatism and realism, or by established and popular religion. Each has its attraction, and Jesus must have realized that.

But Jesus chose another way, a way that draws on the best that these paradigms can offer and yet takes religion and faith to a deeper dimension. This is the way of faithfulness to God. Jesus rejected the way of violent revolution and refused to walk the way of collaboration. He would not accept the option to escape life and be uninvolved, and he saw the pitfalls of superficial religiosity where observance and rituals replace morality and authentic relationship with God.

What is the way of Jesus? It is the way of allegiance to God's kingdom. The way of Jesus is (1) to stand for justice and truth without picking up the sword—that is, to resist evil without using evil methods; (2) to rise above the ways of the world without abandoning involvement and commitment to the poor and oppressed; (3) to seek the humanity of the oppressor without losing integrity by appeasement or collaboration; and (4) to love and worship God without adhering to a strict and closed religion.

Jesus presented God as a loving father/mother who loves and cares for all people equally, a God who is just and merciful. He called into being a distinct community whose basic rule of life is love: the love of God, God's unconditional love of humans, and the inclusive love of neighbor that denies boundaries. He inspired his disciples to walk a path of nonviolence and to accept God's will and rule over their life. Jesus asked his community to be salt and light to all those around them. He modeled his understanding of nonviolence as a path that must be followed even if it leads to suffering and death. And Jesus showed that a person can, at one and the same time, live in the world, in the midst of the community and serve it and heal it, without conforming to the ways of the world. This is the *sabeel* of Jesus.

Could Jesus have looked at the availability of these four ways of life and decided not to choose any of them? He must have seen that none of them agreed with the heart of the faith tradition. He must have felt that while each contained some attractive features, on the whole they strayed from the essence of the faith.

He did not choose the way of armed struggle, which later ended disastrously for the Jewish people with the destruction of Jerusalem by the Romans in 70 CE. He did not choose collaboration with the occupying forces, which was a life of deception and destructive to one's soul. He did not choose escape into the desert, but sought involvement with the poor and wretched of his time. And while Jesus instructed his followers in prayer, he did not choose religiosity, often used to disguise a lack of faith. He chose a different way.

Perhaps Jesus looked back at his tradition of faith. The exile, several hundred years earlier, did not end the suffering and misery of his people. The strong empires of Assyria, Babylonia, and Persia had been replaced by even greater Greek and Roman empires. The people still longed for liberation. Such a passion for freedom seems natural. People talked about their religious tradition that referred to the coming of a messiah who would provide redemption and liberation. The fervor for the coming of such a person must be understood against the conditions of their miserable existence. Jesus surely must have been aware of the many so-called messiahs who had come and gone and yet no liberation had been achieved.

TWO MESSIANIC STRANDS

There were two messianic strands within the Jewish tradition. The first and more attractive and popular one was that of a warrior king, a messiah who would come from the lineage of King David to free his people. Only a king like David could bring justice and peace to the nation (Isa. 9:6-7; 11:1; Jer. 23:5-8; Ezek. 37:24-28). This implied armed struggle. Many people's enthusiasm was based on this religious consciousness: through it they could express their faithfulness to God. The people frequently invoked this popular tradition, and they anticipated its fulfillment in their time.

It is clear in the Gospels that the Davidic strand was strong not only among Jews but also among gentiles. Both the Matthean and Lukan genealogies refer to the fact that Jesus was of the line of David. In Matthew, the emphasis is very clear. The genealogy begins with the words, "An account of the genealogy of Jesus the Messiah, the son of David, the son of Abraham" (Matt. 1:1). The angel addressed Joseph as "son of David" (Matt. 2:20). Blind Bartimaeus called Jesus the son of David (Mark 10:47; see also Matt. 20:30-31). The Canaanite woman from the region of Tyre and Sidon, a gentile, also called Jesus the son of David. According to Matthew, the people who saw his healing and teaching wondered if Jesus was the son of David (12:23). This was a messianic title that clearly implied a royal ancestry and legitimate leadership that could muster an army and employ military force to bring salvation and liberation to those oppressed under Roman rule.

A second strand less familiar, less attractive, and less popular developed a few hundred years before the time of Jesus. It can even be said that it seemed to critique the older and more popular "son of David" strand. This second strand was expressed in the poems of the Suffering Servant (Isa. 42:1-9; 49:1-7; 50:4-9; 52:13-53:12). While some of these words refer to the entire Israelite community, these songs, especially the last one, are also highly personalized as the prophet seems to refer to one chosen individual. Salvation and liberation will be won not through military means but through the servant who suffers on behalf of others. Such an idea was foreign and incomprehensible to the people. The prophet whom we call Second Isaiah was reflecting on the suffering of his people as a result of the repeated tragedies that befell them in the destruction of the kingdoms of both Israel and Judah and resulted in the dispersion and exile of many Israelites. Yet the prophet also expresses new nonviolent, revolutionary thinking about the meaning of suffering: liberation could be won through the sacrificial offering of oneself. Moreover, there is a universal dimension for the mission of the servant that goes beyond the Israelite community.[6]

Second Isaiah offers a new theological reflection on the meaning of suffering and its salvific benefits. In Isaiah 53:4-9 the servant takes the suffering of the people on himself. He dies for their sins and through his suffering brings them healing. This was a new and unexpected role for the messiah.

However, if, as scholar George Mendenhall believes, the book of Job was also written around this time, the writer of Job may also be reflecting on the tragedy of the exile and the destruction of Jerusalem. He also reflects on the meaning of the suffering of the people, concluding that there is a need to discover deeper meaning in a direct encounter with God and not in "traditional doctrines and teachings."[7]

Most people were attracted to the first strand—a triumphant son of David. Their natural inclination was to seek destruction of the enemy, revenge the wrong, and humiliate their opponents. It is not surprising that in a tradition of military leaders and warrior kings, the people preferred the messiah to be a warrior king in the line of King David who would usher in an era of unending peace. It has often been pointed out that "Davidic sonship . . . is so clearly part of the messianic profile in Jewish tradition, going back to 2 Samuel 7."[8]

Furthermore, although Luke refers to Jesus as coming from David's ancestry, he emphasizes the Suffering Servant strand. One of the clearest references is found in Luke 24 when Jesus meets two disciples on the way to Emmaus. In a very clear way the risen Christ says to them that the Messiah must suffer. "Was it not necessary that the Messiah should suffer these things and then enter into his glory?" (Luke 24:26). This is repeated in verses 46-48 when we read, "Then he opened their minds to understand the scriptures, and he said to them, 'Thus it is written, that the Messiah is to suffer and to rise from the dead on the third day, and that repentance and forgiveness of sins is to be proclaimed in his name to all nations, beginning from Jerusalem. You are witnesses of these things.' " In other words, Jesus was reading the tradition from beginning to end, "from Moses and all the prophets" (vv. 26-27, 45-46), not from a Davidic strand but from the suffering servant strand. Does this mean that Jesus was questioning the Davidic warrior strand of the tradition?

The three Synoptic Gospels mention an argument between Jesus and the scribes and Pharisees regarding the relationship between the Messiah and David. Jesus points out that the Messiah cannot be David's son because David calls him "lord." "How can the scribes say that the Messiah is the son of David? David himself, by the Holy Spirit, declared, 'The Lord said to my Lord, Sit at my right hand until I put your enemies under your feet' " (Mark 12:35-37; Matt. 22:41-46; Luke 20:41-44). Does this mean that Jesus was calling into question or even rejecting the Davidic warrior strand of the tradition?

Another important reference that shows Jesus educating his disciples in a different way is found in Mark 8:27-36. Jesus and the disciples were in the vicinity of Caesarea Philippi. Jesus asked them, "Who do people say that I am?" They told him that some said he was John the Baptist, Elijah, or one of the prophets. Then Jesus directed the question to them and said, "But who do you say that I am?" Peter answered, "You are the Christ (Messiah)." Jesus warned them not to tell anyone.

Then the writer Mark adds that Jesus began to teach them that the Son of Man must suffer much and be rejected and be killed. In other words, he was redefining the messiah tradition in a new way and a new light. He was calling into question the traditional concepts. "Then he began to teach them that the Son of Man must undergo great suffering, and be rejected by the elders . . . and be killed . . ." (Mark 8:31). When Peter tried to remind Jesus of the warrior-king tradition, Jesus said to him, "Get behind me Satan! For you are setting your mind not on divine things but on human things" (Mark 8:33).

According to the book of Acts, the early church combined the two strands of the tradition as being fulfilled in the coming of Jesus the Christ, the Messiah. On the one hand, they wanted to show that Jesus was the Messiah. He came from the line and lineage of David the king. He fulfilled all the prophecies. On the other hand, they wanted to show that he suffered death on the cross. He was the Suffering Servant. Yet although he was the son of David, he rejected David's military way. Liberation was not going to be won through wars but through suffering on the cross.

Some of the passages that reflect this approach are as follows:

Acts 2:22-36	Jesus is superior to David because David calls him "my Lord" and prophesies that Jesus will be resurrected.
Acts 3:18	"In this way God fulfilled what he had foretold through all the prophets, that his Messiah would suffer. . . ."
Acts 8:26-40	The story of the Ethiopian eunuch is a direct application of Isaiah 53 to the suffering of Jesus.
Acts 13:23-31	"Of this man's [David's] posterity God has brought to Israel a Saviour, Jesus, as he promised. . . ."
Acts 17:3	Paul in the synagogue is "explaining and proving that it was necessary for the Messiah to suffer and to rise from the dead, and saying, 'This is the Messiah, Jesus whom I am proclaiming to you.'"
Acts 26:22-23	"I stand here, testifying to both small and great, saying nothing but what the prophets and Moses said would take place: that the Messiah must suffer, and that, by being the first to rise from the dead, he would proclaim light both to our people and to the Gentiles."

It is easy to argue that when the two strands are joined together they leave the reader with contradictory messages. In many ways they cannot be reconciled. Jesus is identified as the Suffering Servant and the son of David at one and the same time. Before Christ's death, they were two separate strands. After Christ's suffering, crucifixion, and death, one cannot match them together. It is impossible to think of King David, the warrior king who, according to the Old Testament tradition, was not even allowed to build the temple because his hands shed blood, and match it with the image of a servant who was going to suffer and offer himself on behalf of the people. According to 1 Chronicles 28:3, God tells David, "You shall not build a house for my name, for you are a warrior and have shed blood." David is a "reformed terrorist," a man of violence, while the "Temple on Mount Zion was to be, from its very inception, a palace of peace."[9]

It is clear from the history of the early church that the strand of the Suffering Servant became the most prominent with Christ's followers. It was not the David strand. Indeed, the church saw Jesus fulfilling the prophecies as coming from the lineage of David as well as assuming the role of the Suffering Servant. It was important for the early church to emphasize that Jesus was from the ancestry of David. He came from that royal line and in fulfillment of God's promises. Yet Jesus did not adopt David's way at all. He died on the cross. His suffering, death, and resurrection were in fulfillment of the role of the Suffering Servant and not that of David.

The First Three Hundred Years

For three hundred years, the early believers lived in the shadow of the cross and its meaning. They were persecuted first by the local authorities and eventually by the empire but never considered taking up arms during this time. They were convinced that the way of Christ was the way of the cross. Discipleship for them meant following in the footsteps of Christ, and this could include the way of suffering. "For to this you have been called, because Christ also suffered for you, leaving you an example, so that you should follow in his steps" (1 Pet. 2:21). They were sure that in order to be faithful disciples they must bear the suffering of the present moment even if it led them to death without taking up the sword. Moreover, because of their faith in Christ's resurrection, they were sure that if they died they would be with Jesus Christ and would share in his glory. This can be substantiated over and over again by later New Testament writings like that of 1 Peter as well as those of the early church fathers.

In other words, the early church rejected the Davidic strand. Yet this strand continued to be pursued by the Zealots, and eventually they led their people to another major catastrophe in 70 CE. For the Christians, however, the way of Christ, the way of faithful witness, the way of suffering, proved to be more enduring. In fact, within two centuries, the Christian movement that started with a few weak individuals was able to overwhelm and impact many people inside and outside the Roman Empire.

The Church Makes Peace with Empire

Although it took over two hundred years for the Christian movement to spread throughout the vast domains of the empire and beyond, due to external political changes and internal theological controversies, the church was unable to keep the original flame going. In many ways, the empire co-opted the church and its leaders. So long as the church maintained its life outside the direct influence of the empire, it was able, to a large extent, to maintain its faithfulness and integrity to its founder. It was living and following the footsteps of the Suffering Servant and was indeed a leavening influence in the community. The believers lived in loyalty to Christ as Lord and practiced servanthood and sharing in their daily living. Once the empire co-opted the church, it was not strong enough to convert the empire. In other words, the world went on as if Christ had not even come. Christ was co-opted by the powers and used in the service of the state. Jesus Christ was militarized.

We cannot continue to remain complicit. We must reject and condemn the church's adoption of the warrior messiah image because it is a deviation from the gospel of Christ. We need to rediscover the power of the Suffering Servant. Unfortunately, the church chose to make peace with empire and bless its ways. In essence it went back to the Old Testament concept of the Davidic strand; the dormant Davidic strand that Jesus and the early church rejected was picked up again by the Constantinian church in the fourth century. Tragically, the suffering servant role was suppressed as the church and empire joined forces. Although one can point to the pros and cons in any historical development, the problem remains that the church was unable, by and large, to develop the meaning of discipleship in line with the authentic way of Christ and find power in the cross and vicarious suffering.

With the Davidic strand leading the way, it was easy for church leaders to justify wars and violence again. This has been our history throughout the last seventeen hundred years. We have been stuck with David and what he represents. The David strand is closer to the fallen and broken human nature that has not been redeemed and regenerated by the way of Jesus Christ. It is the way in which military power is glorified and magnified. In today's world, where violence and warfare have increased, it is important for us as Christians to review this history and recognize where we have fallen. We must consciously try to rediscover the way of Christ.

Contemporary Relevance

The dichotomy between the two strands of messianic prophecy has come home to me more forcefully because I have personally seen both the futility of the military power of modern Israel, power used to perpetuate the injustices which Israel has created, and on the other hand the futility of the power of violence that has been adopted by extremist Palestinians. When I look at it all in light of the historical events of the first century, I can clearly see the options for responding. Three groups become obvious. Two are opposed to one another: the power of the Roman Empire with its strong military machinery versus the power of the Zealots' revolutionaries. Both are forces of destruction. One represents the power of empire and the other represents the power of extremists and of guerrilla warfare and violent resistance. Both were based on violence and counterviolence. I can also see, however, a third group that walked a different way. It was a movement among people who, on the one hand, were rejecting the power of empire because they considered it false and transitory, and on the other hand, were rejecting the power of armed resistance that was doomed to destruction. Instead, they were lifting up the banner of the slain lamb—the Suffering Servant through whom they are able to conquer.[10]

According to the book of Revelation, Christians can conquer by two ways: "by the blood of the slain lamb and by the word of their testimony" (12:11). According to Barbara Rossing, "To follow the model of Jesus means that we conquer not by attacking anyone or shedding others' blood—but rather by identifying with Jesus' own blood that was shed when he was crucified by the Romans. . . . Revelation does not advocate the use of violence or bloodshed. Revelation is more a book about terror *defeated* than terror inflicted."[11] Christians can conquer injustice today by the same two methods. In the footsteps of Christ, they can endure suffering rather than inflicting it. At the same time, they can maintain a strong witness for truth, justice, and peace.

In many ways, the political options of these first-century groups continue to live with us. We are faced today with empire and what it stands for. We live with that violence and terrorism that resists empire. But there is another group that refuses to go the way of empire or the way of violent resistance that are both represented in our image of the Davidic strand. These are the followers of Christ who are inspired by his teachings and are willing to walk the way of service and sacrifice, the way of suffering love, to bring healing for their fellow human beings.

Today, in the twenty-first century, Palestinian Christians must also decide which biblical strand of Messianism they will follow. But our strategy cannot be decided by simple references to proof texts that can be taken out of context. We must return, instead, to a paradigmatic understanding of the New Testament.[12] The New Testament was written for the communities of faith that were suffering. The idea that Christ suffered was still very real. They did not experience Christ as a warrior. The letter of 1 Peter gives us a picture of the early church and its life in the world. The writer encourages the readers to persist in their faith even in the midst of suffering. This is why we Palestinian Christians have rejected the way of suicide bombings—that is, the way of violence. The way of violence is the way of empire. We instead have chosen the way of the Suffering Servant. This is also the way chosen by many others, Palestinian or not, Christian or not, perhaps best illustrated in recent times by the tragic martyrdom of human rights activist Rachel Corrie, who gave her life in service to others.[13]

It thus should not surprise us that Christian Zionism arose first in the British Empire and then flourished in the context of the new American Empire in the latter half of the twentieth century. Christian Zionists have deferred the image of a warrior messiah to the last days, placing Christ in this role and thereby changing his basic character. For them, Christ is no longer a Suffering Servant at all but one who will return with wrath and anger to destroy his enemies. Such an approach typically fails to notice the importance of the sword coming from Christ's *mouth* (Rev. 19:15). The way Jesus makes war is significant: "Jesus makes war not with a sword of battle but 'by the sword of his mouth.' The word is Jesus' only weapon."[14]

Today we see in a stark way within the Jewish community a repeat of what the Christians have done in the past. After the suffering of the Holocaust, they have chosen the way of empire. They thought that the Western powers represented the more advanced cultures and progress. They chose to imitate them. They went the way of Christendom. They live today in their own Jewishdom. They established the state of Israel and made it a nuclear nation and the sixth strongest military power in the world. They abandoned their religious tradition, with its strong stand against empire, again.

Today, many Palestinian Christians are the ones who are lifting up the banner of the Suffering Servant. These Christians are the true inheritors of the religious tradition of the Christian faith from both the Old Testament and the New Testament. We say the way of empire is not the way of Christ. It must be rejected. The way of Christ is the way of nonviolence and suffering love.

Chapter 8

Saddam, Sodom, and the Cross

The worst evils are done by those who justify destruction for redemptive purposes.
    —Rosemary Radford Ruether[1]

Many people in the West pronounce Saddam Hussein's name incorrectly. Instead of enunciating it as "*Sud*-dam" with an emphasis on the first syllable, they often pronounce it as "Sodom," thus leaving the conscious or unconscious possibility, especially for those who know their Bible, of associating Saddam with Sodom—an ancient Canaanite city known for its wickedness.[2]

Saddam's name, which in Arabic means "the confronter," the one who confronts and even shocks, is not a common name in the Palestine-Israel region. It is interesting, though, that after the beginning of the Gulf Crisis in 1990 and the occupation of Kuwait by Iraq, many people on the West Bank and especially in the Gaza Strip chose to name their sons "Saddam." At the time, the Israeli occupation authorities, due to their fear and revulsion of Saddam, refused to issue birth certificates to hundreds of newborn Palestinian males whose parents wished to name them Saddam. Parents had to choose other names. At the time, Saddam was seen as a symbol of power and defiance, and thought to be the only Arab leader with the military power to defy the West. He was perceived as capable of liberating the Arabs from Western imperialism and the Palestinians from Israel's colonialism. However, many Palestinians could not justify such a blatant occupation of another country when they were fighting the Israeli occupation of their own country. They were aware that to justify the occupation of Kuwait was to justify the occupation of the West Bank and the Gaza Strip.

In the end, the occupation of Kuwait did provide a significant comparison with the Israeli occupation. Many Palestinians, while rejecting occupation of any kind, did support a linkage between the withdrawal of Iraq from Kuwait and the withdrawal of Israel from Palestine. When Saddam was pressured to pull out from Kuwait, he responded that he would withdraw in compliance with a U.N. resolution, provided that Israel would pull out from the Palestinian territories in accordance with similar U.N. resolutions. He exposed the hypocrisy of the West, especially the United States, calling attention to some essential similarities between the two occupations. However, not all

Arabs liked the comparison, especially the Kuwaitis. Consequently, relations between Palestinians and Kuwait broke down, leading to the displacement of about three hundred thousand to four hundred thousand Palestinians and their families from Kuwait with terrible financial losses.[3]

THE FIRST *INTIFADA*

For many Palestinians the Gulf Crisis was a stimulus for rekindling the first *intifada*. Since its beginnings in December 1987, the message of the *intifada* had been that the occupation of the West Bank, including East Jerusalem and the Gaza Strip, was evil, unjust, and illegal under international law, a clear violation of U.N. resolutions that maintained that the occupation had to be terminated and that Palestinians had the right to self-determination in accordance with international law. This included the right to establish their own state on all the land of the occupied territories.

The *intifada* was a popular liberation movement that won attention and sympathy around the world. Many people who had formerly viewed the Palestinians as terrorists now came to see them as victims of the government of Israel. Until the beginning of the *intifada*, most Western countries had been conditioned to view the Palestinians as poor and miserable refugees who needed humanitarian assistance. The *intifada* succeeded in drawing attention to the basic underlying fact that many people had forgotten or chosen to forget that the Palestinian problem was not just about refugees but about a nation that had been denied its human and political rights. The condition of "refugeedom" resulted from their forced expulsion from their homes and their land. Their poverty was due primarily to the denial of their political rights.[4]

The Palestinians tried their best to keep the flames of the *intifada* burning through nonviolent resistance. The Israeli army, however, intensified its brutal practices while the international community was ineffective in pressuring Israel to implement U.N. resolutions and end the occupation. Thus, after three years of primarily nonviolent resistance, the *intifada* showed signs of slowing down. The stamina of the Palestinian people ultimately wore down. It had become increasingly clear that the *intifada* by itself could not liberate Palestine. In addition, Palestinians placed great hopes in the Madrid Peace Conference in October 1991.

In fact, had the international community (especially the United States and its allies) possessed the political will to peacefully solve the Palestinian/Israeli conflict, it could have done so then simply by implementing the pertinent U.N. resolutions. Had that happened, much future violence and suffering could have been prevented and the lives of thousands of men, women, and children would have been spared. Today Palestinians could be in normalized relations with their Israeli neighbors with both states well on their way to greater stability and prosperity.

The first intifada will remain in the historic memory of the Palestinians as that great period in the history of their struggle when the whole community, young and old, men, women, and children alike, rose up in unity and solidarity to nonviolently shake off the shackles of their Israeli oppressors. Yet those with the actual power to end the suffering of the Palestinians stood by silently and watched Israel flout international law as the agony and anguish of the occupation settled on the Palestinians. How ironic that the United States, which claimed to champion the freedom of the Kuwaitis during the oppressive Iraqi occupation, now chose to support the occupiers. Contrary to the biblical story of the exodus, in this case the pharaohs of this world had won. Palestinians viewed the behavior and conduct of the Americans in their passion and obsession to drive Saddam out of Iraq as enigmatic: while they could see the unjust occupation of Kuwait by Iraq, they were blind to the occupation of the West Bank and Gaza by Israel. They could see an injustice that had lasted less than one year but not an injustice that had lasted for twenty-three years.

THE FIRST GULF WAR[5]

The Gulf Crisis turned into war in the early hours of Thursday, January 17, 1991. As the coalition forces led by the United States were bombarding Iraq, the Israeli army imposed a curfew on Palestinians in the West Bank and Gaza Strip. Millions of people were confined to their homes. While the attention of the world was focused on Iraq, Israel was free to do what it pleased. The Palestinians were left to the mercy of a harsh occupying power. Although every few days the curfew would be lifted for two to three hours, food became scarce and medical needs were not adequately met. The fragile Palestinian economy crumbled while the human rights of Palestinians were violated daily. The curfew persisted for well over forty days in order to break the spirit of the people. For the rest of the world, the Palestinians became invisible and disappeared from the scene.

In contrast, as soon as Iraqi missiles landed in Israel, Western delegations flooded Israel with trips of solidarity and gifts of millions of dollars. Everything the *intifada* had accomplished during the three previous years seemed to be quickly erased as the Palestinians were left to rot under the curfews. How sad when in our human foolishness and ignorance of God's mercy we begin to rank humans in their order of importance. And how tragic when we allow powerful and influential people to condition our ways of thinking until those with power rank higher in human worth and value than other less fortunate human beings. These are signs of a moral and spiritual bankruptcy.

After the third week of fighting, it became clear to many in the region that the Western coalition intended not only to liberate Kuwait but also to crush Iraq. In fact, given the indiscriminate bombing of civilian areas and the rising toll on human life, we could only wonder whether the liberation of Kuwait was ever the primary objective, or if its purpose was only to cover up the more sinister goal of destroying Iraq.

THE SECOND IRAQ WAR

Many in the Middle East believe that the second war on Iraq could have been averted if the United Nations, and not the United States, had had a free hand to pursue negotiations. Although U.S. Secretary of State Colin Powell was himself questioning the wisdom of waging a war against Iraq and the interpretation of much of the intelligence that had been passed along by the White House, he still addressed the United Nations in February 2003, asking the General Assembly to authorize the war. During his presentation, Powell referred to Saddam's possession of "up to a few dozen Scud-variant" missiles, despite the fact that U.N. inspectors had accounted for all but two Scuds. Powell not only played recordings of intelligence intercepts but "had decided to add his personal interpretation of the intercepts to his rehearsed script, taking them substantially further and casting in the most negative light." And despite his own doubts about any connection between Iraq and al-Qaeda, under pressure from the Bush administration he agreed to refer to any links between the two as "potentially much more sinister."[6]

Leading the charge to war was Secretary of Defense Donald Rumsfeld and his deputy, Paul Wolfowitz, who once testified before Congress that a fairly small peacekeeping force of U.S. soldiers would be needed in Iraq since "Iraqi citizens would welcome an American-led liberation force." Wolfowitz suggested that the war could almost pay for itself with Iraq's annual oil exports of $15 billion–$20 billion: "To assume [the U.S. is] going to pay for it all is just wrong."[7] These administration officials and other neoconservatives in the administration and the Congress were enthusiastic to go to war to destroy Iraq. It goes without saying that they were also strong supporters of Israel; the war on Iraq was perceived as good for Israel because it would provide an excuse for Iraq's destruction, eliminating a foe of Israel.

These administration and military leaders knew that one of the strongest arguments for the war would be the threat of weapons of mass destruction, even if evidence of their actual presence was lacking. Such manipulation of basic facts casts real doubt on the integrity and the purity of their motives as they exerted their influence and extracted decisions from the U.S. Congress and the United Nations. These were decisions that adversely affected the destiny and lives of millions of people around the world. How sinister and frightening!

With hindsight the true facts of the situation have become clearer. From the invasion of Iraq on March 19, 2003, to the end of 2006, the United States had spent "roughly $400 billion on the Iraq War, and costs [were] running about $8 billion per month. . . . Estimates run as high as $2 trillion for the final cost of the U.S. involvement in Iraq." Also, "as of December

2006, nearly 2,900 Americans have lost their lives serving in Iraq. Another 21,000 Americans have been wounded, many severely."[8] And these figures do not include the great economic cost to the Iraqi people or the well over 100,000 Iraqi deaths that may have been caused in the early months of the U.S. invasion.[9]

THE IRAQ STUDY GROUP

As mandated by Congress, the Iraq Study Group, led by James Baker III and Lee H. Hamilton, systematically studied the war in Iraq. Its final report made it clear that the group's members advocated a return to negotiations and diplomacy—something that should have been done much earlier.[10] Many of the suggestions and recommendations closely resembled what might be described as a nonviolent, nonmilitary approach to the conflict. It recommended opening the lines of communications with all of Iraq's neighbors, including Syria and Iran. Although the arrogance of power and the cockiness of political leaders prevented negotiations, there would have been no better way of directly addressing points of contention and strife. Unfortunately, this is a policy often ignored by both Israel and the United States, which are quick to brand a person or a group as "terrorists" and then shut the door on any negotiations with them. In the past, many opportunities have been missed because of such misdirected policies.

Nations and leaders who genuinely seek peace are always ready to negotiate—even with their enemies. Those who are dragging their feet or unwilling to negotiate are simply not interested in peacemaking. The *Iraq Study Group Report* spells it out this way: "Dealing with Iran and Syria is controversial. Nevertheless, it is our view that in diplomacy, a nation can and should engage its adversaries and enemies to try to resolve conflicts and differences consistent with its own interests. Accordingly, the Support Group should actively engage Iran and Syria in its diplomatic dialogue, without preconditions."[11]

The report also recognizes that "the United States will not be able to achieve its goals in the Middle East unless the United States deals directly with the Arab-Israeli conflict."[12] The emphasis that the report places on the Arab-Israeli conflict is surprising, considering the obvious double standard the United States brings to relationships with Israel and the Palestinians.

The report mentions two essential issues that must be resolved in order for peace to be achieved. First, negotiations with Syria must resolve a number of issues and lead to "a full and secure peace agreement [where] the Israelis should return the Golan Heights [to Syria], with a U.S. security guarantee for Israel that could include an international force on the border, including U.S. troops if requested by both parties."[13] Second, regarding the Palestinian issue, a two-state solution on the basis of U.N. Security Council Resolutions 242 and 338 must be implemented. The report advocates "sustainable negotiations leading to a final peace settlement along the lines of President Bush's two-state solution, which would address the key final status issues of borders, settlements, Jerusalem, the right of return, and the end of conflict."[14] The conclusions of the report are very clear. The ten members of the Iraq Study Group have pointed to a way forward for Iraq as well as for resolving the Arab-Israeli conflict.

THE DESTRUCTION OF SODOM

The tragic and desperate situations in Iraq and Palestine are often justified by reference to the supposed "wickedness" or "terrorism" of the leaders or people of these places. This justification suggests that we turn back to the story of the destruction of Sodom recorded in Genesis 18. Abraham had become aware that Sodom was going to be destroyed because of its wickedness, so he stood before God and pleaded for mercy because his nephew Lot lived there with his wife and children. In addition, a number of Lot's married daughters and their husbands and children lived in the town. Abraham could not bear the thought that these innocents would be destroyed along with the wicked inhabitants of Sodom, so he pleaded with God for their rescue.

> Then Abraham came near and said, "Will you indeed sweep away the righteous with the wicked? Suppose there are fifty righteous within the city; will you then sweep away the place and not forgive it for the fifty righteous who are in it? Far be it from you to do such a thing, to slay the righteous with the wicked, so that the righteous fare as the wicked! Far be that from you! Shall not the Judge of all the earth do what is just?" (Gen. 18:23-25)

Abraham continued to plead and negotiate with God, decreasing the number of innocents from fifty to forty-five, to forty, to thirty, to twenty, and finally to ten. God's answer each time was basically the same, "For the sake of the innocents, I will not destroy the city."

According to Genesis, Sodom was not spared because not even ten innocent persons were found within it. The implication is that had they been found, the city would have been spared. While Lot and his two daughters escaped, Lot's wife, who disobeyed, became a pillar of salt. And the text of Genesis indicates later on that even Lot and his two daughters were not as righteous as had been thought (see Gen. 19).

According to this Old Testament ethic, the city of Sodom would have been saved for the sake of at least ten innocent people, because the judge of the earth is just and merciful. Suppose we concede that Saddam Hussein was an evil man. Were not the first President George Bush, Prime Minister John Major of Britain, and President François Mitterrand of France aware that there were innocent people in Iraq? Have the world leaders today sunk so low that they are incapable of seeing innocents and hearing their cry? How can the death of thousands of innocents be labeled "collateral damage"? Has the war mentality become so ingrained in the human psyche that leaders still opt for wars in spite of their knowledge of the destruction such wars unleash?

Tragically, since 1991 we have experienced even more devastating wars in the Middle East: there is a second war on Iraq, war in Afghanistan and Lebanon, not to mention the continuous war on the Palestinian people in the West Bank and the Gaza Strip. By the beginning of 2007, according to researchers at the Johns Hopkins School of Public Health, the second war on Iraq alone had resulted in the deaths of over 650,000 Iraqi civilians and 3,000 American soldiers, with an additional 22,000 American soldiers permanently maimed or injured. And the cost of the war approaches half a trillion dollars.[15]

The situation in Gaza is equally desperate. Journalist Rachelle Marshall writes, "UNICEF officials estimate that some 840,000 children in Gaza bear the consequences of Israeli shelling and other attacks. Many suffer from post-traumatic stress disorder as well as from severe malnutrition and disease."[16] The war in Lebanon between Hezbollah and Israel resulted in the death of hundreds with many thousands displaced from their homes. How can national leaders act in this way?

FOUR PARADIGMS

The Bible records four different models that represent the human condition from its worst bestial crimes to its highest possible state. The worst state is represented by the story in the New Testament about the killing of the holy innocents, which is truly one of the worst crimes committed in human history: "When Herod saw that he had been tricked by the wise men, he was infuriated, and he sent and killed all the children in and around Bethlehem who were two years old or under, according to the time that he had learned from the wise men" (Matt. 2:16). This incident represents the very incarnation of evil, yet Herod has been duplicated in human history by dictators who have committed the most heinous crimes against innocent people. The slaughter of the innocents was a crime committed to satisfy the narcissism, sickness, greed, and ambitions of a dictator. This crime serves as a paradigm that represents the depth of human evil. Other heinous tragedies that fit within this paradigm include the genocide of the Armenians,[17] the genocide of Assyrian and Syrian Christians,[18] and the genocide of Jews.[19] These people, who were perceived guilty solely because of their identity, were massacred.

The story of Jericho in Joshua 6 provides a second example. Under the pretext of war, the city of Jericho was destroyed, with no questions asked: "Then they utterly destroyed all in the city, both men and women, young and old, oxen, sheep, and asses, with the edge of the sword."[20] No moral scruples were involved in selecting the targets for destruction; the innocent were destroyed along with the guilty, the combatants along with the noncombatants. Women and children were massacred with the rest of the people. In the story of Jericho and in line with the beliefs of primitive people, war and the killing of enemies was supported, even commanded by their god. Many wars in history can be characterized by the Jericho paradigm. In modern times, the destruction of Hiroshima and Nagasaki during World War II and the wars on Iraq definitely fit this category.

A third paradigm is that of Sodom (Gen. 18:16-33). Some people believe that the destruction in this story should be placed a few steps higher on the ethical ladder because the wicked are killed but the innocent are spared. Many people view this as civilized behavior that reflects sober, logical, and calculated planning. Similarly, today we are told that indiscriminate killing is a thing of the past because modern technology has resulted in "smart" bombs that can be guided to kill the guilty and spare the innocent. Yet, the survivors of recent wars in the Middle East know that the Sodom paradigm lives only in the wishful thinking of presidents and army generals. In modern warfare the numbers of civilian casualties are colossal and the destruction of property is massive.[21] Perhaps no one knows this better than the residents of Qana in Lebanon whose village was struck by Israeli "smart bombs" and guided missiles in 1996 and again in 2006.[22]

The cross is the last model or paradigm. The first three examples include in one way or another most conflicts and wars. Although there arguably is some distinction between one paradigm and another, all three come down to destruction and devastation. For Christians the only remedy is to consider a different paradigm that views conflicts and solutions from a totally different angle. The foundation of this paradigm is God's love for all people expressed in Jesus Christ. It is based on the willingness of love to suffer and to bear pain rather than to inflict it on others. This is love that categorically refuses to use war and violence in order to crush an enemy. It is a love of others that invests itself in inventing and creating ways and methods that can, to a large extent, be successful in vanquishing evil through nonviolence. It is a love that is willing to sacrifice much in order to resolve conflict without resorting to arms.

Modern warfare has an enormous cost today that can run into billions of dollars.[23] Surely it is possible to resolve conflicts at far less expense—provided that world leaders muster the will to commit themselves to finding nonviolent solutions. Yet many of our world leaders approach conflicts with a belief in the necessity and efficacy of war. This belief can only stem from pride, arrogance, greed, domination, and desire for exploitation. Most of these chronic conflicts could be resolved if the international community could learn to overcome these political lusts and work together to find just and fair solutions to the problems and needs of the world.

The paradigm of the cross requires that we choose to serve others rather than to dominate them, to provide for their welfare rather than to participate in their exploitation. It calls us to absorb the pain of negotiations and even insult rather than retaliate with threats and attempts to humiliate the other. It moves us to take risks. The power of Christ shatters the old paradigms. We need not resort to killing the innocents with the wicked, nor the more "civilized" ethic of killing the wicked and saving the innocent. Jesus would condemn and reject these violent paradigms and replace them with a paradigm of love that would pursue the wicked in order to melt their wickedness and turn them toward justice and liberation.

These are responses that are seldom tried today. Yet in probably 95 percent of the conflicts in the world today, it may be possible to find solutions without resorting to war. An empowered United Nations should be able to prevent any individual state, and particularly the strongest powers, from imposing its will on the international community. The United Nations should be able to use political and financial power to develop and build peace in the various regions of the world. It can also exert economic pressure on states that are unwilling to comply with international law.

In order for such an endeavor to be successful, the United States must place its political and economic power, its prestige, and its influence in the service of the United Nations and allow the United Nations to make decisions in compliance with the demands of justice and fairness as enshrined in international law. The United States must abandon its path of unilateralism and work cooperatively with the international community. If the United States could be seen as a champion of the poor and oppressed of the world, the threat of violence and terrorism would be significantly reduced. A paradigm of servant leadership would require state leaders, especially those of the wealthy and strong states, to express national love for their own citizens as well as love for all the people of the world and to commit themselves to work for their well-being.

This would be a love that exerts moral power evenly with no double standards, a love that recognizes that all world leaders and their countries stand under God's judgment. Is this love too hypothetical, too utopian, and too imaginary? Have we all succumbed to the notion that war, strife, and violence are more realistic methods for dealing with conflict resolution than demonstrating love for one's neighbor? Have we truly tried servanthood and love of neighbor in international conflict resolution and failed, or does the arrogance of power and a war mentality prevent us from even trying?

Surprisingly, it was Saddam Hussein who, in an interview with CNN's Peter Arnett after the first war on Iraq, accused the United States and its coalition of focusing only on how to reduce the casualties of the coalition forces. Saddam said that he had always warned that a war would extract a heavy toll on all those involved and not only on the Iraqis. It would be better to sit together and negotiate a political settlement.[24] Yet the American people were (at least initially) very supportive of President Bush's position on Iraq. A Washington Post/ABC News poll on November 27, 2001, found that 78 percent of Americans supported going to war against Iraq.[25] A poll conducted a year later found that 60 percent of Americans supported the use of nuclear weapons against Iraq.[26] Even more incredibly, a May 1, 2003, Gallup poll for CNN and USA Today reported that 79 percent of Americans believed that the war with Iraq was justified even if weapons of mass destruction were never found.[27] With such a mentality, how can we hope for a better world?

THE WAY OF EMPIRE

At a time when most people realize how small our world is through our communication systems and our interdependency, the two wars on Iraq and the unresolved Israel-Palestine conflict have widened the gap between the Middle East and the West, and especially with the United States, driving deep wedges between the two. They have created new animosities, exacerbated resentment, and added many new fears of an American Empire that threatens to dominate, exploit, and humiliate the people of the Middle East.

In the world today, it is apparent that the United States sees itself as the only country that is entitled to use force anywhere in the world. The U.S. National Defense Strategy states, "Our strength as a nation state will continue to be challenged by those who employ a strategy of the weak using international forums, judicial processes and terrorism."[28] It is tragic that this statement equates international forums with terrorism. Such a strategy gives the United States an exclusive right to "preventive" military intervention all over the world. Commitment to the United Nations is rejected as a restriction of the freedom of the United States to act. While the United States talks repeatedly about the importance of helping democracies to emerge, according to this grand strategy democracies abroad are regimes that support and follow America's dictates.[29]

Such a strategy brings to mind the saying among the ancient Athenians: "Everyone knows that justice is relevant only among those who are equal in power, while the strong take whatever they can, and the weak concede whatever they must."[30] Such a strategy cannot bring justice or peace to our world. The United States, indeed, has an important role to play. Its role, however, must be within the community of nations to support the United Nations and to help the United Nations enforce the demands of international law. This is the only way to enhance the standing of the United Nations so it can bring about justice and peace.

In his autobiography, Lincoln Steffens mentions a dramatic incident at the Paris Peace Conference in 1919 when Clemenceau of France confronted the heads of the countries present and asked them if they really wanted a permanent peace in the world. They all nodded their heads affirmatively. Clemenceau then began to list the cost of peace.

> "If we want to give up war," he said, "we must give up our empires. You, Mr. Lloyd George, will have to come up out of India. We French will have to come out of North Africa. And you Americans, Mr. President,

will have to relinquish your dollar rights in the Philippines, Mexico, and Cuba. We, the dominant powers, will have to give up our empires, tear down our tariff walls, free our colonies, and open up the world."

The heads of states looked at each other in astonishment and informed him that this is not the peace that they had in mind. Then Clemenceau banged his fist on the table and roared at them "then you don't mean peace, you want war."[31]

Tragically, history proved Clemenceau right: twenty years later World War II started.

Most of the problems in our world today stem from the fact that people of power want to impose peace on their own terms and for their own interest without regard to justice firmly based on international law. Such peace will always be short lived and cannot prevail.

The ideology of empire is the ideology of military and economic power. It fills its leaders with hubris and arrogance. Empire might preach democracy, peace, and freedom but its actual practices tend to suppress and enslave others. Whereas God's power is shown through love and mercy, justice and peace, empire's power is shown through domination and exploitation. In the twenty-first century what is at stake is the way people of power behave. The challenge before them is whether they can use their power with humility in the service of justice and peace for all, especially for the oppressed of the world. This is the greatest challenge that faces world leaders today.

Chapter 9

Samson, the First Suicide Bomber

The issue of Palestinian suicide bombings has become a familiar topic to many people throughout the world. It is easy for people, whether inside Israel-Palestine or outside, either to quickly and forthrightly condemn suicide bombing as a primitive and barbaric form of terrorism against civilians,[1] or to condone and support it as a legitimate method of resisting an oppressive occupation that has trampled Palestinian dignity and brutalized their very existence.

As a Christian, I know that the way of Christ is the way of nonviolence. Therefore, I condemn all forms of violence and terrorism, whether coming from the government of Israel or from militant Palestinian groups. This does not mean, however, that all Christians believe in nonviolence. On the contrary, "Christian" nations in the West have waged some of the bloodiest wars in history and have been responsible for the worst atrocities and violations of human rights.

With this point clearly established, it is important, nonetheless, to help readers understand the phenomenon of suicide bombings that has tragically arisen from the deep misery and torment of many Palestinians. When healthy, beautiful, and intelligent young men and women set out to kill and be killed, something is basically wrong. Why has the world not heard their anguished cry for justice? These young people deserve to live, as do all their victims. This chapter, therefore, is addressed to all people of conscience, urging them to work for the liberation of the Palestinian people.

THE BACKGROUND

Palestinian resistance to the Israeli occupation of the West Bank and the Gaza Strip took an important turn after 1993. Young Palestinian men, and more lately women,[2] began to strap themselves with explosives and make their way to Israeli Jewish areas often crowded with soldiers or civilians and then to blow themselves up, killing and injuring dozens of people around them. From the first suicide bombing in Afula in April 1994 to the beginning

---

This chapter has been adapted in part from the Sabeel booklet on suicide bombers: Naim Ateek, *What Is Theologically and Morally Wrong with Suicide Bombings? A Palestinian Christian Perspective* (Jerusalem: Sabeel, 2003).

of the second *intifada*, 120 Israelis were killed in suicide bombings.[3] Between the beginning of the second *intifada* in September 2000 and until Wednesday, June 19, 2002, Palestinian militants carried out 56 suicide bombings, killing, according to Israeli statistics, 225 Israelis, including soldiers and civilians—men, women, and children.[4] In the same period, the Israeli army killed 1,645 Palestinians, including police, men, women, and children. By 2005, there had been 165 suicide bombings.[5] According to the Israeli human rights group B'tselem, 452 Israeli civilians have been killed by suicide bombs between September 2000 and March 2008.[6]

History reveals the root causes of the suicide bombings. In October 1991, after the first Gulf War, Secretary of State James Baker III called for a peace conference. The Madrid Conference was attended by a number of the Arab states and Israel. Since the PLO was still considered a terrorist organization, the Palestinians attended as part of the Jordanian delegation. It was hoped that the conference would lead to the implementation of U.N. Resolutions 242 and 338. Instead, the negotiations took a circuitous route and opened the way to the Oslo Peace Process in 1993. With enthusiasm on the part of many and skepticism on the part of others, most Palestinians entered the Oslo Peace Process with the hope that it would lead into a negotiated settlement with their Israeli neighbors. People expected that the presence of the democratically elected leadership of the Palestinian Authority would enhance that process. Instead, Oslo resulted in the entrenchment of the Israeli system of domination and control, deterioration of Palestinian economic life, fragmentation of the occupied territories through hundreds of checkpoints, an increase in the confiscation of land, expansion of the Israeli settlements (illegal under international law), and intensification of oppression.

THE UNDERLYING CAUSES: AN ATTEMPT
TO UNDERSTAND BUT NOT TO JUSTIFY

Historically speaking, although the occupation of the West Bank and the Gaza Strip began in 1967, the first suicide bombings happened after the Oslo Peace Process in 1993. In other words, for the first twenty-six years of the occupation, Palestinian resistance was not "suicidal." The later suicide bombings resulted from the despair and hopelessness that set in when an increasing number of Palestinians became frustrated by the deepening Israeli oppression and humiliation, and when it became clear that the international community was powerless to implement its own resolutions regarding the occupation of Palestine.

This point is well illustrated by the story of Abdel Baset Odeh, a young Palestinian who blew himself up in the Park Hotel in Netanyah in March 2002, killing twenty-eight Israelis and tourists and sparking Operation Defensive Shield, the largest Israeli incursion in the West Bank since 1967. Six months earlier, the Israeli authorities had prevented Odeh from crossing into Jordan to marry his fiancée from Baghdad. The Israeli Shin Bet (security intelligence) repeatedly summoned him to the military governor's office. He refused to go because he suspected, as often happens, that they would blackmail or pressure him into becoming a collaborator.[7] He was twenty-five years old, ready to get married, start a family, settle in Jordan, and enjoy life. When his future plans were shattered by the Israeli army, he turned to suicide bombing. His father attributed his son's action to humiliation and a broken heart. His family first heard about the bombing from a report on television.[8]

Such stories abound in the Palestinian community. They include one or more basic elements: humiliation by the army, a desire for revenge for the killing or injury of a relative or a friend, desperation and frustration from the oppressive Israeli occupation, unemployment and confinement, imprisonment and torture, hopelessness, racism, and discrimination. In other words, these young people were not born "terrorists." Like us, they were born in the image and likeness of God, human beings with a love of life and freedom. All of them, with no exceptions, were born under the Israeli military occupation. The only Jews they knew were Israeli soldiers who carried guns and threatened and dehumanized them. They were shaped and formed in the crucible of the occupation. If Israel labels them as terrorists, they are, after all, products of the Israeli occupation.

These young Palestinians did not blow themselves up because they wanted to commit suicide. Before 1993, they resisted the occupation of their country but through few overt actions. Then Israel increased its oppressive and punitive measures against them, including using helicopter gun ships to assassinate Palestinian leaders, F-16 fighter planes to kill people and destroy their homes, mushrooming military checkpoints to control and humiliate people, and closures and sieges of towns and villages. Suicide bombings came to be perceived as a more potent tool of resistance and one that would reciprocate the pain and hurt they were experiencing. As they were driven more deeply into despair, their desire to strike back in any way possible grew in intensity. From a Palestinian perspective, therefore, the real sequence of the cycle of resistance has been this: the Israeli occupation was met by Palestinian resistance, greater Israeli oppressive measures were met by greater attempts on the Palestinian side to increase the resistance, and the cycle of violence continued unabated.

MUSLIM PERSPECTIVES

The suicide bombings became a more powerful phenomenon when their religious underpinnings were emphasized. Hamas leader Khaled Mash'al outlined three main reasons for suicide bombing: the religious, the nationalist or patriotic, and the humanitarian. The last is a case where a suicide bomber sacrifices himself so his people may live.[9]

It is difficult to determine whether the religious dimension followed and enhanced the political decision for its use or whether the religious significance preceded and prompted it. More likely both went hand in hand since any Palestinian killed by Israel, whether a militant or an innocent bystander, was regarded as a martyr. Consequently, groups like Hamas referred to these acts not as suicide bombings but as "martyrdom operations" and "martyrdom weapons." Nationalism and faith have become fused together and imbued with greater power. Many Muslim Palestinians regarded the suicide bombers as martyrs, and believed that paradise awaited them. Their rewards included forgiveness, companionship with the prophets and God in heaven, and intercession on behalf of their families on the Day of Judgment.

Martyrdom was described in a sermon preached by Sheikh Isma'il al-Adwan and broadcast on Palestinian TV: "When the *shahid* [martyr] meets God, his sins are forgiven with the shedding of the martyr's first drop of blood; he's saved from the grave's confines; he sees his seat in heaven; he's saved from judgment day; he's given seventy-two dark-eyed women; he's an advocate for seventy members of his family."[10] The martyrs do believe they are fighting for the cause of God and that their place in heaven is, therefore, guaranteed. An important quote from the Qur'an in this regard is, "Count not those who were slain in God's path as dead, but rather living with their Lord, by Him provided" (Qur'an 3:169).

In an interview on Al Jazeera satellite television on June 29, 2002, Khaled Mash'al said that had the international community done justice to the Palestinians, there would have been no reason for it to resort to martyrdom operations. He considered these operations very effective for several reasons, noting first the cumulative number of casualties and losses that Israel could not continue to sustain. Then he listed their impact in causing the emigration of Jews out of Israel, the rise of unemployment in Israel and the worsening of its economy, the low morale of the people, but most of all, the fact that the Israeli army does not have a weapon that can deter these operations.

In other words, militant Islamic groups see the suicide bombings as a powerful weapon that inflicts not only a heavy human toll but also a psychological trauma that affects a large segment of Israeli society and exposes Israel's vulnerability. Indeed, the suicide bombings shook the Israeli state and caused widespread panic and fear. Consequently, Israel heightened its media warfare against the Palestinians, locally and internationally, comparing its predicament to that of the United States in its fight against terrorism, and comparing Palestinian terrorism with that of Osama bin Laden and his al-Qaeda network. Israel does not mention its illegal occupation of the Palestinian territories and its domination of an entire nation. Many people in the West, especially in the United States, who have fallen into the Israeli trap cannot distinguish between what happened in the United States on September 11, 2001, and what is happening to a people who are subjected to a harsh and brutal occupation.

Some Palestinian militants have commented that, given the tremendous imbalance of military power of the Palestinians and Israel, the suicide bombings have created a relative balance of fear. The casualties on the Palestinian side have been approximately four times higher than on the Israeli side but the suicide bombings have equalized the spread of fear and terror within Israel and also increased in a dramatic way the number of Israeli casualties. Those who support armed struggle believe the suicide bombings demonstrate that the weak are not as weak as they seem to be, and the strong are not as strong as they think they are.

Hamas leader Mash'al mentioned that 120 persons have already given themselves up for the sake of God and the homeland. Half of them were university graduates, and most of the others were high school graduates; only a few had only finished primary school. Another Hamas leader reported on television that 75 percent of all the Israelis killed by Palestinians were killed through suicide bombings. He added that if Israel wanted to call it "terrorism," so be it. Did not Yitshak Rabin, the late prime minister of Israel, himself call terrorism the "weapon of the powerless?"[11]

Other Muslims argue strongly that Islamic law forbids the killing of noncombatants and, therefore, that the killing of innocent Israelis is wrong. Imam Yahya Hendi, a Qur'anic scholar who is the Muslim chaplain at Georgetown University in Washington, D.C., describes a Qur'anic view of *jihad*, martyrdom, and terrorism and violence on his Web site.[12] He emphasizes the personal form of *jihad*, which is the intimate struggle to purify one's soul and spirit from sin. This *jihad* takes precedence over the physical *jihad* in which Muslims wage wars against oppression and transgression. Hendi comments on the verse, "Fight in the cause of Allah those who fight you, but do not transgress limits; for Allah loves not transgressors" (Qur'an 5:32). This verse speaks of a defensive war that is waged to stop aggression but not to go beyond it: "The idea is that justice prevails. You don't fight because you enjoy fighting, but because there is oppression."[13] The emphasis on justice implies that civilians are not to be killed.

Imam Hendi says clearly that those who die in the service of God are martyrs, "though that service needs to be of a different sort than that provided by terrorists."[14] He provides a number of illustrations:

> Suppose I'm on the pulpit teaching and giving my sermon, if someone shoots me because of what I'm saying about God, the Qur'an says I'm not really dead because I'm with God. If I'm feeding the poor, and calling for justice, I can't be called dead. My soul is alive and God sustains me. . . . So to claim martyr status, all terrorists have to do is convince themselves that they are fighting for "justice," which is, of course, highly subjective. . . . [Terrorists] think if they hurt Americans, they serve the cause of justice. They use these [Qura'nic] verses.[15]

Imam Hendi notes that the Qur'an has many verses about martyrdom that indicate that a person must not cause harm to others. He quotes Prophet Muhammad as saying, "Do not attack a temple, a church, a synagogue. Do not bring a tree or a plant down. Do not harm a horse or a camel."[16]

Finally, Imam Hendi and many other Muslims believe that the Qur'an prohibits terrorism:

> The Qur'an doesn't condone terrorism, though Muhammad was the leader of a military force and therefore used violence. . . . While there are passages in the Qur'an, like the Old Testament of the Bible, that celebrate military victory, the overall gestalt of the Qur'an promotes a more restrained view. . . . We ordained for the Children of Israel that if any one slew a person—unless it be for murder or for spreading mischief in the land—it would be as if he slew the whole people: and if anyone saved a life, it would be as if he saved the life of the whole people [Qur'an 3:169].[17]

This passage places a great value on the sanctity of a single life. "If you kill one person it's as if you kill all humanity," says Imam Hendi.[18]

PALESTINIAN CONDEMNATION OF SUICIDE BOMBINGS

Although the harsh conditions of the occupation and the desire to strike back against the daily killing of Palestinians led some in the Palestinian community to justify suicide bombing, other Palestinians, including members of the Palestinian Authority, condemned them. While the American government rushed to condemn suicide bombings and expected the same from the Palestinian Authority, Israel's killing of Palestinian leaders and ordinary civilians did not abate; it passed as self-defense and remained free from public condemnation by the United States.

It is important to reiterate clearly that many in the Palestinian community do not support the suicide bombings. Although there are Palestinians who are sympathetic, many have denounced them. On June 16, 2002, fifty-eight Palestinian leaders, men and women, Muslims and Christians, signed a public statement published by the most widely read Arabic daily, *Al-Quds*, asking for an end to all suicide bombings. They made it clear that such operations only widen and deepen the hate and resentment between Palestinians and Israelis and destroy the possibility for the two peoples to live in two states side by side. The signers were against suicide bombing based on moral principles. The statement also argued that the suicide bombings are counterproductive and will not lead to the fulfillment of the Palestinian national aspirations; instead they allow Israel to justify its increasing vicious attacks on Palestinian towns and villages.

The statement was published in the paper on five consecutive days before it was transferred to a Web site and gained hundreds of additional signatories. Over five hundred people expressed their desire to see the termination of any suicide operations.

The Palestinian community stands in even stronger opposition to suicide bombing today. Most Palestinians have rejected these bombings as unjust, against moral principles, and ineffective.

ISRAELI REACTION

There are voices inside Israel calling for more drastic and severe measures to curb the suicide bombings. One of the loudest was Gideon Ezra, the then-Israeli deputy public security minister who on August 19, 2001, openly called on his government to execute the families of Palestinian suicide bombers. He argued that if potential suicide bombers know that their families would be killed they would then refrain from committing the act. Apparently, Ezra based his suggestion on a Nazi practice of arresting or inflicting suffering on the families of those who were suspected of undermining the state. Historian Moshe Zimmerman of Hebrew University has stated that under the Nazis, if someone shot a German soldier and was not caught, fifty people would hang. It was shocking to learn that Ezra's words drew no protest or criticism from the Israeli government.[19] Fortunately, not all the voices inside Israel are as extreme as Ezra's.

By contrast, courageous voices within Israel call on the Israeli government to examine its harsh policies against the Palestinians, as it is these policies that breed suicide bombers. In one case, Rami and Nurit Elhanan's fourteen-year-old daughter was killed by a Palestinian suicide bomber in September 1997. In spite of their tragic loss, the parents became actively involved in peacemaking. They placed responsibility for their daughter's death on the Israeli occupation, calling it "a cancer that is feeding terror": "Israel is becoming a graveyard of children. The Holy Land is being turned into a wasteland. . . . Our daughter was killed because of the terror of Israeli occupation. Every innocent victim from both sides is a victim of the occupation." Although Rami's grandparents, aunts, and uncles had perished in the Holocaust, he said, "The pain of losing our beautiful daughter is unbearable, but our house is not a house of hate." Nurit added, "Hamas takes power from the anger of people. If you restored people's dignity, honour and prosperity by ending occupation, Hamas would lose power." The couple established the Bereaved Family Forum with Izzat Ghazzawi, a Palestinian whose sixteen-year-old son Ramy was killed by Israeli troops.[20]

On June 27, 2002, Shamai Leibowitz, an Orthodox Jew, wrote a letter entitled "An Israeli Officer's Response to President Bush." He began, "I am an Orthodox Jew and a criminal defense attorney in Tel Aviv. I am also a tank gunner in reserve duty, and part of a group of 1,000 soldiers who have refused to serve in the occupied territories. Many of them were imprisoned in military jails in the past few months." Then he added:

Now that President Bush has enlightened us with his new "Plan" for the Middle East, we can only wonder how long it will take him to realize that his plan is useless and meaningless. . . . [Bush's] failure to understand that no progress can be made while a whole nation [Palestinian] is being brutally occupied is the basic flaw in this policy. . . . Bush fails to comprehend that the suicide bombings are a product of mass starvation and humiliation of the Palestinian people. Bush's aides are doing us so much harm by refusing to acknowledge that only an immediate end to the Israeli occupation will bring an immediate end to the Palestinian uprising.

We are now witnessing a situation in which 3.5 million people have no future, no hope, no vision, other than to become terrorists and avenge the continued harassment and shelling by the Israeli army's helicopters, tanks and artillery. While Bush has never set foot in this region, we have been living here, watching how the Palestinians were trampled and denied basic rights on a daily basis, besieged and occupied in every possible way. Our Jewish sources teach us that where there is no justice, there is no peace. . . . Most Israelis know deep in their hearts that once we stop humiliating and oppressing this nation, we will return to become a safe and secure democratic Israel living next to a viable Palestinian State.[21]

A CHRISTIAN RESPONSE

A dictionary's definition of martyr is "one who chooses to suffer death rather than renounce a religious principle; one who makes great sacrifices for a cause or principle; one who endures great suffering." From their political and religious perspectives, the suicide bombers have made a supreme sacrifice, the offering of themselves for their faith (in the way they understand God) and for their homeland.

In Arabic, the verb *shaheda* means to witness. *Shahid* is a martyr, a person who has suffered death as a witness to one's faith or the principles that he or she stands for. In the Palestinian struggle, this word has been used to refer to those Palestinians killed by the Israeli army as well as for those who voluntarily sacrifice their life for Palestine. The death of a *shahid*, including the suicide bombers, is a cause of pride for the family, though that in itself does not lessen the pain and grief of their loved ones.[22]

In English the word for martyr is derived from the Greek *martus* and, like the Arabic, simply means a person who has given up herself or himself as a witness. It was first used in the early Christian centuries to indicate the witness for Christ of the early apostles. When Christians began to be persecuted, the word was used to refer to those who underwent some form of suffering for their faith. Eventually, it was used exclusively for those who died for their faith.[23]

In viewing suicide bombings from a religious perspective, it is worthwhile to reflect on the story of Samson, which occupies four chapters in the book of Judges (13-16). Many Christians have been spellbound as they, whether as children or adults, listened to its fascinating details. It is a story of a strong young man who rose up to save his people who were oppressed by the Philistines, their powerful neighbor on the coast.[24] The Israelites regarded Samson as a hero and a freedom fighter who struggled for their liberation, while the Philistines, the people of power at the time, saw him, using today's language, as a terrorist.

Samson fought very bravely against his enemies. Eventually, he was captured by the Philistines and tortured. They pulled out his eyes and kept him in jail. In order to celebrate their victory over Samson, their archenemy, the Philistines brought him to a big event attended by three thousand men and women, including their five kings. His final act of revenge took place when he pushed the two main columns of the building, bringing it down on himself and everyone present. Samson's final prayer seems very similar to the last prayer of a suicide bomber: "Lord GOD, remember me and strengthen me only this once, O God, so that with this one act of revenge I may pay back the Philistines for my two eyes" (Judg. 16:28).

Read in the light of the suicide bombers of this century, the story poses a barrage of questions. Was Samson a suicide bomber? Was he acting on behalf of the God of justice who wills the liberation of the oppressed? Was God pleased with the death of thousands of men and women of the Philistines? Are we confronted with many similar stories today in the experience of suicide bombers? Is it legitimate to tell the story of Samson by substituting Ahmad for his name? Can it be said that the God of justice is active in working out the liberation of the oppressed Palestinians through the likes of Ahmad? Is the dynamic under which God operates that of Jews versus other people or is it that of oppressor versus oppressed? Do we see the divine involvement of God in one story and not the other? Is the story of Samson more legitimate (because it is written in the Bible) than the story of Ahmad? Do we have the courage to condemn both as acts of violence and terror or to condone both as acts of bravery and liberation? Are the acts of the ancient Philistines against the Hebrews and the actions of the state of Israel against today's Palestinians comparable? Does God always stand with Israel, whether right or wrong?[25]

From our position of faith as Christians we must condemn violence and terrorism whether it is recorded in legendary stories or in history being written today. Although some people in our Palestinian community admire the sacrifice of the suicide bombers and view it as an ultimate offering for the sake of the homeland and the liberation of the people, and although we understand its deeper motivation and background, as Christians we must condemn it as an illegitimate method for resisting the occupation:

1. We condemn suicide bombings as a crime against God. Ultimately, it is God our creator who gives us life and who can take it. Therefore, the Sixth Commandment, "You shall not murder," applies as much to killing oneself as it does to killing others. If it is a crime to shed another person's blood, it must

be equally criminal, if not more so, to shed one's own blood. If the second greatest commandment is to love our neighbor as we love ourselves, then to kill oneself is a greater sin since it eliminates any possibility for loving the other. Suicide is a sin against God who has blessed us with the gift of life.[26] Those who love God do not kill themselves. Moreover, those who love God do not kill themselves for the sake of God. Indeed, they should be ready to die and even be killed for God's sake, but not to kill themselves.

Christian history is full of examples of people who suffered torture and death rather than renounce their faith and love of God. In the New Testament, we have only one case of suicide, and that was Judas Iscariot (Matt. 27.5). Although we understand the reasons behind his suicide, we believe that he committed a sin. If he had instead repented of his crime of betraying Jesus, he would certainly have received forgiveness. While the Bible contains no overt condemnation of suicide, it is clear that it is God, and only God, who gives and takes life. Later, the church condemned suicide, based on passages such as 1 Corinthians 6:19-20, wherein Paul writes, "Do you not know that your body is a temple of the Holy Spirit within you, which you have from God, and that you are not your own? For you were bought with a price; therefore glorify God in your body." The text from Ephesians 5:29 reads, "For no one ever hates his own body, but he nourishes and tenderly cares for it, just as Christ does for the church . . ." (cf. Rom. 14:7-9). Taking one's own life was considered a sin against a loving, creator God, which was probably why traditionally the church did not allow those who committed suicide to have church burials.

According to the Gospels, Jesus Christ knew that he would die in Jerusalem: "The Son of Man must undergo great suffering, and be rejected . . . and killed" Mark 8:31; Matt. 16:21; Luke 9:22). Yet he did not seek to escape the danger but set his face toward Jerusalem where he would be killed. Christians believe that he voluntarily offered himself for the sin of the world in a death that was vicarious and redemptive. He said, "No one has greater love than this, to lay down one's life for one's friends" (John 15:13). In other words, giving oneself on behalf of others is the greatest sacrifice of all. Christians believe this is precisely what Christ has done. He was open to sacrificing himself for the world but he was not the one who killed.

2. We condemn suicide bombings as crimes against our neighbors. From a Christian point of view, the tragedy lies in the fact that when these young men and women kill themselves, they cause the death of others, many of whom are innocent civilians. Similarly, Christians must condemn the government of Israel's killing of innocent Palestinians, which constitutes the underlying cause of the conflict. From a position of faith, even when the cause for which a person kills oneself is noble, nothing justifies the killing of innocent people. Christ accepted suffering for himself but did not inflict it on others. When we intentionally inflict suffering and death on others, we inflict untold suffering on their relatives and we sin against God and neighbor.

In fact, from a New Testament perspective, Christians who suffer should become more compassionate toward the suffering of others rather than bitter and vengeful. The greatest form of bravery is to bear suffering rather than to inflict it. In the struggle for civil rights in the United States, Martin Luther King Jr. recognized the heavy price to be paid for freedom but refused to accept violence to achieve it. In King's words, "Rivers of blood may have to flow before we gain our freedom, but it must be our blood." It has been noted that "King insisted on the teaching of Jesus and Gandhi that unearned suffering is redemptive. The willingness to suffer is the utmost expression of human freedom."[27] If the choice is between inflicting suffering on others or bearing suffering, it is better to accept suffering rather than inflict it on others. For Christians, suffering endured can serve as evidence of Christ's victory over suffering and death (2 Cor. 4:14-18). It can also be a way of exposing the evil and the injustice that must be resisted.

3. Christians condemn suicide bombing from the belief that injustice and evil must be resisted without resorting to evil or injustice. We must endure suffering inflicted upon us by unjust governments. *We bear it but we do not accept, submit, or succumb to it.* Some Christians have developed nonviolent direct action to resist unjust governments and systems. Martin Luther King Jr. expressed it well when he wrote:

> The ultimate weakness of violence is that it is a descending spiral begetting the very thing it seeks to destroy. Instead of diminishing evil, it multiplies it. Through violence you may murder the liar, but you cannot murder the lie, nor establish the truth. Through violence you murder the hater, but you do not murder hate. In fact, violence merely increases hate. Returning violence for violence multiplies violence, adding deeper darkness to a night already devoid of stars. Darkness cannot drive out darkness; only light can do that. Hate cannot drive out hate; only love can do that.[28]

The Israeli occupation of Palestinian land is evil and unjust and must be resisted for the sake of both oppressed and oppressors. Faithfulness to God drives us to work for justice and for ending the occupation of Palestine, but our actions must be carried out through nonviolence, no matter how long it takes. Only the methods of nonviolence can uphold the humanity of Jew and Palestinian alike when the conflict finally ends. Moreover, because nonviolent resistance does not impinge on or violate the human dignity of people, it contributes later to more effective reconciliation and healing.

4. For Christians, the supreme example is Christ. "When he was abused, he did not return abuse; when he suffered, he did not threaten; but he entrusted himself to the one who judges justly" (1 Pet. 2:23). This is not passive resignation. It is total surrender to the God of justice who established this world on justice and who will not let injustice have the last word. This does not mean, however, that we must not resist or combat injustice and resist it; it means, instead, total surrender and faith in the God who will ultimately

vindicate us. Archbishop Desmond Tutu has often pointed out that this is a moral world and that God will not allow injustice to continue.[29]

Christians condemn suicide bombings because they are trapped in the same violent logic exercised by the Israeli government. This logic is based on the law of revenge expressed in "an eye for an eye and a tooth for a tooth." Although it is not easy for us to do, we are taught as Christians to seek a higher law: "Beloved, never avenge yourselves, but leave room for the wrath of God; for it is written, 'Vengeance is mine, I will repay, says the Lord.' No, 'If your enemies are hungry, feed them; if they are thirsty, give them something to drink; for by doing this you will heap burning coals on their heads.' Do not be overcome by evil, but overcome evil with good" (Rom. 12:19-21).

5. Some Israeli religious leaders, including many of the religious settlers, believe that the war against the Palestinians can be justified biblically because it is similar to Joshua's campaign in the Old Testament. If Joshua's actions pleased God, why would not the actions of Israel's leaders today? Similarly, the suicide bombers believe that with their actions they are fighting for God's cause by ridding their land of the injustice inflicted on it by "infidels" and so earning a place in paradise.

Our basic problem with both interpretations lies in their concepts of God. Christians must reject any understanding of God that reflects war, violence, or terrorism. The God that we have come to know in Jesus Christ is a God of peace, mercy, and love. Moreover, our God is a God of justice, whose actions are expressed supremely in love, peace, and forgiveness.

6. In the midst of the injustice, suffering, and death inflicted on the Palestinians, we believe that God in Christ is there with us. Christ is not in the tanks and jet fighters, fighting on the side of the oppressors (although many Jewish and Christian Zionists believe that); God dwells in the city of Gaza, in the Jenin camp and in the old cities of Hebron, Nablus, Ramallah, and Bethlehem, suffering with the oppressed.[30] God has not abandoned us. As Christians we reject suicide bombings because they reflect feelings of total despair and hopelessness. We must never lose hope, and our hope must be anchored in God who is ultimately our savior and liberator. The words of the psalmist are very apt:

> I say to God, my rock, "Why have you forgotten me? Why must I walk about mournfully because the enemy oppresses me?" As with a deadly wound in my body, my adversaries taunt me, while they say to me continually, "Where is your God?" Why are you cast down, O my soul, and why are you disquieted within me? Hope in God; for I shall again praise him, my help and my God. (Ps. 42:9-11)

7. We condemn suicide bombings because they practice, in essence, collective punishment against people, many of whom are civilians. When suicide bombers commit collective punishment, they become what they loathe, what Palestinians detest about the Israeli government. One of the most despised

and feared acts of the Israeli army is its exercise of collective punishment against the Palestinians. While suicide bombers might say that collective punishment is not intentional, but an unfortunate collateral that comes with the resistance, this is basically the same rationale Israel uses when it imposes curfews, siege, and closures of checkpoints. In the end innocent people are harmed and killed. When the Israeli army incarcerates whole towns or when a suicide bomber blows himself or herself up in a marketplace, both actions result in the collective punishment of largely innocent people. Consequently, we must affirm the basic principle that it is unjust and immoral to punish people collectively.

Moreover, the fact that the Israeli government carries out collective punishment frequently should not be an excuse for Palestinians to follow suit. The question expressed by Abraham to God regarding the destruction of Sodom and Gomorrah still hovers today: "Will you indeed sweep away the righteous with the wicked?" (Gen. 18:23). Punishing people indiscriminately, including the elderly and the sick, women and children, is one of the most savage and brutal behaviors exercised by people of power in the past as well as in the present.

There are examples in the Old Testament where God warns the ancient Israelites that he will punish the "children for the iniquity of parents, to the third and the fourth generation" (Exod. 20:5). In another story, Achan disobeyed Joshua's order and out of greed took some of the spoils of war, which was forbidden. Although Achan confessed his sin, he was taken, at the command of God, "with his sons and daughters, with his oxen, donkeys, and sheep, and his tent and all that he had . . . and all Israel stoned him to death; they burned them with fire, cast stones on them" (Josh. 7:24b-25). Tragically, such acts of collective punishment have been wrongly attributed to God by humans in order to justify their own evil behavior against their fellow human beings. Such acts radically contradict our concept of the God of mercy and love. God's justice always includes mercy.

At the time of the exile, several hundred years later, many people believed that God did not deal with them justly; that they were suffering for the sin of others. They could only express their sorrow in the words of a popular proverb, "The parents have eaten sour grapes, and the children's teeth are set on edge" (Ezek. 18:2). However, both Jeremiah and Ezekiel began to articulate a different theology that said, essentially, only "the person who sins shall die" (Ezek. 18:20; Jer. 31:29-30). This was a reversal of long-held beliefs. Unfortunately, throughout history, people in power, whether religious or not, have continued to exercise the indiscriminate punishment of people and justify it as divinely sanctioned.

In modern times, the Fourth Geneva Convention clearly prohibits collective punishment. Article 33 of the Convention makes it clear that "No protected person may be punished for an offence he or she has not personally committed. Collective penalties and likewise all measures of intimidation or terrorism are prohibited." It is clear that today the government of Israel practices collective punishment in order to control and bring the Palestinians into submissiveness, including through extended curfews, the detention of large numbers of people for lengthy periods for alleged offenses, the destruction of homes, and many other techniques. Suicide bombings, whether deliberate or not, perpetrate collective punishment, punishing all Israelis for the evil policies of their government. Some Palestinians, as already indicated, might justify their actions by the heavily oppressive nature of Israel's occupation or refer to human nature's propensity to seek revenge. Nonetheless, the moral and ethical principles of international law must reign supreme: collective punishment is wrong and must be stopped.[31]

8. Although people may be ready to die for their faith or even for their country they need to do everything they can to stay alive and witness in their lives, remaining faithful until death (Rev. 2:10). As long as they are alive, they have the opportunity to witness to the truth. Their life is a gift from God and they must not destroy it. Christ has come so that we might have life and that we might have it abundantly (John 10:10). To end one's life abruptly is to end the opportunities God gives us and the possibilities to contribute to building a better society. Standing before Pilate, Jesus said, "For this I was born and for this I have come into the world, to bear witness to the truth" (John 18:37). When those in power tried to kill the truth by killing him, he did not kill himself. Even when they killed him, the truth could not be silenced, but was revealed and exposed much more widely.

Christians reject suicide bombings because we believe in life before death as well as life after death. Often, even though life can be difficult and frustrating, we can still give and receive joy and love with family and friends. Even in the darkest of hours, it is possible to find some beauty and inner peace and to find some contentment in the service of others. Life, God's gift to all, always offers new opportunities to each of us.

CONCLUSION

Our faith motivates and drives us to act justly, love mercy, and walk humbly with God (Mic. 6:8). We cannot condone suicide bombings or any use of violence and terror whether perpetrated by the government or militant groups. We must not allow ourselves to succumb to hate or to walk the road of vengeance and malice. As we continue to struggle for justice, peace, and reconciliation in Israel-Palestine, we must continue to lift up the prophetic vision of a world without violence: a world where people (Israelis and Palestinians) will "beat their swords into plowshares, and their spears into pruning hooks; [where] nation shall not lift up sword against nation, neither shall they learn war any more" (Isa. 2:4; Mic. 4:3-4). This is an achievable vision. Israelis and Palestinians can live together in peace if Israel is willing to share the land and accept the establishment of a viable Palestinian state.

Unfortunately, given the intransigence of the government of Israel, this does not seem possible at the present time. In fact, Israel is creating *bantustans* (homelands, reservations) for the Palestinians that seem more dehumanizing than what was practiced in South Africa under apartheid. Today the occupation of the West Bank, East Jerusalem, and the Gaza Strip continues to be the root cause of the violence and terror that is killing not only the present but the future as well. We must guard the future from such hate.

Ultimately, there can be no room for hate if we want to live together, and live together we must. Before Samson pulled down the house on his enemies, he prayed, "Lord GOD, remember me and strengthen me only this once, O God, so that with this one act of revenge I may pay back the Philistines for my two eyes." It was a prayer of hate and revenge that contrasts strongly with the prayer of Jesus on the cross, "Father, forgive them, for they know not what they do." It is not through acts of violence and revenge that we can achieve the justice we seek, but in the work of nonviolent resistance and in the spirit of sacrificial love that was exemplified by Jesus Christ himself. It is this spirit that can help us vanquish injustice and overcome evil with good. Ultimately, justice will prevail, the occupation will end, and peace will be achieved, not through blind revenge like that of Samson, but through the endeavors of all those who walk the way of Jesus Christ.

Chapter 10

Daniel or Judah Maccabeus

In spite of the plethora of violence and terrorism that marked the beginning of the twenty-first century, voices of nonviolence are gaining strength and momentum. The history recorded in the Bible provides abundant evidence that the work of nonviolence is the best means for resisting the illegal occupation, the injustice, and the oppression of the Palestinians. According to the book of Judges in the Old Testament, the twelve tribes of Israel enjoyed periodic peace with their neighbors. Sometimes they were conquered and ruled by stronger neighbors like the Canaanites, Philistines, Midianites, and others, and at other times they were able to muster enough unity and power to rally behind a strong leader and achieve a period of liberation and independence. This situation continued until the emergence of the ancient empires. From that point on, small kingdoms could survive only through alliances with others or as vassal states that paid tribute to an empire and thus received its protection. With the exception of short periods of time, the two small kingdoms of Israel and Judah did not experience much security or peace.[1]

Eventually, the northern kingdom of Israel could no longer survive the onslaught of the Assyrians, one of the early empires, and was destroyed in 722 BCE. There is no record that it was able to reemerge. The southern kingdom, Judah, was able to survive with the help of alliances for an additional 136 years, but in the end it was destroyed by the Babylonian Empire and many of its people were taken into exile. Although there is no record after this time of the ten tribes of the northern kingdom, there were serious attempts, after the exile, to restore political independence to the southern kingdom of Judah. Many southerners lived with the belief in God's promise that David's kingdom would stand forever.

With the coming of the Persian Empire, the exiled Jews were permitted to return. The Persians showed greater tolerance for religion than the Babylonians and allowed their subjects to practice their religions and customs quite freely. The records of this period indicate that there was excitement and vitality among some Jews who wanted to return to Jerusalem to restore the glory of the past. They wanted to rebuild the city of Jerusalem, its walls and the temple, and protect the returning Jewish community. Some, who attributed their exile to their disobedience of the laws of God, wanted to establish strict religious observance of the Mosaic laws.

The new leadership, including Ezra, Nehemiah, Zerubbabel, and others, could see that the country had undergone drastic changes. A good number of people from different ethnic and racial backgrounds now lived in the country in greater numbers. Some had moved from across the Jordan while others had been settled by the successive ruling empires. Some returning Judeans harbored resentment against the new inhabitants of the land, and others expressed hostility against their fellow Judeans who were exploiting the poor. In order to protect the small Jewish community, some of the leaders opposed any mixed marriages between the Jewish population and the inhabitants of the land. A new nationalist streak was becoming apparent.

In other words, at a time in which serious demographic changes were taking place, new theological reflections (both progressive and conservative) were being articulated: What was God's relationship to the land and to other people who were not Jewish? Prophets like Haggai advocated for an exclusive nationalist position that was opposed to foreigners. If, as some scholars maintain, the Torah was to some extent being finalized during this time, then the stories in Genesis about God giving the land to Abraham, Isaac, and Jacob and their seed forever would have had a great influence on the returning exiles as they observed the growing number of non-Jews in the land. Ezra and Nehemiah demonstrate the growing presence of xenophobia.

Some scholars believe that the book of the law that Ezra read to the people could have been the Torah itself in its earliest collected form. If this was the case, then the Jewish audience would have learned of an ancient tradition that God's will was to drive out or exterminate the inhabitants of the land because God had given the land to them alone. Although such ideas clearly implied the use of military power, the returning exiles lacked such power. If for Ezra and Nehemiah the exile resulted from the people's sin against God, then it was of prime importance to strictly adhere to the law in order to prevent another national disaster.

Ezra and Nehemiah demonstrate the beginning of the establishment of a religious tradition that leaned toward traditionalism, conservatism, exclusivity, and xenophobia. Eventually these materials, collected, revised, and edited, became the most authoritative text of Judaism, the Torah.

However, at the same time, there were other people who expressed new theological reflections concerning the meaning of exile and faith, suffering and renewal, and the people's relationship with God. What lessons could they learn from their exile? What was God saying to them?

According to George Mendenhall, Jeremiah, Ezekiel, Second Isaiah, and Job expressed at least four different responses to the exile.[2] These prophets, each in his own way and time, reflected on the tragedy of 586 BCE when the Babylonians destroyed Jerusalem and the southern kingdom. What did it mean? What was God saying through this disaster? What should they do?

FOUR RESPONSES

For Jeremiah, the exile meant a new covenant and a new relationship with God. The new covenant was not to be based on state and military power but on people who had God's law written on their hearts. It was to be a relationship with the community that "would embrace the commitments and receive the benefits of the covenant relationship with Yahweh."[3] "But this is the covenant that I will make with the house of Israel after those days, says Yahweh: I will put my law within them, and I will write it on their hearts; and I will be their God, and they shall be my people . . ." (Jer. 31). The fact that Jeremiah spoke of a new covenant implies that the older one was no longer operational. Although Jeremiah seemed to be looking to a new covenantal relationship with God, the Jewish leadership of the returning exiles was emphasizing an even stricter return to the old covenant.

Mendenhall writes:

> [B]ecause the law of the new covenant is "written on the heart," the undelegated will of Yahweh is once again regarded as the actual determinant of behavior. As in the formative period of the faith, the internalization of Yahweh's will makes unnecessary the entire machinery of external enforcement and religious indoctrination. The "knowledge of Yahweh" does not reside in an accumulated written corpus of religious traditions or doctrines, maintained by scribes and theologians. Instead, it is an aspect of personal character; as such, it exists irrespective of social distinctions altogether, whether class, rank . . . or moral reputation.[4]

For Ezekiel, the way to deal with the disaster was to suggest a new division of the land for the twelve tribes. Ezekiel's idealized vision "accommodates a Judean government, it does not simply envision the return of the political state."[5] This vision was significant because it included a new idea of sharing the land with the non-Israelites who inhabited the land. This was totally different from the exclusive manner in which the Torah reserved the right to the land solely for the ancient Israelites. That covenant called for them to drive out the inhabitants of the land or eliminate them. The new covenant called for the land to be shared:

> So you shall divide this land among you according to the tribes of Israel. You shall allot it as an inheritance for yourselves and for the aliens who reside among you and have begotten children among you. They shall be to you as citizens of Israel; with you they shall be allotted an inheritance among the tribes of Israel. In whatever tribe aliens reside, there you shall assign them their inheritance, says the Lord GOD. (Ezek. 47:21-23)

The book of Job also dealt with the disaster of 586 BCE, although recent scholarship suggests that this book was written after the exile. It did not focus primarily on the question of theodicy, "the eternal and fruitless attempt to justify why God allows injustice to prevail and righteous people to suffer,"[6] but attempted to answer some very basic questions: Why should we continue to worship Yahweh when he failed us by allowing the destruction of Jerusalem and our whole land? Has it happened because we are wicked? How do you find religious meaning in this? Job's basic thesis is that he would not abandon his faith in God, although his friends begged him to repent and return to the established doctrines and religious traditions of the day:

> [But] he simply has no confidence in conventional religious teachings. Instead, he repeatedly demands from Yahweh a face-to-face explanation for his current suffering. He finally arrives at the answer that "religious meaning . . . does not lie in established religious traditions . . . but in a dynamic encounter with the reality of God . . . even in the midst of suffering."[7]

Throughout, Job proclaimed his commitment to God no matter what happened: "Though he slay me, I will yet trust in Him."

In other words, Job's future with Yahweh did not require deference to established religious teachings or systems. This remarkable work illuminates a unique concept of the Yahwist faith: that the preservation of familiar traditions, doctrines, and forms alone cannot ensure a religion's future. Furthermore, in another stroke of genius it profoundly insists that a commitment to God must not be based on the expectation of reward. It must be grounded in the intrinsic value of faithfulness. The role of faith is to affirm that value, not to seek a reward.[8]

Second Isaiah speaks of Cyrus, the king of Persia, as God's messiah. It is as if the author of Second Isaiah is saying that it is not important to have an Israelite state with political power; God can call and work through other rulers to bring about his purposes even if those rulers are not Jewish. Jewish survival does not depend upon the establishment of their own exclusive political state.

At the same time, Isaiah delegates to the whole community the work and responsibilities that belonged to the Judean kings, but he redefines the community in nonpolitical terms. The community becomes Yahweh's servant who must break away from its parochial boundaries and relate to foreigners (Isa. 49:6). Whereas kings and states characteristically exercise coercive force, the servant community must not, even to the point of submitting to the attacks of others (50:6):

> Second Isaiah's so-called universalism sees the Israelite community existing for some purpose other than preserving its own cultural traditions within its own traditional boundaries. . . . This is a vision of the unity of all humanity that draws deeply on religious emphases found in pre-monarchic Yahwism. Second Isaiah thus foresees the worship of Yahweh accomplishing religiously and substantively what the Persian Empire could only do politically and superficially.[9]

INCLUSIVE VERSUS EXCLUSIVE

These four responses seem to imply deeper religious thought about God. Some of these great prophets were beginning to move toward understanding God in a more progressive, inclusive, and universal way. The tragedy of exile was clearly evoking diametrically opposing views among the Jewish leaders. It was driving some people to a narrow, fanatic, and militant theology, while leading others to a more open and inclusive theology of God and others. While some prophets were beginning to emphasize ritual, with strict observance of laws and traditions, other great prophets could see God's passion for justice and morality. While some went back to clinging to a warrior messiah in the line of David and a restored monarchy, other prophets were emphasizing the futility of war and the importance of a community of faith under the sovereignty of God. While some were ready to use violence and force God's hand in military campaigns, others began to see God's passion for justice and nonviolence.

As the movement began, the division seemed clear. Both movements were convinced that each possessed the authentic religion and an authentic understanding of God. One claimed its divine origins and authenticity through a return to dogmatic traditions and exclusionary laws, while the other understood authenticity to arise from the guidance of God's spirit and out of the lessons they learned from the disaster of the exile. One concept of God was fixed and limited by the past, while the other was influenced by the God of the future who journeys with God's people through the disasters of life and teaches them new lessons of faith. One enclosed God in the past, and the other kept the future open to be shaped by God's everyday interactions with God's people. In many ways the tension between the past and present needs to remain dynamic. The past is important but faith cannot be fossilized by the past. We believe in a living God who met us in the past but will meet us and be with us in the future. We believe in a God who is behind us and ahead of us. It is also important to remember that the earliest traditions for Jews and Christians alike refer to God as the creator of the whole world and to ancient Israel as a community of faith dependent on God rather than a monarchy "like other nations" (1 Sam. 8:5) based on coercive military force.

We must move forward in history with God to discover God's love for all people. God has always been and will be forever the same God of all, a loving, merciful, and compassionate God. It is human beings who can be the bigots, narrow-minded, exclusive, fickle, and changeable. Humans are in trouble if they attempt to create a god in their own image.

DANIEL VERSUS JUDAH

In its turn, the Persian period fell to Alexander the Great in 335 BCE. After Alexander's premature death, his vast empire was divided into smaller kingdoms and awarded to his generals. Two of these kingdoms were ruled by the Ptolemies and the Seleucids. In 167 BCE, Antiochus IV Epiphanes was the head of the latter, and his kingdom included Syria and Palestine. Antiochus was determined to thoroughly Hellenize his kingdom. While there were Jews who were willing to accommodate the new Hellenistic ways and consider it progress, others regarded Hellenization as a desecration of their religious tradition. Jewish resistance met severe and vicious reactions on the part of Antiochus, who savagely cracked down. Their insolence to his rule led him to offer a pig on the altar inside the temple to prove his power over them, a supreme insult to the Jews.

In another incident, when a Jewish man was about to offer a sacrifice to a Greek god, a Jewish zealot named Mattathias stepped out with great courage and killed him. This event ignited the Maccabean uprising against the Greek occupation. Its most prominent leader was Judah Maccabeus, a son of Mattathias. This armed resistance went on for a number of years and actually won independence for the Jewish community that lasted approximately 130 years (see the first book of Maccabees).

Increasing numbers of biblical scholars believe that the book of Daniel was also written around the same time. Whereas Maccabees glorifies the armed resistance of the Jewish people against the Seleucid kingdom and the vicious dictatorial rule of Antiochus, Daniel offers a different approach. The writer of Daniel gives "an alternative plan of response to the oppression to which the Maccabees respond with armed violence."[10] Biblical scholars Howard-Brook and Gwyther believe that Mattathias was defending "the *culture of Judaism* not obedience to the living God . . . What has been narrated is the struggle of human beings to maintain the tradition of their ancestors in the face of enormous pressure from the dominant culture."[11] For the writer of Daniel, God demands faithfulness even to the point of martyrdom rather than violent resistance or cultural accommodation.

Howard-Brook and Gwyther further note that, "This is the first key point of difference between the Maccabean and Danielic programs: whereas Mattathias and his sons take upon themselves the prerogative of destroying Israel's enemy, the apocalyptic vision insists that Israel's salvation lies in the power of God."[12] Daniel maintains that the seemingly unstoppable and undefeatable evil of Antiochus will be defeated, not through the sword but by God and "without human hands."

Some scholars have suggested that the book of Daniel was written as a critique of the Maccabean revolt. Whereas Judah lifted up the sword, Daniel was promoting a nonviolent resistance. Daniel emphasizes the importance of faithfulness to and trust in God. So the six beautiful stories of the book of Daniel show how he and his friends Shadrak, Mishak, and Abednego were saved repeatedly, not by the power of the sword but by prayer and loyalty to God.

When considered from this perspective it appears that the two strands that developed after the exile were becoming even more evident just before the close of the Old Testament period. Even within the Old Testament the separation between the two movements begins to accelerate. While the Maccabean revolt reinforced the building of faith in a God that marches to war using violence, arms, and bloodshed, Daniel turned to building a faith with which God's followers can resist evil through nonviolent resistance.

JESUS AND NONVIOLENCE

Jesus, who was born under the Roman Empire and lived all his life under empire, chose the Daniel strand. Like most Palestinians today, he was born during an occupation, and all his travels and teachings were carried out under the Roman occupation. It was also the forces of the occupation that killed him. The spirit of the Maccabees continued in the Zealots, and it is likely that some of his disciples belonged to the nationalist Zealots. There are indications in the Gospels that some disciples pushed Jesus to assume the role of a military leader and lead the uprising against Rome. The Davidic strand was real and appealing, yet Jesus refused it and chose the path of Daniel. It was not the way of escape of the Essenes who fled to the desert, nor was it the way of blind religious observance, nor was it a path of collaboration and accommodation. Jesus involved himself in the affairs of life but in total obedience to the will of God. Jesus chose a different ethic—that of Daniel and the Suffering Servant. It was an ethic of a total trust in God, even in the lion's den or in the fiery furnace.

Whereas the stories in the book of Daniel validated and celebrated those who were faithful to God, Jesus was confronted with the cross. In the eyes of nonbelievers, Jesus' death was a failure: "He trusted in God, let God save him." In their eyes, because God did not save him Jesus died a shameful death on the cross. While the forces of evil, both religious and political, colluded to put Jesus on the cross, Christians believe that the cross became God's instrument for the defeat of evil powers and, consequently, for the salvation and liberation of all humanity.

Jesus, who stands in the midst of empire, provides us with an ethic. It is an ethic of nonviolence, even if it leads to his death on a cross. Using three short verses from Matthew's Gospel, scripture scholar Walter Wink presents the nonviolent way of Jesus. These three examples constitute three important paradigms for all those who follow Jesus and believe in the power of nonviolence.[13]

The first verse is recorded in Matthew 5:39:

"If anyone strikes you on the right cheek, turn the other also." The only way to strike someone on the right cheek is to apply the strike by the back of the right hand. In many societies, including the Middle East, such a strike expresses insult and humiliation. It is the way a master strikes a servant. It is the way one shames and dishonors another. The person who turns his/her cheek is effectively saying, "Try again. Your first blow failed to achieve its intended effect. I deny you the power to humiliate me. I am a human being just like you. Your status does not alter that fact. You cannot demean me."[14]

This is Jesus' personal paradigm for nonviolent resistance. When insulted and humiliated by the occupation forces, a person can maintain his or her human dignity by a response that baffles and confounds the striker.

The second example has to do with the economic system of the day: "If anyone wants to sue you and take your coat, give him your cloak as well" (Matt. 5:40). The economic system in Palestine at the time could strip the poor of their property and even their clothes. As a way to resist the system and expose its unjust structures, Jesus suggested a total unmasking of it. So if a person had to give up his outer garments because he could not pay his debt, he was to take off his inner garments as a way of exposing and unmasking the oppressive economic system. The poor person had no chance of winning the trial because the laws were against him. In a society where nakedness was shameful, when a debtor was forced by law to give up his outer garment, he exposed the cruel system by taking off his inner garment as well. In effect he was saying, "Here, take everything." It is the debtor who has seized the initiative. As Wink sees it,

> This message, far from being a counsel of perfection unattainable in this life, is a practical, strategic measure for empowering the oppressed. . . . Here is a poor man who will no longer be treated as a sponge to be squeezed dry by the rich. He accepts the laws as they stand, pushes them to the point of absurdity, and reveals them for what they really are. He strips nude, walks out before his compatriots, and leaves the creditor and the whole economic edifice he represents, stark naked.[15]

The third example has to do with the political system of the day: "If anyone forces you to go one mile, go also the second mile" (Matt. 5:41). According to Roman law at the time, a soldier could ask any person to carry his gear one mile. The occupied people considered this a very humiliating task. Undoubtedly one of the basic questions facing people at the time of Jesus was how they could resist empire, as any armed revolt against the Romans would be futile. But Jesus counseled the people to resist the occupation by maintaining their human dignity and by taking the initiative by nonviolent means. Offering or even insisting on carrying a soldier's bag, which could weigh from sixty to eighty pounds (over thirty-five kilograms), would throw the soldier off balance. "If he has enjoyed feeling superior to the vanquished, he will not enjoy it today."[16] Walter Wink summarizes Jesus' way of nonviolence whereby evil can be opposed without being mirrored:

- Seize the moral initiative.
- Find a creative alternative to violence.
- Assert your own humanity and dignity as a person.
- Meet force with ridicule or humor.
- Break the cycle of humiliation.
- Refuse to submit or to accept the inferior position.
- Expose the injustice of the system.
- Take control of the power dynamic.
- Shame the oppressor into repentance.
- Stand your ground.
- Force the Powers to make decisions for which they are not prepared.
- Recognize your own power.
- Be willing to suffer rather than to retaliate.
- Cause the oppressor to see you in a new light.
- Deprive the oppressor of a situation where a show of force is effective.
- Be willing to undergo the penalty for breaking unjust laws.
- Die to fear of the old order and its rules.[17]

We have not walked the way of Jesus and have not lived by his ethic. This we must do.

THE CONFLICT OVER PALESTINE

In the conflict over Palestine, Palestinians have followed the way of Judas the Maccabee in resisting the occupation of their country and seeking independence. Indeed, the Israeli occupation represents empire with its vicious oppressive system. Extremist Palestinians know, as did the Maccabeans and later the Zealots, that they cannot conquer empire by military means. The empire, its formidable war machinery, is much stronger. While they might win some battles, they cannot win the war. Nevertheless they have decided to take up the sword and fight, believing that God fights on their side. We must declare loudly and clearly that this is not the way of God. God is not a god of war. We must champion and follow the deeper biblical tradition that presents the nonviolent way of God.

Since the beginning of the *intifada* thousands of people from both sides—Israeli and Palestinian—have been killed, most of them innocent women and children. History has not taught its lessons well enough, or we have been very slow learners. We must put down the sword to lift up the banner of peace. The evil of the occupation will eventually collapse from its own internal corruption and injustice. Injustice always carries within it the seed of its own destruction; however, in the meantime we must struggle nonviolently to bring about peace, never condoning injustice, or collaborating with it, or attempting to justify it. It must be opposed and detested at every turn.

In 2004, the Sabeel Ecumenical Liberation Theology Center produced a document with the title "Morally Responsible Investment."[18] This document encourages Christian denominations everywhere to look carefully at their investments and decide if they meet the moral and theological criteria of their Christian faith. Any investments in companies that work within the occupied territories (including the settlements) and that profit from the injustice and oppression of the Palestinians are immoral and should not be condoned by Christians. The document, which challenges Christians to be faithful stewards of God's gifts, invites a nonviolent means of resisting the occupation.

Many Christian, Muslim, and Jewish groups as well as secular organizations are committed to nonviolent peace activities. The Christian Peacemaker Teams (CPT),[19] the Ecumenical Accompaniment Program in Palestine and Israel (EAPPI) organized by the World Council of Churches,[20] the International Solidarity Movement (ISM),[21] the Israeli Committee Against House Demolitions (ICAHD),[22] and the nonviolent direct action of Palestinian groups such as the weekly demonstrations in Bil'in[23] and the work of the Palestine Solidarity Project in Beit Ommar[24] are a few examples of the many groups hard at work engaging in nonviolent resistance against the occupation.

Despite the important work of all of these organizations, we have a long way to go to create a national movement of nonviolence powerful enough to make a difference. Instead of training people in the use of military force and violence, we must work to create an "army" trained in nonviolence that is able to stand up against the forces that oppress and dominate others. We need people, trained people, who are ready to suffer rather than inflict suffering on others.

Long ago, some of the prophets had a vision of a day in which people would not learn war anymore, when they would beat their swords into plowshares and their spears into pruning hooks. They had a vision of God who "makes wars cease to the end of the earth; he breaks the bow, and shatters the spear . . ." (Ps. 46). We work and pray for the advent of such a day.

Chapter 11

Whose Jerusalem?

There can be no peace, no holiness in Jerusalem, without justice.
    —Karen Armstrong[1]

A few years ago while on a British Airways flight I watched the movie *Kingdom of Heaven*. The climax of the film depicts Salah el-Din (Saladin) fighting the Crusaders and conquering the city of Jerusalem. Just before the final battle, Balian of Ibelin, commander of the Crusader force spoke to the people of Jerusalem:

> It has fallen to us to defend Jerusalem, and we have made our preparations as well as they can be made. None of us took this city from Muslims. No Muslim of the great army now coming against us was born when this city was lost. We fight over an offence we did not give, against those who were not alive to be offended. What is Jerusalem? Your holy palaces lie over the Jewish temple that the Romans pulled down. The Muslim places of worship lie over yours. Which is more holy? The Wall? The Mosque? The Sepulchre? Who has claim? No one has claim.

Then he raised his voice and said, "All have claim!" The patriarch of Jerusalem who was standing by said, "That is blasphemy!" Balian of Ibelin continued, "We defend this city, not to protect these stones, but the people living within these walls."[2]

GUIDANCE FROM THE SCRIPTURES

The background is clear. Jerusalem has been the military spoil of armies and kingdoms. It has been ruled by powerful conquerors until a more powerful empire emerged that was able to reconquer it. The history of Jerusalem has been written with blood. The city has been demolished and rebuilt on at least eighteen occasions, and it has been conquered and reconquered more than thirty-seven times. The latest conquest was by the Israeli army in 1967. After the war Israel "took in not only the five square kilometers of Arab East Jerusalem—but also 65 square kilometers of surrounding open country and villages, most of which never had any municipal link to Jerusalem. Overnight they became part of Israel's 'eternal and indivisible capital.' "[3] Jerusalem has been controlled throughout history by war and blood.

The tragedy of Israel is that it has walked the way of previous empires, regarding Jerusalem in an exclusive way while denying it to its equally legitimate children. Israel has never taken the opportunity to make Jerusalem a symbol of peace. Even today the Israeli government cannot pride itself on being any better or different from the Crusaders or the Muslim caliphs or other conquerors from history. The city is being Judaized daily, marginalizing and isolating Christian and Muslim adherents.

As with other issues, it is possible to exploit the Bible for a particular purpose, including exclusivity. However, since the core message of the Bible is not about an exclusive god—although many religious Jews and Christian Zionists would disagree—the Bible does provide general guidance on the complex issue of Jerusalem.

In using biblical texts, there's always the danger of a "clothesline" hermeneutic: one grabs certain verses from different parts of the Bible and pins them together, interpreting them to support one's own agenda or to justify a variety of beliefs. Similarly, there is a danger in removing certain texts from their original context (whether historical, theological, or spiritual), which also detracts from the true message of scripture. Furthermore, if one is not faithful to the heart of the message of the Bible and the criteria of interpretation—for Christians, this is our knowledge of God revealed to us in and through Jesus Christ—one cannot expect to arrive at a sound theological conclusion. As mentioned before, the Bible has been used to condone and sanction many atrocities, including slavery, polygamy, the silencing of women, war, ethnic cleansing, and many others.

However, if we search more deeply in the Jewish and Christian traditions, the God we believe in is an inclusive and loving God. The primary sources in both the New Testament and the Old Testament witness to one God who reigns over all. It behooves us, therefore, to find within the scriptures the principles to be used to arrive at just solutions to conflict. And it is important to remember that the principles that can be deduced from the Bible regarding justice and morality do not, nor should they, contradict those of international law. We must also remember that everything needs to be judged according to the principle that the loving creator and liberator God deals with us as a divine parent on an equal basis.

FOUR BIBLICAL TEXTS ON JERUSALEM

Four different biblical texts focus specifically on the city of Jerusalem: two from the Old Testament and two from the New Testament. There are texts that can seem exclusive and be used to contribute to and enhance the perpetuation of the conflict in Israel-Palestine, and there are texts that lend themselves to peace and reconciliation. Which texts constitute the heart of the biblical message from God that agree with God's revelation in Jesus Christ and correspond to the commandment to love our neighbor as ourselves?

An Exclusive Text: Nehemiah 2:19-20

> But when Sanballat the Horonite and Tobiah the Ammonite official, and Geshem [Jasem] the Arab heard of it, they mocked and ridiculed us, saying, "What is this that you are doing? Are you rebelling against the king?" Then I replied to them, "The God of heaven is the one who will give us success, and we his servants are going to start building; but you have no share or claim or historic right in Jerusalem."

Exegesis of this text requires a look at the political background reviewed in the previous chapter. Under Nebuchadnezzer, king of Babylon, the kingdom of Judah was destroyed in 586 BCE and many Judeans were taken into captivity. The Persian Empire overtook and succeeded Babylon. The Persians were more tolerant in religious matters than their predecessors, and Cyrus, king of Persia, allowed Jews to return to Judea. "He [Cyrus] and his successors actually encouraged the distinctive religions and customs of their subject peoples to flourish, with the hope that by directing their energies inward to the cultivation of their respective cultures, they would accept Persian control of the political arena."[4] Around 445 BCE the Persians appointed Nehemiah as governor of Judea to administrator its civil affairs. Some time later, they appointed Ezra, a Judean priest and scribe, to administer the religious affairs of the Judean community. Nehemiah and Ezra worked together to bring about civil and religious reform in the community, and their most important project was to rebuild the city of Jerusalem and the temple.

As previously noted, life in Palestine had undergone many changes during the years of the exile. Although many of the elite were taken to exile, the country was never empty, and various ethnic and racial groups had moved in from the surrounding lands to form a multiethnic and multiracial society. Nehemiah mentions the presence of the Samaritans, Arabs, Ammonites, and Philistines (3:34; 4:1). One instance that Nehemiah records (2:19-20) is of a conflict that arose over the building of the walls of Jerusalem. Apparently, Sanballat, governor of Samaria, Tubia the Ammonite, and Jasem the Arab expressed opposition to the building of the walls of Jerusalem, fearing that it could be the beginning of a regional control establishment or even a rebellion against the Persian Empire. Nehemiah told them frankly that they had no right or share in Jerusalem: "The God of heaven is the one who will give us success, and we his servants are going to start building; but you have *no share or claim or historic right in Jerusalem*" (v. 20) [emphasis mine]. The implication is clear: Nehemiah and his fellow Jews, and no one else, had the sole right to Jerusalem. The fact that the dispute was between Nehemiah the Jew and strong local officials, including Jasem the Arab, sharpen the text's relevance for today.

Ezra records a similar incident. Whereas the conflict in Nehemiah was spurred by the building of the walls of Jerusalem, the rebuilding of the temple itself prompted Ezra's event. In this case, some of the people of the land came to offer help in the construction but Zerubbabel, a descendant of the line of David, turned them down: "You shall have no part with us in building a house to our God; but we alone will build to the Lord, the God of Israel . . ." (Ezra 4:1-4).[5]

What happened around the mid-fifth century BCE is being repeated in our times when the Nehemiahs of today claim exclusive rights to Jerusalem and deny the rights of others to live there. Today the political leaders of Israel show total unwillingness to share Jerusalem. They reiterate the same words: "No share or claim or historic right." These exclusivist texts in Nehemiah and Ezra sum up the argument that is promulgated by the government of Israel and its friends. It denies the historical rights of others, refutes any other claims to Jerusalem, and rejects the idea of sharing the city with others.

These texts exemplify a mind-set that is closed and narrow, that considers itself above others, and refuses to accept people as they are. Such a position expresses a theology that is exclusive, narrow, and xenophobic and it can never lead to peace, whether in its historic setting or in our contemporary context.

An Inclusive Text: Psalm 87

On the holy mount stands the city he founded;
The LORD loves the gates of Zion
more than all the dwellings of Jacob.
Glorious things are spoken of you,
O city of God.

Among those who know me I mention Rahab and
Babylon;
Philistia too, and Tyre, with Ethiopia—
"This one was born there," they say.

And of Zion it shall be said,
"This one and that one were born in it";
for the Most High himself will establish it.
The LORD records, as he registers the peoples,
"This one was born here,"

Singers and dancers alike say
"All my springs are in you."

This psalm is usually referred to as a hymn of Zion, with its focus on Jerusalem. Because a simple reading of this psalm does not obviously reveal its deeper meaning, some context must be given.

The perceived significance of Jerusalem began to crystallize after the exile—most likely in the fifth century BCE. Given the loss of the monarchy and the unlikelihood of its restoration, religious leaders began to take on greater significance than kings and princes. Greater attention was paid to the stipulations of religious laws and to organizing the community on religious grounds. The people were caught between the idealized glories of the past that spoke of kings and kingdoms and the realities of the present as they lived under foreign rules. For some, this meant agitating intermittently for independence through uprisings and resistance. Others, however, sang of God, who puts an end to war. The theology of Jerusalem was directed more and more to what God could continue to do rather than what a former king was able to do.

There is much debate in scholarly circles about this psalm. Some scholars believe it must refer to Jews living outside Palestine or to converts to "Judaism." I prefer to think that it is one of those rare texts from Hebrew scripture that is more progressive theologically and reflects the kingdom or reign of God as very inclusive. It can be compared with certain texts in Micah or Isaiah, or even the text par excellence of the book of Jonah. In many ways, this psalm critiques Nehemiah's and Ezra's exclusive concepts of Jerusalem.

The hymns of Zion reflect the belief that God's presence provides people with physical protection and military security. Some commentators have observed that, "In a world shredded by war and violence, the city of God becomes the symbol and the reality of the possibility of peace."[6] Psalm 48 declares that "Within its citadels God has shown himself a sure defense" (48:3), and another psalm states, "God is in the midst of the city; it shall not be moved" (Ps. 46:4-5). It is God who provides security in the face of enemies. It is God who "makes wars cease to the end of the earth; he breaks the bow, and shatters the spear; he burns the shields with fire" (Ps. 46:9). God brings peace to Zion, and since God dwells in Zion, Zion is the city of God. Without God, there can be no lasting peace or security.

The image presented in Psalm 87 is of God standing at the gate of Jerusalem, welcoming all into the city, including Israel's worst enemies. Rahab, a mythological beast, represents Egypt, and then Babylon, Philistia, Tyre (representative city of Phoenicia), and Ethiopia. The mention of Babylon but not Assyria suggests an early postexilic date, perhaps after the rebuilding of the temple (520-516 BCE). The fifth verse of Psalm 87 says that all who know God are born, or have their life begin, in Zion. Jerusalem is the spiritual mother of all of God's children. The Lord has recorded that they were born in it. Even those empires or nations perceived to be enemies of Jerusalem are invited by God to worship and be renewed in the holy city.

It is interesting to note that all who worship God in Jerusalem become residents of the city as if they are reborn there: "Worship in Zion has the power to transform the distant pilgrim into a person reborn within the gates of Zion, the city of God. It is very much similar to the vision of Isaiah and

Micah, a vision of peace, a vision of a God who puts an end to war. . . . The Hymns of Zion help the community to discover that it is the God in the city, not the king in the palace, who brings well-being and peace to the world outside Zion's walls."[7]

If our interpretation of this psalm has credence, it must have been written by a theologian/poet with a wonderful inclusive vision of Jerusalem that embraces all people. This vision is certainly the antithesis of Nehemiah's view. Furthermore, if this psalm is postexilic, it demonstrates the profound effect of exile. On the one hand, exile made the people narrow, resentful, and hard, as appears to be recorded in Nehemiah and Ezra. Yet, on the other hand, exile can help people become open, inclusive, and softhearted. Exile can lead to exclusive attitudes and theology, but it can also create people who look to embrace others. This appears to be the theological insight about God recorded in Psalm 87.

It is important to emphasize that the texts from Nehemiah and Ezra, the exclusive and the inclusive, both come from the Old Testament. Yet, for all those who work for a shared and open Jerusalem, Psalm 87 is much closer to the spirit of justice and peace that embraces the other rather than shuts them out.

These two texts demonstrate the tension and the struggle on the question of Jerusalem. Since 1967, Israel has claimed exclusive sovereignty over the city, refusing to share it equitably with the Palestinians. Psalm 87 provides a basis for sharing. There is a constant pull between these forces of exclusion and inclusion. Yet, because exclusion negates the rights of others, we need to work for an inclusive paradigm that can guarantee a future of peace for all of Jerusalem's inhabitants.

Beyond Jerusalem: John 4:21-24

"Our ancestors worshiped on this mountain, but you say that the place where people must worship is in Jerusalem." Jesus said to her, "Woman, believe me, the hour is coming when you will worship the Father neither on this mountain nor in Jerusalem. You worship what you do not know; we worship what we know, for salvation is from the Jews. But the hour is coming, and is now here, when the true worshipers will worship the Father in spirit and truth, for the Father seeks such as these to worship him. God is spirit, and those who worship him must worship in sprit and truth."

The context of this passage is the discussion between Jesus and the woman of Samaria. Jesus and his disciples passed through the region of Samaria, a journey most Jews of that time would have avoided because of the hostility between Jews and Samaritans. Yet, according to John, this was the path Jesus intended to follow. There, stopping at Jacob's well, he began a conversation with a Samaritan woman, asking her for a drink. She was obviously surprised that a Jewish man would make such a request of her, a Samaritan woman. Jesus then raised the level of their exchange, speaking with her about living water.

The conversation turned personal when Jesus asked the woman about her spouse. This was a sensitive issue since she had been married on multiple occasions and was then living with a man who was not her husband. She quickly attempted to change the subject by turning the conversation to a religious topic, Jerusalem. She explained that for Samaritans the holy place for the worship of God was Mount Girizim while for Jews it was Jerusalem. Which was the right place for worship? Jesus responded: "Not here nor there, God is spirit and those who worship God must worship in spirit and in truth."

As seen above, the two texts from the Old Testament view Jerusalem as a physical city populated by people, but they represent two different theologies of land: one exclusive and the other inclusive. The New Testament theology of land goes beyond that of the Old Testament. In fact, it is clear in the New Testament that Jesus is not concerned with the issue of land—his focus is the reign of God. The city of Jerusalem and other physical places, then, lose their significance. Every piece of land is part of God's world because the coming of Jesus Christ has sanctified all land. The incarnation of God in human flesh has consecrated the world and all of humanity. While it is true that Christ suffered and died on the cross in Jerusalem and was resurrected in Jerusalem and that the church came into being there by the power of the Holy Spirit, yet Jesus told the disciples to go into the whole world and preach and teach all nations. "You shall receive power when the Holy Spirit will come on you and you will be my witnesses in Jerusalem, Judea, Samaria and to the end of the earth" (Acts 1:8). Jesus, who transcends all, points us beyond geography. God can be worshiped anywhere in spirit and in truth. God's reign is not limited to one area or one people. It is for all.

During the first three hundred years of the Christian faith, no special status was accorded to Jerusalem. In fact, the greater centers of the faith were Antioch, Alexandria, and Rome. Later, Constantinople became a fourth important faith-center. It was not until 451 CE that Jerusalem was recognized as a patriarchate. Until then, the emphasis had been on the missionary thrust of the church through spreading the gospel. This focal point is best seen in the teaching and preaching of the metropolitan bishop of Palestine, Eusebius, whose see was in Caesarea, not Jerusalem.[8] Eusebius did not emphasize the significance of Jerusalem, as he believed that the holiness of the place was substituted and replaced and transformed by the holiness of Jesus Christ. What was important was not the holy city but the holiness of Christ. The focus was not on Jerusalem but on what Christ has done and continues to do offering redemption to the entire world: "The Divine Presence is to be experienced in Jesus . . . and his spirit is not geographically conditioned."[9]

It is important to point out that when Jesus was talking to the Samaritan woman, he did not say *where* Jews or Samaritans should worship, but that people shall worship God in spirit and in truth. Once again, he reiterates that all people, not one segment of humanity (whether they are Jews or others) will worship God, and the physical place is no longer important.

Only after the fourth century and the building of the Church of the Resurrection in Jerusalem did the church leadership—initially, Bishop Cyril of Jerusalem—emphasize the holiness of the place. While many Christians still cling to the significance of Jerusalem (is this part of human nature?), the words of Jesus to the Samaritan woman indicate clearly that true worship of God transcends any physical geography.

The New Jerusalem: Revelation 21:1-5

> Then I saw a new heaven and a new earth; for the first heaven and the first earth had passed away, and the sea was no more. And I saw the holy city, the new Jerusalem, coming down out of heaven from God, prepared as a bride adorned for her husband. And I heard a loud voice from the throne saying, "See, the home of God is among mortals. He will dwell with them as their God; they will be his peoples, and God himself will be with them; he will wipe every tear from their eyes. Death will be no more; mourning and crying and pain will be no more, for the first things have passed away." And the one who was seated on the throne said, "See, I am making all things new."

In the book of Revelation, the author John saw the city of Rome as the embodiment of the evil city of ancient Babylon. He pointed out the great contrast between life in the New City of Jerusalem and life in Babylon. To live in the New Jerusalem is to experience life with God because God lives in the midst of God's people. The characteristics of Babylon—its injustice, misery, wretchedness, and everything that oppresses—are no more. Even death is wiped out. In its place is life with God, an experience of beauty and love. The contrast is very striking, as Wes Howard-Brook and Anthony Gwyther describe in their book on Revelation: "Babylon exists wherever sociopolitical power coalesces into an entity that stands against the worship of YHWH [God] alone," while the "New Jerusalem is found wherever the human community rejects the lies and violence of empire and places God at the center of its shared life."[10] John saw that the real struggle in the world is between Babylon/Rome and the metaphoric New Jerusalem, between the city of the Beast and the city of the Lamb, the Dragon's empire and the kingdom of God where the faithful followers of Jesus live.

The book of Revelation is a call to "Come out of Babylon" (18:4) that both encouraged and warned the churches. Those who were faithfully resisting Rome were encouraged to persist in their resistance. Those who were colluding with empire were warned that it was time to abandon Babylon. Revelation called them to discern the true character of their faith and to distance themselves from the imperial seduction of their time and place.

They were exhorted to live in the New Jerusalem, a community of faith that would resist the ways of empire in order to place God at the center of its life:[11] "The downfall of Babylon is not brought about by a passive waiting on God. Rather, it is won by joining forces with God and the Lamb in active resistance to empire and creative participation in New Jerusalem."[12]

In her book, *The Rapture Exposed: The Message of Hope in the Book of Revelation*, Barbara Rossing comments on the way Martin Luther King Jr. contrasted the vision of the New Jerusalem (Rev. 21) with what he saw in Memphis, Tennessee, in the 1960s:

> It's alright to talk about "streets flowing with milk and honey," but God has commanded us to be concerned about the slums down here, and his children who can't eat three square meals a day. It's all right to talk about the New Jerusalem, but one day, God's preacher must talk about the new New York, the new Atlanta, the new Philadelphia, the new Los Angeles, the new Memphis, Tennessee. This is what we have to do.[13]

Rossing writes, "Revelation gives us God's urgent message of hope for all the world's cities and communities. It promises a vision for our life in God after we die. But even more importantly, New Jerusalem holds promise for this world, giving a vision for 'what we have to do' in the words of [Martin Luther] King."[14]

The challenges of Israel-Palestine should always recall for us the New Jerusalem. Although whatever God has promised lies in God's hand, as people of faith we have work to do now. We must continue to work to establish the reign of God here and now; we must continue to work for justice and truth; and we must continue to resist the evil of empire.

According to Revelation the sins of Babylon/Rome and empire were (and are) whoring, murder, economic exploitation, and arrogance. "Whoring" signified infidelity and idolatry. People who are seduced by empire become evil in their ways. Howard-Brook and Gwyther ask, "Why is empire able to enlist so many into its service? Why do so many good people cheer for empire and give their lives for it? Why do those willing to seek peace, justice, and community always seem so few? The answer resides in the seductive character of Babylon."[15]

"Murder" connotes violence and imperial terrorism. Empire violently kills those who obstruct its power. Biblical scholar John Dominic Crossan describes the imperial theology of Rome as consisting of "religion, war, victory, and peace . . . easily summarized as 'peace through victory.' "[16] The *Pax Americana* maintains its dominance in the same fashion, as articulated in documents such as the "Project for a New American Century"[17] and through such actions as the war in Iraq. Such "peace" achieved through military victory is a myth.

Empire as described in Revelation is also an economic exploiter. This describes well the power of global capital today. David Korten writes that "free market ideology has been embraced around the world with the fervor of a fundamentalist religious faith. . . . [T]he economics profession serves as its priesthood . . . to question its doctrine has become virtual heresy." Some of its dogmas are: "1. Economic growth is the only path to human progress. 2. Unrestrained free markets are the best mode of trade. 3. Economic globalization is beneficial to almost all. . . ."[18]

Arrogance is a fourth characteristic of empire mentioned in Revelation:

In his vision of Babylon, John sees that the activities of seduction, coercion, and exploitation in which Babylon specializes are all underpinned by an attitude of imperial arrogance. . . . In Revelation, this sin is expressed by the inability of imperial actors to envision the end of empire. . . . Empire never admits its fragility or its finitude in time or space. In this respect Rome was no different from its predecessors. The Roman myth of Eternity, which held that Rome would last forever, was a manifestation of that shortsightedness. . . . Arrogance at the top of sociopolitical structures blinds rulers to the fallout from their actions. Where the citizenry see this arrogance as a sign of power, the blindness is intensified. Yet the Bible contends that such arrogance is self-destructive: by its very nature it is bound to fall.[19]

Palestinian life under Israeli occupation experiences the presence of similar sins. And the message of Revelation applies equally to our own people as it is so easy to be tainted by life in Babylon. Palestinians must constantly heed the call to remove themselves figuratively from empire and to make their home in the New Jerusalem with a community that centers its life on God: "Those who faithfully reject empire and embrace the way of God are the residents of the New Jerusalem. It is with these people that God lives: 'Behold, the dwelling of God is with the people, God will dwell with them and they will be God's people . . .' " (Rev. 21:3).[20] In New Jerusalem is found the tree of life whose leaves are for the healing of the nations: "while Ezekiel saw the leaves of the trees as being 'for healing,' John sees that they are 'for the healing of *the nations.*' "[21] This picture is of an inclusive community of faith that centers its life in God and looks to God's embracing love, healing, and care.

MOVING TOWARD THE "NEW JERUSALEM"

The heart of the Middle East conflict is the conflict over Palestine, and the heart of the Palestine conflict is the city of Jerusalem. Tragically, the government of Israel has chosen the exclusive paradigm of Nehemiah, a paradigm that will never lead to peace. Nothing but perpetual conflict will lie in its wake because it is built on selfishness and greed, on control and negation of others. Slogans such as "Jerusalem is Jewish" or "Jerusalem is Islamic" reflect this narrow, exclusive, and xenophobic paradigm. With it in place, future reconciliation does not seem possible.

This ugly, destructive picture of Jerusalem must be rejected. Jerusalem cannot and should not be the exclusive claim of one nation or one religion. Before David conquered it by force, it was a Canaanite town inhabited by Jebusites. According to the book of Joshua, written most likely during or after the exile, "But the people of Judah could not drive out the Jebusites, the inhabitants of Jerusalem; so the Jebusites live with the people of Judah in Jerusalem to this day" (Josh. 15:63). The prophet Ezekiel also recognized the non-Israelite origin of Jerusalem: "Thus says the Lord GOD to Jerusalem: Your origin and your birth were in the land of the Canaanites; your father was an Amorite, and your mother a Hittite" (Ezek. 16:3). There have been a number of attempts to make Jerusalem exclusive for one group throughout history, but they have never lasted. The city seems to vomit out exclusion. The Crusaders who tried to make it Christian failed, and today the government of Israel is doing everything it can to Judaize it, yet it will not succeed.

The archetype of Psalm 87 is much more favorable to peace. It presents a vision of Jerusalem that embraces all people, including enemies, in an inclusiveness that knows no exceptions. All the people and religions of the region are welcome as well as those who arrive from far away. After all, Jerusalem does not belong only to all the people of Israel-Palestine, it belongs to the world. Psalm 87 reminds us that "Jerusalem at peace cannot belong exclusively to one people, one country or one religion. (It) should be open to all, shared by all."²²

We must keep in mind that although humans tend to cling to places—especially so-called holy places—and are willing to shed blood to guard and protect them, God is not limited in this way. God is bigger and greater than all that we humans create for God. We do have a need to sacralize the material—we need things that we can see and touch—but we must remain aware that it is through the Spirit that we worship God. We must transcend material things and physical places and encounter God in the love and service of our fellow human beings. When the place becomes more important than the human being who is present there, we have strayed far from the knowledge and love of God.

Ultimately, we must build the New Jerusalem here and now. We live today in the midst of empire, and it demands our allegiance at every turn. Because empire can exist only through violence and domination, we must rely on our faith in Jesus the Christ to reject the deceptive nature of empire. When faced with empire, we must remember that "the societies that have lasted the longest in the holy city have, generally, been the ones that were prepared for some kind of tolerance and coexistence in the Holy City. That, rather than a sterile and deadly struggle for sovereignty, must be the way to celebrate Jerusalem's sanctity today."²³

PART III

THE PEACE WE DREAM OF

Chapter 12

Israel's Predicament

All that is needed for the triumph of evil, is that good people do nothing.
—Edmund Burke

Before turning to the prospects for the future, a major obstacle needs to be addressed that obstructs the way to peace, and that is Israel's desire to be recognized as an exclusively Jewish state. This goal takes precedence over peace. Because of it, Israel demonstrates no desire to genuinely pursue peace.

Many precious opportunities for peace have been missed over the years. Even today countless people think that the Palestinians and the Arabs are the real obstacles for peace. People say: if the Palestine Liberation Organization (PLO) would only recognize Israel, Israel would make peace; if the Palestinians would only stop the violence, Israel would make peace; if the Palestinians would only stop the suicide bombings, Israel would make peace; if the people of Gaza would stop launching the *qassam* rockets, Israel would make peace; and so on.

Some of these steps have been accomplished completely or partially, and yet the desired peace has not been achieved. Even more significantly, the Palestinian Authority (since 1988) and the Arab states (since 2002) have officially extended their hands, expressing their eagerness to make peace with Israel, yet Israel has spurned these offers. In fact, the Palestinians and the Arabs have made three bold advances.

1. In 1988, the Palestinians, through accepting U.N. Resolution 242, implicitly recognized the state of Israel within the 1967 borders and expressed willingness to enter into discussion. Israel did not reciprocate.

2. In 1993, at the beginning of the Oslo Peace Process, the Palestinians, through the Palestine Liberation Organization, gave a more formal recognition of Israel's right to exist. However, the Oslo Peace Process did not produce the desired peace.

3. In 2002, the Arab League expressed its willingness to recognize and make peace with Israel provided it withdrew to the 1967 borders in line with U.N. Resolutions 242 and 338. The government of Israel did not even consider the offer.[1]

The Palestinians are not the real obstacle to peace. Although Israel talks about peace continuously and gives the impression that it is seeking it, in actual fact, Israel is not ready for peace. To begin with, Israel is unwilling to abide by international law to resolve the conflict. However, a deeper problem lies in Israel's perception of the nature of its own state. No matter how peaceful the Palestinians are or how much they show willingness to submit to Israeli demands, Israel will not enter into a peace agreement except on its own terms and to achieve its own objectives. What are the implications of Israel's intransigence?

ISRAEL AS A JEWISH STATE

Israel insists that Arabs, including the Palestinians, must recognize Israel as a *Jewish* state. The implications of such recognition might not be immediately clear. When Israel is recognized as a Jewish state, then all those Israeli citizens who are not Jewish will find themselves basically disfranchised. There are 1.3 million Palestinian Arabs who are citizens of the state of Israel. They have no other citizenship; they live in their homeland, and that is where they want to stay, but they are not Jewish. They comprise over 20 percent of the population of the state of Israel. The recognition of Israel as a Jewish state closes the door on them as well as on the right of return of any Palestinian.

From the perspective of Israel, one of the greatest threats that faces the state is demographic.[2] Before too long the Arab Israelis will compose a quarter of the population and their numbers will continue to increase. A number of Israeli officials have already issued warning signals. If Israel is officially recognized as a Jewish state by the Palestinians, then as non-Jewish citizens they will have no place in it except as aliens or unwanted guests. But these Palestinian Arabs are the indigenous people of the land whose presence predates the establishment of Israel. Why should they be stripped of their citizenship and be susceptible to transfer as some extremist Jewish ministers and government officials advocate? The refugees who long for return are also seen as a demographic threat by Israel. They are denied the right of return to their homes guaranteed by international law and U.N. Resolution 194.

The demographic threat to Israel is not new, and the debate surfaces periodically. It has been dealt with primarily by distinguishing between citizenship and nationality. Only Jews can be nationals of the state, Arabs can only be citizens. Usually citizenship and nationality are one and the same. It is possible that some religious Jews think of the differentiation in Leviticus 19:33 between the alien in the land and the native Israelite.[3] The implication is that these citizens will never enjoy equality with their Jewish counterparts. After all, Israel's basic law of return does not apply to non-Jews. The concept of transfer, unfortunately, is not new either: while the word "transfer" may have a mild sound, in essence it means expulsion and forced removal.[4]

Although Arab Israeli citizens have been treated as second-class citizens, many have thought that it would only be a matter of time before the Israeli government would see the illegality of that discrimination and rectify the injustice. But this has not happened; instead a more sinister form of discrimination is surfacing. With audacity, Israel maintains that it will not enter into any peaceful agreement with the Palestinians and the Arab states unless the

Palestinians, all Arabs, and the world recognize the Jewish character of the state. This, of course, is supported by the United States. The insistence on an exclusively Jewish character for Israel is thus a major obstacle that shuts the door to peace.

THE ABSENCE OF A CONSTITUTION

It is interesting to note that to date Israel does not have a constitution. Many problems have stood in the way. The first major problem is the definition of who is a Jew and what defines Jewishness. While some Orthodox groups would define being Jewish in a very narrow way, a broader definition is problematic. Would it include Messianic Jews, meaning those Jews who have become Christians? Or secular Jews who may be atheists or who may have converted to Buddhism or Christianity? Are they still Jewish? It should be noted that the vast majority of the Jewish citizens of Israel are secular, nonobservant, or atheist. Does Jewishness include religion and ethnicity? If Israel perceives itself as the state for all the Jews in the world, what does that mean for Jews who are citizens in their own countries and are happy where they are? In the view of Israel, all Jews in any part of the world are eligible citizens and potential nationals.

The second problem concerns the non-Jews. If the state is Jewish, what is the legal standing of its Arab citizens? Long before the state of Israel was established, Arab Palestinians—Muslims, Christians, and Jews—were living in the land. Is it conceivable that with the stroke of a pen, the Muslim and Christian citizens of the land could lose their rights and become disfranchised? Thus, forming a constitution for Israel must begin with this complex issue of citizenship.

ETHNIC NATIONALISM

Closely connected with the concept of the Jewish state is the question of nationalism. The world is moving toward internationalism and the abandonment of narrow nationalism, as indicated by movements of economic and regional cooperation such as the formation of the European Union. Israel, however, stresses a form of nationalism that is obsolete and past-oriented rather than future-oriented.

While fear prompts Israel to emphasize an ethnic form of nationalism, such an emphasis cannot be justified in our contemporary world. Today Israel's concept of nationalism is considered racist. Yet, Israel has been able to market its narrow nationalism to many Western countries and gain support.

Many countries, especially in the West, view Israel as the only democracy in the Middle East. Not everyone sees the stark contradiction that is Israel. If Palestinian Muslims were to insist that Palestine must be a Muslim state, would people consider it a true democracy? Although Israel has successfully used its propaganda in the West, the Israeli façade is beginning to crumble as many Palestinians and an increasing number of Jews now see the discriminatory and racist nature of the Israeli state.

THREE JEWISH TESTIMONIES

Avraham Burg is an Israeli who sensed the inherent dangers in Israel's identity. For many years he was a member of the Knesset (Israel's Parliament) and also served several years as its elected speaker. In that capacity, in 2000 he served as interim president of Israel for twenty days. Throughout his public life in Israel, while holding prominent positions in both the Israeli and world Zionist establishments, he began to detect the dangerous trends in the structure of the Israeli state. On September 15, 2003, he wrote in *The Guardian*:

> The Israeli nation today rests on a scaffolding of corruption, and on foundations of oppression and injustice. As such, the end of the Zionist enterprise is already on our doorsteps. There is a real chance that ours will be the last Zionist generation. There may yet be a Jewish state here, but it will be a different sort, strange and ugly.[5]

Burg contrasted the situation in Israel with that of Germany in the 1930s, explaining that there are two different types of nationalism, liberal and ethnic. Liberal nationalism finds its roots in the French Revolution where the masses cried for liberty, equality, and fraternity; in a system characterized by liberal nationalism, all citizens stand equally under the rule of law. Ethnic nationalism, on the other hand, which has its roots in German Romanticism, views the state as belonging to or bestowing privileges on a particular ethnic group while denying them to other ethnicities. Indeed, ethnic nationalism preceded Nazism in Germany. Burg notes that Israel has chosen ethnic nationalism and that Israel is becoming racist when it refuses to be the state for all its citizens:[6] "The horror of the Holocaust created a paranoia that sees every gentile as anti-Semitic; and 40 years of maintaining a brutal occupation have spawned a militaristic spirit and widespread contempt for universal norms."[7]

Eventually Avraham Burg left Israel to live in France. His book, written in Hebrew, is entitled *Victory over Hitler*.[8] Burg maintains that the only way to transcend the ethnic nationalism of Hitler is to create "a vision of a new Israel in which every citizen, Jew and Palestinian, stands equal before the law."[9]

Jeff Halper, an Israeli professor of anthropology and head of the Israeli Committee Against House Demolitions (ICAHD), addresses the "ethnocracy" of Israel. Israeli ethnocracy, he asserts, based on tribal nationalism and maintained by a security paradigm, is an obstacle to any vision of peace based on justice and inclusion. He defines ethnocracy as follows:

It arises when one particular group . . . seizes control of the government and armed forces in order to enforce a regime of exclusive privilege in what is in fact a multi-ethnic or multi-religious society. Ethnocracy, or ethno-nationalism, privileges *ethnos* over *demos*, whereby one's ethnic affiliation, be it defined by race, descent, religion, language or national origin, takes precedence over citizenship in determining to whom a country actually "belongs."[10]

Halper argues that "Israel presents itself as a Western democracy . . . and, on the surface, it resembles one. In fact, it is something quite different, an ethnocracy based on an Eastern European tribal nationalism."[11] Halper believes that Israeli ethnocracy has been able to maintain a façade of democracy because ethnic cleansing and demographic manipulation of borders, which have removed Palestinians, has left Israeli Jews the majority of the population. Arabs can be granted a certain level of Israeli citizenship and rights without upsetting the balance of the ethnocracy. However, there are "serious . . . structural inequalities inherent in any ethnocracy," such as the marginalization of Arabs in the Knesset, the Law of Return, land issues, housing and education, house demolitions aimed at Arabs, religious laws governing marriages, and burial codes.[12] Furthermore, with the population of Palestinian citizens in Israel now at 20 percent, "ethnocracy, always present but concealed, is beginning to assert itself."[13] Halper maintains that any future peace will have to overcome the obstacle of ethnocracy within Zionism in order to truly be just and inclusive.

Joel Kovel, a Jewish American activist and psychiatrist and Green Party candidate for U.S. president in 2000, published a book entitled *Overcoming Zionism*[14] in which he maintains that with Israel one is contending with a settler-form of colonial racism that follows two strategies to justify their action against the indigenous people of the land through land confiscation and domination. The first strategy is to present an a priori claim to the land ("God gave us the land") and by invoking past suffering ("Look at how much we have suffered"), and the second is to denigrate the indigenous people by referring to them as subhuman or congenital terrorists, in contrast to the more civilized and ethically superior Jews. Israel's capable propaganda machine has long worked to create myths and stereotypes to undermine and humiliate the Palestinians.[15]

Thus racism is set into motion, and remains so, grounded in an exclusion based not on what the Other does but entirely on what the Other *is,* or to be more exact, *is not,* namely, Jewish. By this one gesture, no matter how one rationalizes a Jewish state as owed to the Jews by virtue of their sufferings, or ethical superiority, or promises made to ancestors, or generations of landlessness, or a Covenant with God, or cultural genius, or just because it feels good to have a state for one's own kind—one violates the whole law by which humanity has risen above the muck of narrow self-interest and cyclical vengeance.[16]

These testimonies represent a growing number of Jewish academics who have become disenchanted with Israeli injustice and oppression of the Palestinians. Indeed, many have left Israel and emigrated to the West.

THE ACRI REPORT

In 2007, the Association for Civil Rights in Israel (ACRI) released a report entitled *The State of Human Rights in Israel and the Occupied Territories.*[17] It analyzes a disturbing trend—that "Racism toward Arab citizens among the Jewish public continues to rise"—and presents the following statistics:

- Fifty percent of the Israelis interviewed do not think that Jews and Arabs should enjoy full equal rights.
- Fifty-five percent of the Israeli Jews surveyed support the idea that the government should encourage Arab emigration.
- Seventy-eight percent are opposed to Arab political parties joining the governing coalition.
- Fifty percent of the Jewish population report feelings of fear when hearing Arabic spoken on the street.
- Seventy-five percent of those questioned would not agree to live in the same building as Arabs.
- Over half of the Israeli population agrees that Arabs and Jews should have separate recreational facilities.[18]

The ACRI report adds that it "does not take very much for feelings of fear, hatred, and racism to be translated into actions."[19] It records discrimination against Arab citizens of Israel in the form of popular racism, stereotypes in media portrayals, draft legislation in the Knesset regarding mandatory military service and land usage for "Jews only," racism in airport security checks, allocation of development funds, and restrictions on freedom of expression and political activity. To this list can be added the Law of Return and the laws that determine nationality. Visitors from South Africa have said that the clear and disturbing tendencies noted in the ACRI report resemble their own experiences under apartheid.

SOUTH AFRICAN TESTIMONIALS

Farid Esack, a South African Muslim theologian who has visited Israel-Palestine a number of times, made the following remarks at a conference in Boston in October 2007.

If anything, I think the apartheid analogy is often a weak analogy in relation to how the Palestinians are experiencing Zionism. In apartheid

South Africa we never had the walls that we see in Israel. We never had separate roads for black people and for white people as we see in Israel and in Palestine. We didn't have separate number plates for Arab cars. No, our courts never sanctioned collective punishment. Our courts never sanctioned torture, as the Israeli courts have. No, the apartheid regime never singled out for particular abuse the land, the destruction of the olive groves and their fruits. . . . Our engagement in solidarity with the Palestinians is not for the Palestinians. We are really doing this for ourselves. . . . Desmond Tutu often said that this struggle against apartheid was a barometer of our humanness. Our humanness is measured by the extent to which we are moved by the suffering of other people.[20]

John Dugard, a special *rapporteur* on human rights in the occupied territories to the U.N. Council of Human Rights, also spoke at the Boston conference.

What is happening in the Palestinian territory is that Israel is practicing apartheid but in a very dishonest and concealed manner. At least South African apartheid was open and honest. There were notices to indicate that certain facilities were for blacks and certain facilities were for whites only. In Israel you cannot easily access the law. You just have to take it from some member of the IDF that this is the law for a particular day.[21]

Dugard cited an incident that happened in the occupied West Bank:

A former Israeli cabinet minister Shulamit Aloni said that she confronted a member of the IDF when he was confiscating a Palestinian vehicle for driving on a settler road. She said, "What is the legal justification for this action?" He said, "This is the practice, what do you expect us to do? To put up a sign saying settlers only or Palestinians only? If that happens everyone will start taking photographs and we will be seen to be like South Africa."[22]

THE WAY OF RACISM

The turning point in Israel's movement toward apartheid was building the wall in the West Bank, now known to many as the apartheid wall. Although Israel claims it is a security fence, it is clear that it was built to confiscate additional Palestinian land, to separate the Palestinians from each other, to humiliate them and oppress them, to make their lives miserable to encourage emigration, and to create safer boundaries for Israel. The convoluted route of the wall also relieves the demographic threat of an increasing Palestinian population, which haunts the state of Israel. For example, "Approximately

25% of the 253,000 Palestinians living in East Jerusalem have been cut off from the city by the Barrier," separating them from work places, schools, and neighbors, but also keeping them outside of the demographic balance in Jerusalem.[23] At the same time, the Wall plunges into the West Bank to keep the population of Israeli settlements, illegal under international law, "inside" the Wall and with easy access to Jerusalem.[24] It is not surprising that the International Court of Justice has advised that the wall is illegal.[25] In light of the deteriorating situation within the Palestinian occupied territories, John Dugard made the following suggestion:

> [I]t would be helpful to start talking about the occupation as an aggravated occupation, one which has elements of colonialism and elements of apartheid. I think it would be very helpful if the International Court of Justice were to be asked for a further advisory opinion on the legal consequences of prolonged occupation, the consequences for the occupied people, the consequences for the occupying power, and the consequences for third states, because third states like the United States also have obligations in respect of the occupied people. . . . One of the sad things . . . is that the United Nations has handed over everything to a quartet . . . [that is] totally dominated by the United States and is giving its unashamed support to Israel at the expense of the Palestinian people.[26]

Many Israeli Jews used the Hebrew word *hafrada* in expressing their desire to separate themselves from the Palestinians. This word, which means separation, is comparable to the Afrikaner word *apartheid*. Although in its origin apartheid also meant separation, over the years it began to acquire a more sinister and racist connotation. This can easily be the future of the word *hafrada*. However, today many South Africans and Jews of conscience feel that the word *hafrada* does not do justice to Israel's action against the Palestinians. Jeff Halper has suggested that a more appropriate Hebrew word is *nishul*, which means dispossession. The government of Israel is going beyond separation from the Palestinians; its goal seems to be outright dispossession in the form of total ethnic cleansing.

It is important to point out that peace is not possible as long as the government of Israel walks the way of *hafrada* and *nishul*, which inevitably lead to racism. Racism can never lead to peace. As noted in the book of Proverbs, "Sometimes there is a way that seems to be right, but in the end it is the way to death" (16:25).

There are many good people in Israel who would reject the way of racism, but many give up and emigrate instead of staying and working for transformation. Unfortunately, once racism sets in, neither the one-state nor the two-state solutions can succeed. Joel Kovel believes that today a racist state cannot be a legitimate state; it must change, as did South Africa.[27] For Israel to survive and live in peace and security—and many Palestinians willingly accept Israel as a state—Israel has to abandon racism and must become a democratic state for all its citizens—Jewish and Arab alike.

IS TRANSFORMATION POSSIBLE?

Since 1967, Israel has not completely won any of its wars. While Israel has been good at making war, it has been a failure at making peace; experience shows that Israel is more willing to go to war than to do justice and live in peace. In spite of all its military strength, its nuclear capability, and its alliance with the United States, the one global power today, Israel continues to live in fear and insecurity. Israel faces serious problems because, as Avraham Burg describes it, "It rests on the foundation of oppression and injustice."[28] In order to gain peace and security, transformation is necessary in two different areas.

A Transformed Zionism

First of all, Israel must transform Zionism. Since its inception at the end of the nineteenth century, Zionism has captured the imagination of millions of Jews around the world. It inspired many Jews who rallied together to build an "impressive" state on most of the land of Palestine. However, it does not seem possible that Zionism, as conceived by Herzl and the early Zionists, is capable of leading the modern state of Israel to peace. Zionism was conceived in the womb of colonialism and imperialism and thus largely used violence and military power to bring the Zionist dream to fruition. But Zionism's ideology and its natural disposition are a hindrance and a liability today.

Israel is now a state and likes to think of itself as a state in the European sense. If Israel would like to model itself after Western European democracies, it must begin behaving like a European state. It must stop its discriminatory practices and respect the human rights of all people. It cannot continue to think in colonial terms. As long as it continues to confiscate other people's lands to expand its borders, it still lives in a colonial and imperialist framework. This is the paradigm in which Zionism was born and bred. Israel today needs a new paradigm that can lead to peace. If Zionism cannot be transformed, it must be abandoned.

Israel needs to realize that it lives in a different era today. In order to have peace, it must respect and implement international law. It must return to the Palestinians some of the land it has confiscated in the name of Zionism. It has to accept the Palestinians as partners and sharers of the land. If it is going to continue as an ideology, it must be totally transformed as it presently contains no seed or germ of peace. Its "ingredients" of violence, war, conflict, deception, dispossession, terrorism, and expulsion can never add up to peacemaking.

This does not mean that Israel must give up all of its previous successes. It can still live in peace on three-quarters of the land of historic Palestine, but it must have a new vision of peace, a transformed vision of neighbor, and a transformed vision of land. It is possible that in fifty years many Jews will look back at Zionism and consider it a shameful stage in the long history of the Jewish people.

A New Theology

Israel's Declaration of Independence states:

[The state] will promote the development of the country for the benefit of all its inhabitants; will be based on the principle of liberty, justice and peace as conceived by the Prophets of Israel; will uphold the full social and political equality of all its citizens, without distinction of religion, race, or sex; will guarantee freedom of religion, conscience, education and culture.[29]

Such a vision has never been realized. On the contrary, the state of Israel is moving further away from the vision expressed in its Declaration of Independence. In addition to transforming its political goals, Israel needs a new theology, one "based on the principle of liberty, justice and peace as conceived by the Prophets of Israel; [that] will uphold the full social and political equality of all its citizens . . ." Israel, in fact, has been living by an antiquated tribal theology, based on exclusive claims, that has brought insecurity and misery. As previously noted, such a tribal theology has been abandoned by many people, including many Jewish theologians. And the seeds of inclusiveness for Israel lie within its own Hebrew scriptures.

One text from the heart of the Torah was used in the American struggle for independence in the eighteenth century. The inscription around the Liberty Bell in Philadelphia comes from the book of Leviticus: "and you shall proclaim liberty throughout the land to all its inhabitants" (25:10). At the time these words from Leviticus were written, the ancient Israelites were not alone; many ethnic groups inhabited the land. While the text may have been addressed to one sector of the population, we have a choice today. We can interpret it to apply exclusively to Israeli Jews or it can embrace all the people of the land, whether Jewish, Muslim, Christian, or secular. Any group that chooses to interpret it exclusively is guilty of practicing racial or discriminatory behavior and attitudes. Such tendencies must be rejected. Liberation must be for all the people of the land regardless of their ethnic or racial backgrounds.

Israel's theology has also been fed and influenced by the exclusive and narrow biblical outlook of American Christian Zionists. When President George W. Bush visited Jerusalem to share in Israel's celebration of its sixtieth Day of Independence and addressed the Knesset, he noted that the establishment of the state of Israel "was more than the establishment of a new country. It was the redemption of an ancient promise given to Abraham and Moses and David—a homeland for the chosen people Eretz Yisrael."[30] His words, which may have disastrous political implications for peace in Israel-Palestine, raise many questions. Was he the victim of a Zionist script writer? Had he weighed the full impact of his words, or did they reflect a Christian Zionist exclusive theology on his part? With such a theology, does he really see himself capable of being an honest broker in mediating and brokering peace between Israel and the Palestinians? President Bush mentioned the promise of the land to Abraham, Moses, and David, but had he read the commandment God gave to Moses regarding the land for the fulfillment of the promise?

> In the plains of Moab by the Jordan at Jericho, the LORD spoke to Moses, saying: Speak to the Israelites, and say to them: When you cross over the Jordan into the land of Canaan, you shall drive out all the inhabitants of the land from before you, destroy all their figured stones, destroy all their cast images, and demolish all their high places. You shall take possession of the land and settle in it, for I have given you the land to possess. . . . But if you do not drive out the inhabitants of the land from before you, then those whom you let remain shall be as barbs in your eyes and thorns in your sides; they shall trouble you in the land where you are settling. And I will do to you as I thought to do to them. (Num. 33:50-53, 55-56)

Was President Bush suggesting such a resolution to the conflict today? Was he promoting the idea of the transfer and ethnic cleansing of the Palestinians? Does this reflect his concept of God? Does he know that this is precisely the solution promoted by a number of Israeli Jewish leaders including ministers and Knesset members and American Christian Zionists? Did he realize that he was citing some of the most ancient and primitive tribal theologies about the land and glossing over the more inclusive, universal, and enlightened theologies of the great prophets of the Old Testament? Did he intentionally ignore texts that could have contributed to justice and the making of peace between Israelis and Palestinians?

The Hebrew scriptures contain many inclusive texts that can inspire and promote a new theology that can lead to peace. Its pages include inclusive teachings about election and chosenness, God's mercy for all people, and God's demand for justice and righteousness. In fact a model for a new theology could be the message of the book of Jonah, which challenges leaders and people to see the inclusive nature of the one God, an inclusive theology of the people of God that embraces all of humanity, and an inclusive theology of land that opens the way for the sharing of the land between Israelis and Palestinians.[31] Israel must, however, abandon its exclusive tribal theology if it is serious about bringing about a genuine peace with the Palestinians. Only a transformed theology can lead to peace.

In the United States, the Liberty Bell is an icon of freedom. A tourist brochure that describes it reads, "To Americans who demanded independence on this site, and to those who even now seek self-determination, [the bell] still declares 'Proclaim Liberty throughout All the land unto All the Inhabitants Thereof.' Its crack is a reminder that liberty is imperfect, hopefully evolving to include those who have been denied full participation in a democratic society." This last phrase—those who have been denied full participation in a democratic society—describes the situation of the Palestinian people today, and it also describes the exclusionary nature of the Israeli "democracy." A true democratic Israel would guarantee liberty for all the people of the land—Israelis and Palestinians alike.

Chapter 13

The Two-State Solution Is Not Enough

O Lord, help us to disagree without being disagreeable, to differ without being difficult, to be honest without being tense, and to be frank without being offensive.
—Peter Marshall

With this advice of Peter Marshall, the goal before us all is to devise the best possible vision for peace and the best possible solution to the conflict in Israel-Palestine today.

NATIONALISM AND THE CONSTITUTION OF MODERN STATES

The historic Palestinian position from the end of World War I has been that Palestine belongs to its people who have lived there for millennia. It belongs to all those Muslims, Jews, and Christians who were born there and consider it their homeland. Even before modern concepts of nationalism were articulated in the nineteenth and twentieth centuries and national boundaries of states were defined, many indigenous peoples' self-identity included their ethnic and religious background as well as their geographic roots. They perceived themselves as belonging to a family, a tribe, a *hamoola* ("clan"), a village, a town, and a region. They spoke a language and were part of a culture that connected them with others. This cultural cohesion aligns with Adeed Dawisha's definition of a nation: "a human solidarity, whose members believe that they form a coherent cultural whole, and who manifest a strong desire for political separateness and sovereignty."[1]

Before World War I, many countries in the world were not constituted as nations and states in the modern sense of the word. Many had no set boundaries. In fact, many of the boundaries of states were fixed by the colonial powers. There are states today that still suffer from poorly determined and marked boundaries. This has been the cause of civil strife, military clashes, and instability with neighbors. Therefore, when the concept of "self-determination" was set out by President Woodrow Wilson, Palestine, as well as the entire Arab region, was in this category. However, the entire area was divided and apportioned between France and Britain and placed under colonial rule. Eventually the colonists carved out the borders of the modern states of Iraq,

Syria, Lebanon, Jordan, as well as the Gulf states. Sometimes, the boundaries were purely arbitrary; other times they were quite fluid. On some occasions the colonial powers took into consideration some political, tribal, ethnic, or religious factors. In many places, though, such decisions contributed to the pain and distress of many people.

The first Zionists did not conceive of two states in Palestine. As described earlier, Theodor Herzl, the founder of Zionism, had a vision of driving the Arab Palestinians across the border and replacing them with Jews. His vision was of a purely Jewish state, as can be seen in his diary entry from June 12, 1895:

> We must expropriate gently the private property on the state assigned to us. We shall try to spirit the penniless population across the border by procuring employment for it in the transit countries, while denying it employment in our country. The property owners will come over to our side. Both the process of expropriation and the removal of the poor must be carried out discretely and circumspectly. Let the owners of the immoveable property believe that they are cheating us, selling us things for more than they are worth. But we are not going to sell them anything back.[2]

The first draft of the Balfour Declaration, prepared by the British Zionists for endorsement by the British government, had no provision for two states. Since the creation of Israel in 1948, the reality on the ground showed clearly that Israel was not in favor of two states. It believed in the vision of Zionism that promoted one Jewish state. Along those lines, a leading Zionist declared in Jerusalem in April 1930, "We must continually raise the demand that our land be returned to our possession. . . . If there are other inhabitants there, they must be transferred to some other place. We must take over the land. We have a great and nobler ideal than preserving several hundred thousands of Arabs *fellahin* (peasants)."[3]

The Zionist argument that Israel accepted the Partition Plan of 1947 and the Palestinians rejected it is not proof that Israel believed in a two-state solution. Israel accepted the partition plan of the United Nations because it provided what seemed to be a legal basis for a claim on Palestine. Jewish Zionists could not approach the United Nations and claim that, because their ancestors had lived in Palestine two thousand years before, they possessed a historic right to claim the country back and drive out its inhabitants. Such an argument would have been naïve and certainly not tenable in a court of law. It would have been equally ridiculous to say that the Balfour Declaration gave Jews a legal right to Palestine. After all, Palestine was not English property to be disposed of by England.

Legally speaking, the Zionists could not claim a divine or a historic right to Palestine. In fact, after the establishment of the state of Israel in 1948, agents of the Israeli government were pressuring and manipulating its new Palestinian Arab citizens to accept compensation for the land that Israel confiscated from them. Some Palestinians who did sell received very low return for their land and property. In fact, it was rumored that the purchase transactions, although carried out after the establishment of the state, were actually dated prior to that. "Land was to be acquired by every means possible; [the World Zionist Organization] officials were to have no compunction about using persuasion, bribery or deception as long as the end was achieved."[4] Backdating the acquisition of this purchased property allowed Israel to claim that the land belonged to it legally through purchase. It was only after 1967 that Israel generally abandoned this practice. Its military strength obviated any need to purchase land. The Israeli government simply confiscated it at will, expropriating it from the Palestinians.

Israel's basic policy has been to prevent the emergence of a Palestinian state, and so its motives regarding the Palestinians have never been pure. One of the myths promulgated by the Zionists and later by the government of Israel is that historically there was never an independent and sovereign state called Palestine and that Palestine thus has no right to exist. Based on this logic, then most of the modern states of today's world could not have been constituted because they did not exist in ancient times, and the United States would certainly be included.

However, some people have believed and still believe this myth that would rule out Palestinian rights. Zionist myths seem to appeal in particular to those who are ignorant of historical and modern realities and to those already prejudiced against the Palestinians. It is important to point out that many intelligent and conscientious Jews have seen the fallacy of Zionism because of the absurdity of these myths. It is also important to indicate that after World War I, Palestinians took quite a different approach to immigration. Palestinians did not negate the right of Jews to live in Palestine, as some Jews have always lived there. Any Jew following a legal immigration process was allowed to live in the land.

The history of the region since the end of World War I shows quite clearly that there have been two possible but contradictory solutions to Palestine. On the one hand, the indigenous Palestinians wanted to exercise their right to self-determination and establish a sovereign state in Palestine for all of its citizens—Muslims, Jews, and Christians alike. The Zionists, on the other hand, wanted to turn Palestine (as well as a much larger area around it) into an exclusively Jewish state. These two goals and two nationalisms inevitably clashed.

Since the 1967 war, Israel has been trying once again to achieve the Zionist dream to forge one state under Jewish control. In spite of major successes in confiscating most of the Palestinian land and building settlements, the government of Israel has been unable to force the Palestinians to accept such an expansion. Moreover, the international community is unwilling to sanction such a clear violation of international law. The only way the government of Israel can reach such a goal is by the outright expulsion of the Palestinian indigenous population, a form of ethnic cleansing that is actually promoted by some right-wing Israeli politicians.

This is not a formula that Israeli experts have invented as it appears in the Torah. It is, therefore, important to reiterate that at no time throughout history have the ancient Israelites lived alone in the land. According to the Old Testament record, when the Israelites entered the land, it was already inhabited by many Canaanite tribes. The Israelites settled among them, and never achieved their ideal of being the sole possessors of the land. The land that they believed to be set aside for them was flowing not only with the proverbial milk and honey but also with many indigenous people.[5] After many millennia, this is still the case today. It becomes a question then of how these peoples can live together in peace.

THE TWO-STATE SOLUTION

A two-state solution has been proposed as the only way out of the political and violent impasse. With the benefit of hindsight, it seems that the idea of partitioning Palestine into two states was another masterful trap in which the Palestinians fell. On the one hand, if they accepted the Partition Plan, they would have voluntarily relinquished most of their homeland to the Zionists. On the other hand, if they rejected it, they would have had to stop the Zionists' onslaught; if they failed to stop the Zionists, they would be blamed for their own weakness. This is exactly what happened. The Palestinians misjudged and miscalculated the military power and preparedness of the Zionists. The Palestinians could not evade either trap. In the end they could not even retain the share of the land allotted to them by the Partition Plan.

Most Palestinians, including their leaders, trusted in the justice of their case and that the United Nations was strong enough to bring about justice for them. However, the United Nations proved weaker than they thought, and the Arab states were also too weak and fragmented to have any real impact. Several Palestinian organizations came into being and used armed resistance to attack Israel and reverse the injustice. In retrospect, they had minimal success and, instead of gaining the world's sympathy, many countries began to perceive the Palestinians as terrorists. The most successful act of Palestinian resistance was the first *intifada* in late 1987. This uprising in which the entire Palestinian community participated was by and large nonviolent.

In the late 1980s when the Palestinian people and leaders took a good look at their struggle, many of them, but certainly not all, realized that Israel could not be defeated through armed struggle. They had to turn to negotiations. By then the government of Israel had become a formidable military power in the world and had developed a strongly cemented bond with the United States. Israel's matrix of control over the Palestinians in the West Bank and the Gaza Strip was unyielding and firm. At the same time, its confiscation of Palestinian land and its expansion of the settlements was unstoppable.

The Palestinian leadership began to explore peace through a two-state solution while Israel was on its way to creating a one-state solution under its sovereignty. Israel was the major player, holding all the key cards, and calling all the plays, while the Palestinians had little or no influence. The government of Israel was not ready for peace. While the Palestinians were ready to seek peace on the basis of U.N. resolutions, Israel wanted peace on its own terms. It would not accept the demands of international law. Moreover, Israel refused to allow any country to interfere in the negotiations other than the United States, its protector and its strongest and most loyal ally. With America's clear bias toward Israel, the negotiations have lacked the presence of an honest broker. Everything hinges on the United States, and yet peace continues to be frustrated.

In the meantime, many Jewish and Palestinian peace activists have begun to see that Israeli government policy, especially by devouring Palestinian land and expanding the settlements, was rendering a two-state solution impossible. Because these activists felt that the government of Israel dealt a deathblow to the two-state solution, they began to advocate for and champion the one-state solution—one democratic state in the whole of Israel-Palestine where all citizens, Israelis and Palestinians, would live under the same and equal rule of law.[6]

Why Pursue a Two-State Solution Now?

Sabeel has always maintained that one democratic state is the ideal solution for resolving the conflict. However, we have reason to believe that a two-state solution is a more realistic and practical solution today. We still cling to a two-state solution, but not at any price.

This solution would give Palestinians sovereignty and independence and restore their human dignity and respect. An independent Palestinian state would place them on a par with Israel. Any future relations between Palestinians and Israelis would take place between two equally sovereign states.

One state that is not democratic, without full equality, would keep Palestinians subservient to Israeli Jews. They would become worse than second-class citizens. Israel is conditioned to oppress and dominate the Palestinians; it would not be easy for Israel to regard the Palestinians as equal citizens. In reality, both the Palestinians and the Israelis need healing. The Palestinians need to be healed from their enslavement and oppression, to recover their God-given humanity and dignity stripped away by Israel. Similarly, the Israelis need to be healed from the spirit of arrogance, superiority, and racism. They need to remember their own history when they were oppressed: "Remember that you were slaves in Egypt?" (Exod. 20:11). Perhaps a phrase with more contemporary relevance would be, "Remember the suffering of the Holocaust." Peace does not come by inflicting oppression on others. If Israelis want to live in peace, they need to show humility, for as the Hebrew scriptures proclaim, "Pride goes before destruction and a haughty spirit before a fall" (Prov. 16:18).

The two-state solution can work only with the full implementation of international law regarding the Israel-Palestine conflict based on U.N. Resolutions 242 and 338. It can work only when Israel withdraws totally from the West Bank as it did from the Gaza Strip. The Palestinians must have the West Bank in toto as one contiguous entity, in addition to the Gaza Strip, as their state. Moreover, once an autonomous and sovereign Palestinian state is formed, no interference from the Israeli government will be permitted.

The only solid foundation for a lasting peace is that of justice: this cannot be repeated often enough. Yet, consistent with our faith as Christians, we are not talking about absolute or strict justice, but are promoting a justice tempered by mercy and compassion. There are certain essential principles that we must affirm.

1. *The God who is worthy to be adored and worshiped is one who loves and cares for all people equally.* Each human being is equally special and precious in God's sight, and no group is more "chosen" than another; God uses the same moral standard to judge all. As God's children we are to live in peace with each other. Tragically, many of us create a God in our own imagination, a deity who might be a bigot, who conforms to our own racist and unjust inclinations and desires. We must cease being creators of a god in our own image and accept that all of us have been created by the One God who expects us to live a life of love and faith, justice and truth, mercy and compassion, humility and peace.

2. *Under international law, the Palestinians have the right to exist in peace within internationally recognized borders.* Likewise, under international law, Israel has the right to exist in peace within internationally recognized borders.

3. *There is no perfect or easy solution to the conflict.* What one side perceives as ideal and just is to the other side reprehensible and unjust. However, international law and the U.N. resolutions provide a compromise that satisfies the basic demands of peace, justice, and security for both sides. Any attempt to circumvent the United Nations and international law will not lead to a lasting peace.

4. *The conflict will never be resolved through military power or armed resistance.* It can be resolved only through earnest negotiations on the basis of international law, which guards the rights of both sides and limits any unjust or unlawful greed.

5. *This vision takes into consideration the basic human and political rights of both Israelis and Palestinians.* Palestinians must have a just peace, and Israelis must have a secure peace. Justice and security are not mutually exclusive: justice alone can produce a lasting peace and security, and there can be no security without doing justice.

6. *Injustice must not be rewarded.* Where it is possible, what is unjust must be undone. Where it is difficult, creative and dynamic ways must be found to satisfy the demands of justice and lean toward the side of the oppressed.

These principles must be applied to each major issue of the conflict.

THE MAJOR ASPECTS OF THE CONFLICT

The Two-State Solution

As already discussed, the Palestinian state must be built on the foundation of international law and the statutes of the United Nations. The approved U.N. resolutions constitute the minimum requirement for justice for the Palestinians. It is clear that the demands of justice take precedence over the demands of security, because it is justice that produces security, not the reverse. This was recognized long ago by the prophet Isaiah: "The effect of justice will be peace, and the result of justice will be security and trust forever" (Isa. 32:17).

We must, therefore, affirm the foundation in international law for the two-state solution: the state of Israel will live in peace and security on no more than 78 percent of the land beside a Palestinian state that is living in peace and security on no less than 22 percent of the land. Both states will be sovereign and independent. Any border adjustments must be in favor of the oppressed Palestinians because they have already yielded so much of their land for the establishment of the state of Israel.

The Settlements

According to international law, all the settlements that have been built on Palestinian land—the land Israel occupied during the 1967 war—are illegal. Strict justice requires the dismantling of all the settlements. Because billions of dollars have been spent building these settlements, it would be foolish to demolish them, as happened in the Gaza Strip when the Israeli settlers were evacuated from there.[7] Since all these settlements were built on Palestinian land, they must become an integral part of the Palestinian state. They can be considered as a small part of the compensation the government of Israel owes to the Palestinian people. In addition, the following factors should be considered:

- All Israeli Jewish settlers living in these settlements must be given the option to remain there and become Palestinian citizens with the same rights as Palestinian counterparts.
- Settlers who do not wish to change citizenship may move back to Israel or continue to live in the settlements according to the laws and regulations that would be set between the Palestinian and Israeli governments.
- Israel must compensate those Palestinians who lost their land to the settlements.
- Since the settlements are part of Palestine, Palestinians can have access to them. Priority must be given to the returning Palestinian refugees.

The Refugees

In 1948, there were almost eight hundred thousand refugees who were displaced.[8] In 1967, two hundred thousand more joined them. Today the estimated number of Palestinian refugees, according to the U.N. Relief and Works Agency (UNRWA), is over 4.3 million people.[9] They constitute the largest group of refugees in the world and the longest in the duration of their displacement.[10]

In seeking a solution to the refugee issue, the following points must be considered:

- The Law of Return is an international law: "Everyone has the right to leave any country, including his own, and return to his country."[11] Furthermore,

The [Palestinian] refugees wishing to return to their homes and live at peace with their neighbors should be permitted to do so at the earliest practicable date, and compensation should be paid for the property of those choosing not to return and for loss of or damage to property which, under principles of international law or in equity, should be made good by the Governments or authorities responsible.[12]

- Israel must admit that the Law of Return applies to Palestinian refugees.
- Israel must admit that it has done an injustice against the Palestinian people and bears responsibility.
- Refugees, whether they wish to return or not, must be compensated.
- All refugees, including those who remained inside what became the state of Israel and received Israeli citizenship, are entitled to compensation.
- Priority needs to be given to the Palestinian refugees who reside in Lebanon.[13]

Jerusalem

Peace in Jerusalem is key for the peace of the whole country. It is impossible to imagine peace for Palestine if Jerusalem is ignored, as Jerusalem belongs to the Palestinians as much as it belongs to Israelis. Jerusalem is as equally holy for Muslims and Christians as it is for Jews.

There are two ideal approaches to the question of Jerusalem. According to the 1947 U.N. Partition Plan, Jerusalem was to be extracted from the formula of the two-state solution and made a *corpus separatum*—a separate entity that would be governed by the United Nations, which would serve to protect fairly and impartially the holy places for the three religions. Although some people still favor such a solution, others believe that the passage of history has rendered the U.N. proposal obsolete.

A second approach is that of the sharing of Jerusalem by the Palestinians and the Israelis. After years of study, the ecumenical center of Sabeel has concluded that the sharing of Jerusalem presents the only way to move forward to peace. If genuine peace is the goal, the control of Jerusalem cannot be left to any one side. History has tested the adherents of the three major religions to control Jerusalem in the past, and all were found wanting. None was capable of acting impartially toward those not affiliated with their own faith tradition. Unfortunately, human nature often expresses itself foolishly in the hubris of power. Jerusalem's destiny should not be subject to the whims of military power. If we have not learned this lesson from all of our histories—Christian, Muslim, and Jewish—we are, indeed, fools.

The question of Jerusalem can be solved once and for all by sharing it in a way that would satisfy the demands of justice, opening Jerusalem to the adherents of the three religions that recognize it as their spiritual home. It can be said that God is entrusting us—Palestinian and Israeli leaders together with other world leaders—with the unique privilege of finding a solution that will truly establish Jerusalem as a paradigm of peace and goodwill.

Any solution for Jerusalem must satisfy the political and the religious needs of the Palestinians and the Israelis. While it is both a religious symbol and a political symbol, the religious significance of Jerusalem has always surpassed the political. Once the principle of sharing is affirmed mentally, emotionally, and psychologically, a solution may be possible. Such a solution will have to take into consideration that Jerusalem is composed of three sections: the Old City, within the walls; East Jerusalem (outside the Old City), which Israel has occupied since 1967; and West Jerusalem, controlled by Israel since 1948.

The Old City

Many of the holiest recognized sites for the three religions lie within the walls of the Old City. The Old City of Jerusalem, within the walls, should be set apart as a "special holy zone" to satisfy the religious needs of the three faiths. If an international charter were to govern this zone, it would not be under the exclusive sovereignty of any one political or religious entity. Equal representation of Muslims, Jews, and Christians—political and religious—with representatives of the international community, religious and political, could form its governing council.

At this juncture, it is best not to talk about specifics but to lift up a vision that would give these three religious communities equal legal rights. This strategy would protect and guarantee their rights, privileges, relationships, and mutual responsibilities for maintaining their holy places and for protecting and supporting the lives of the inhabitants of the Old City without discrimination or prejudice.

The Old City could then be developed in a way worthy of its status and the respect and holiness accorded it by the adherents of the three religions. Special funds could be raised from around the world by the three faiths in order to make the Old City a fitting place for its residents and a spiritually enriching and meaningful place for pilgrims.

Furthermore, if the Jewish community would want to build a temple, it should be encouraged to do so as long as it does not encroach on the Muslim *Haram* area, which encompasses the Dome of the Rock and the Al-Aqsa mosque. A temple could, for example, be built on the plaza of the Western Wall. (Obviously Jewish leaders would have to agree that God would approve the temple being built a few hundred meters from what is believed to be its original site.) The building of a Jewish temple away from the *Haram* area would put Muslim minds at ease and deter extremist Jews from threatening to blow up the Dome of the Rock and the Al-Aqsa Mosque in order to build their temple there.

The three religions would then live side by side, hopefully with less fear and more trust. The Old City could gradually become a model for peace and coexistence for the three faith communities. It would belong to the world. With such a vision, the walled Old City of Jerusalem would be lifted above political and military intrigues and accorded the religious holiness and respect it deserves.

It goes without saying that all unjust practices and expansions within the Old City that have encroached on the Muslim, Christian, and Armenian quarters by the government of Israel and Jewish religious settlers since the occupation of 1967 would have to be reversed to implement this vision on the basis of justice and fairness.

Yerushalayem—Alquds

The territory outside the walls of the Old City can then be used to satisfy the political aspirations of Israelis and Palestinians. At this point in time, it is futile to argue which group has greater claim on the city. We need to accept that the city of Jerusalem belongs equally to Israelis and Palestinians. Any exclusive claim that stems from religious, political, or national arrogance and bigotry can be maintained only by the power of armed strength and not by the power of truth and justice, which would be detrimental to peace. The sharing of political sovereignty seems to be the only option with the capability to guarantee peace and to satisfy the approved U.N. resolutions regarding the city.

In order to honor Palestinian needs for justice, the eastern part of the city, *Alquds* (which Israel occupied in 1967 except for the Old City), must come under full Palestinian sovereign rule, including all the Jewish settlements built on confiscated Palestinian land that lie within it. *Alquds* could become the Palestinian capital. Jews who want to live under Palestinian rule would be free to do so, while those who want to leave for the Jewish part of the city would have that option. The Israeli government would be responsible to compensate Palestinians for any unjust and illegal actions in contravention of international law.

The western part of Jerusalem, *Yerushalayem*, would become the capital of a sovereign Israeli state. It would include the western part of the city that Israel controlled before the 1967 war and any subsequent expansions within the pre-1967 borders of Israel.

Obviously such a division of sovereignty would require much coordination, cooperation, and interdependence on the part of the leaders of Israel and Palestine. But the basic thrust of the vision is clear: for the sake of justice and an enduring peace, the sovereignty of the city of Jerusalem must be shared and the Old City must be protected as a holy site.

Such an approach would satisfy the legitimate religious and political needs of Israelis and Palestinians. An international charter would protect the special holy zone of the Old City and guarantee the rights of the three religious traditions. The eastern and western parts of Jerusalem, outside the walls, would satisfy the political rights of the two states.

This vision contains the seeds for justice, peace, and security; it will also restore the dignity and humanity of every person, whether lost by being oppressors or oppressed. The vision would also establish principles of democracy on which both states must be built. Peace and security are, ultimately, the fruits of justice; peace will open the way for reconciliation and forgiveness.

Confederation

Sabeel believes that peace can move beyond the establishment of a two-state solution by linking the two states in a more dynamic relationship. One possibility would be a confederation in which each state would remain sovereign, but maintain close economic interconnections. They could cooperate in developing the region so it would prosper, increasing employment and reducing poverty. Within a confederation, the two countries of Israel and Palestine would remain open to all of their citizens without walls or checkpoints. Israelis and Palestinians could live, move, and work within the two states while retaining their separate citizenship. This would, of course, require a bill of rights that would respect the human and political rights of all the people of both countries. This would serve to alleviate Israeli fears of the perceived "demographic threat" posed by an increasing Palestinian population. Such a proposal would require extensive negotiations and compromises. It is but a vision at this time, but a vision with the potential to increase trust and the possibility of peace and security that would be long-lasting.

A MIDDLE EAST FEDERATION OF THE HOLY LAND

Looking into the future, and assuming that peace between Israel and Palestine has come about, it is possible to envision a time when the sovereign countries of Israel and Palestine, along with Jordan and Lebanon (and possibly others), might move from their present status as small independent states to form a federation of states—a United States of the Holy Land with Jerusalem as its federal capital. This is a vision that would demand further concessions and a broader sharing of Jerusalem. It might even demand that both Palestine and Israel build their capitals outside Jerusalem in order to set it free from political intrigues. Jerusalem would then be free from any narrow exclusive claims and become God's gift to not only the people of the region but beyond to the billions of faithful believers all over the world. In the city of Jerusalem, God has touched the lives of millions of people of these three religions in a special way. It should be a city of God in which justice reigns and peace is an experienced reality.

CONCLUSION

This proposal has tried to base a resolution of the Israeli-Palestinian conflict on the principles of justice and fairness. For it to work, a majority of people on both sides need to perceive its fairness. Obviously, many extensive negotiations and compromises will keep politicians and world leaders busy, but throughout the United Nations must lead by championing the principles of justice. Compromises, adjustments, and concessions must always benefit the oppressed, and aggressors and oppressors must not be rewarded for injustice.

Success will be contingent on the answers the government of Israel gives to the following four basic questions:

1. Is the government of Israel willing to accept the principle of sharing the land with the Palestinians on the basis of justice and fairness as defined by international law?
2. Is Israel willing to accept the Palestinians as equal partners in peacemaking?
3. Is Israel willing to accept the fact that Palestinians have equal rights to the land?
4. Is Israel willing to share Jerusalem?

Peace is within easy reach if the answer to the above questions is a resounding "yes."

After thousands of years of living under the paradigm of dominator and dominated, we have a responsibility to move our world into a paradigm where partnership replaces domination. Any government or any power that wishes to perpetuate principles of domination must be resisted. Ultimately it will not find victory.

In the final analysis, Jerusalem belongs to God, and our merciful and wise God has placed Muslims, Jews, and Christians as its stewards. Instead of claiming that Jerusalem belongs to this group or that group, we all belong to Jerusalem. A plan for permanent peace will be our way to honor God by the doing of justice and to returning Jerusalem to God as a city of peace. As the following legend demonstrates, it is possible to vanquish arrogance and exclusive inclinations.

Four thousand years ago, two brothers lived near each other on a hill by Jerusalem. They each had their own farm, but they shared a threshing floor. Every year they would bring in the harvest and divide it equally between them. Then they would take the grain to their farms and sell it in the market place.

One of the brothers was wealthy but had no family; the other had a family but was poor. One night after the harvest had been divided into equal measures and taken to each brother's home, the wealthy brother lay awake in his bed, thinking, "I need just enough grain to pay for my food and servants. But my poor brother, he has so many mouths to feed. He needs the money more than I do." He rose up out of his bed and went down to his granary. He lifted up as many sacks as he could carry and started to walk toward his brother's farm. Just around that time, the poor brother was lying in his bed, unable to sleep: "I have a wife and children who will take care of me and the farm if anything happens to me. But my poor brother—if something happens to him, he will have to pay to be cared for. He needs the money more than I do." Quietly, so as not to disturb his wife and children, he rose up out of his bed and tiptoed down to his granary.

He lifted up as many sacks as he could carry and walked toward his brother's farm. The two brothers met midway between their farms, their arms laden with the sacks of grain they were carrying to each other. The full moon shone down upon them as they dropped their bundles and ran to embrace each other. And God looked down and smiled.[14]

According to the legend, on this site Jerusalem was built. With this kind of a spirit, Palestinians and Israelis can move together toward a just peace.

Chapter 14

From Justice to Forgiveness

I like to believe that people in the long run are going to do more to promote peace than our governments. Indeed, I think that people want peace so much that one of these days, governments had better get out of their way and let them have it.
—Dwight Eisenhower

It can be helpful to reiterate some significant basic principles dealt with throughout these pages as they are fundamental to the overriding argument of the book.

1. Chronic injustice has plagued the Palestinians for many years, and no one has been able to stop it because Israel is protected by the world's only superpower, the United States. The perpetuation of this injustice dehumanizes the oppressed Palestinians as well as their Israeli oppressors. The long-extended occupation has created a culture of violence that has ruined the moral fabric of the Palestinian society and, to a large extent, has destroyed the beautiful traditional mores Palestinians had previously enjoyed.

On the Israeli side, the long, extended occupation—maintained by an iron-fisted policy and the suppression of the Palestinians—has made the Israeli establishment, including its military and police, more inhumane and oppressive. Racist feelings have intensified on both sides, and the entire community has lost its moral and spiritual health.[1]

2. Given the absence of a power that can halt this injustice and faced with so much state violence and terrorism, the Palestinians, in turn, have resorted to violent resistance. Instead of contributing to the solution of the conflict, such a strategy has exacerbated the problem, making the situation even more tragic and hopeless. There is a need for a different strategy to replace armed struggle, not only because armed struggle is ineffective, but because it is, in principle, wrong. Such a change demands a conversion. The perspectives of international law and our faith traditions show clearly that the only way forward is through nonviolent resistance.

3. The world began the twenty-first century on the wrong foot: if this same pace continues, this century will prove to be more violent than the twentieth. Hopefully, most countries of the world will recognize the futility of war and begin to emphasize the importance of disarmament, beginning with the elimination of their nuclear arsenals. Furthermore, we hope that masses of

people at the grassroots level will put greater pressure on their governments to shun wars and military conflicts and turn to more peaceful and nonviolent means to resolve conflicts.

4. The cost of modern warfare is becoming so prohibitive that the cry of people will get louder about the insanity of such adventures. In 2007, as the United States was caught in the quagmire of Iraq, its military spending was at the rate of $8 billion a month, and the projected expenditure by the end of the war will exceed $2 trillion. This is a crime, given all the human problems that could be solved through use of these funds. The time will undoubtedly come when world public opinion—starting in the United States and Europe—will limit governments' avarice for wars.

5. This book is a plea for the use of nonviolence in conflict resolution. If only the president of Palestine would announce through the media that the Palestinian people will officially abandon their armed struggle and adopt a nonviolent struggle. A massive campaign would then follow to train the Palestinian community in the techniques and tactics of nonviolent resistance. This call should mobilize the entire nation. Such an action would restore the dignity and humanity of the Palestinians and boost their morale. It would involve the entire community, as did the first *intifada*, substituting nonviolence for the armed struggle of the second *intifada*. Palestine needs a new peaceful and nonviolent *intifada* that is willing to accept suffering rather than inflict it on others.

6. Giants of peace have preceded us. In the struggle for racial justice in America, Martin Luther King Jr. said:

> World peace through nonviolent means is neither absurd nor unattainable. All other methods have failed. Thus we must begin anew. Nonviolence is a good starting point. Those of us who believe in this method can be voices of reason, sanity, and understanding amid the voices of violence, hatred, and emotion. We can very well set a mood of peace out of which a system of peace can be built.[2]

Bishop Desmond Tutu, a leader against the apartheid system in South Africa, maintained,

> We must not allow ourselves to become like the system we oppose. We cannot afford to use methods of which we will be ashamed. . . . We must remember, my friends, that we have been given a wonderful cause. The cause of freedom! . . . We will say, "We used methods that can stand the harsh scrutiny of history."

Mohandas Gandhi, who served as an inspiration for both King and Tutu, proclaimed:

> Non-violent resistance implies the very opposite of weakness. Defiance combined with non-retaliatory acceptance of repression from one's op-

ponents is active, not passive. It requires strength, and there is nothing automatic or intuitive about the resoluteness required for using non-violent methods in political struggle and the quest for Truth.[3]

7. Those of us who are Christians must return to the strategy of Jesus Christ. Today, many Christians have never been exposed to the revolutionary politics of Christ, and many still think that Jesus was neither interested nor involved in politics. On the contrary, Jesus was very much immersed in the lives of people in his time. Rejecting the strategies of the revolutionaries of his day, he chose a different way. He was fully aware of the power of the Roman Empire and not foolish enough to think that it could be overcome by armed revolutionaries. Rejecting the injustice of empire, he believed it was possible to resist its unjust laws. He counseled his disciples that "If anyone forces you to go one mile, go also the second mile" (Matt. 5:41). Jesus advised the people to seize the initiative: "He was telling them how to turn a humiliating experience into an assertion of their own power and humanity."[4] Evil can be resisted without violence.

JUSTICE, NONVIOLENCE, AND PEACE

Three prongs are essential to complete the cycle of a genuine and enduring peace: justice, peace, and reconciliation. These prongs respond to the prophetic call that God requires all of us to do justice, to love mercy, and to walk humbly before God (Mic. 6:8). The doing of justice is at the center of God's demands. Some people choose to reverse the order in the formula: they choose doing mercy and kindness and loving justice. They are generous in giving to philanthropic activities and being involved in acts of mercy, but they hold back from the direct work of doing justice. They love justice from afar. However, the prophetic formula is clear: we must do justice.

Similarly, Jesus said, his followers are to make peace ("Blessed are the peacemakers" [Matt. 5:9]). Doing justice and making peace are foundational requirements for people of faith. Indeed, loving mercy makes the doing of justice palatable. Justice needs the companionship of mercy and kindness. Doing justice is not taking revenge, but setting things right so that reconciliation and healing are possible.

In the conflict over Palestine, Israel has a clear record now of refusing to do justice and, sadly, the international community is unable to make it comply. At times, Israeli intransigence and stubbornness seem to increase each day. Even many levelheaded Jewish minds are unable to steer it from its destructive course. The Palestinians have tried the way of violence and failed to bring about anything but disaster and misery. Now they must turn to nonviolence.

A new strategy of nonviolence should call on the leaders of the world to do their utmost to stop Israeli injustice. While the Arab states could use their "oil power," the Europeans and other countries of the world can take up sanctions and boycotts. Churches and various institutions can participate to use their investment power to make Israel accountable to the demands of justice. It is important, however, that the nonviolent revolution begin in Palestine and be led by the Palestinians. Gandhi, Martin Luther King, Mandela, Tutu, and others recognized that the first principle of nonviolent action is noncooperation with everything that humiliates. Their prophetic call can become our call.

I believe that Palestinian women and children can lead the struggle in a more effective way. Many men have blundered by committing themselves to the strategies of violence and terrorism. They have reacted to Israeli violence with a similar violence, and met terror with terror. Now Palestinian men need to step aside and allow Palestinian women to take the lead. Throughout the struggle, it has been the women who have been in the forefront of the nonviolent struggle. They have organized the demonstrations, the marches, and the sit-ins. They have showed great courage in facing the Israeli occupation forces boldly and with determination.

There is also a need to look at our educational system to see how our children are being nurtured. Are we adults teaching them violence? We need to develop a culture of peace and sharing both for children and adults, in our schools and in our homes.

In his book *Gandhi's Way*, Mark Jürgensmeyer lays down ten basic rules for conflict resolution that can help in the struggle for justice and peace in Palestine.[5]

1. "*Do not avoid confrontation. Avoidance simply prolongs the underlying conflict between principles. Instead, you should welcome an encounter between positions, and the clarity it brings.*" This refers of course to nonviolent confrontations. Many discussions have taken place between Israelis and Palestinians over the years, but there have been many more interruptions and breakdowns, sometimes at crucial moments. What has often been lacking on the Israeli side is the will to resolve the conflict on the basis of international law. The international community must find a way to insist that continuous discussions take place, regardless of changing events on the ground, until the two sides reach an agreement.

2. "*Stay open to communication and self-criticism. Each side in a conflict has only a partial view. It needs the critical perspective of the other to sort out truth from untruth.*" This can be done only through the presence of strong arbitrators who can determine the truth from the untruth clearly and unashamedly.

3. "*Find a resolution and hold fast to it. Once a harmonious alternative becomes apparent, you should seize onto it and base your strategy on it— but be willing to challenge and change it as well.*" Courageous visionaries, whether Palestinian or Israeli, who are willing to work toward a method of consensus should be involved and raised up by both sides. In seeking a viable resolution to this long-entrenched conflict, commonalities and connections

should be highlighted and differences must be discussed and overcome based on justice and international law.

4. *"Regard your opponent as a potential ally. Do nothing to harm or alienate your opponent. Remember your goal is to join forces to struggle together against untruth."* This is of extreme importance. The two sides need to keep in mind that they will ultimately have to live together as neighbors. Therefore, instead of exacerbating the enmity, they must find ways to transcend it.

5. *"Make your tactics consistent with the goal. Use the goal itself as the weapon for fighting, when possible. When not, use only those actions that are consistent with it."* The Gandhian approach treats the means as the goals. In other words, using nonviolence as the means to reach the goal should help ensure that the emerging Palestinian state will be a nonviolent society.

> If you attempt to use violent means to achieve a peaceful end, Gandhi argued, you will fail. You cannot justify destroying a country in order to save it. Gandhi thought that the purest goals could "never justify impure or violent action." Actions are habit-forming. If you use coercion once, you increase the likelihood that you will use it again, and with every coercive act you build up a store of ill will in your opponent that decreases the possibility of a genuine resolution. Harmony, in such cases, recedes farther and farther from sight.[6]

6. *"Be flexible. Be willing to change tactics, alter proximate goals, revise your notion of who your opponent is, and even reconsider your conception of the truth."* Many times, the occupied are forced to play by the rules of the occupiers. In the Israel-Palestine conflict, the occupied have been dragged and pushed into side issues that are not relevant to the central struggle, and they become distracted and lose their focus. It is important to be always aware of the changing dynamics.

7. *"Be temperate. Escalate your actions by degrees. The idea is to keep your opponent from feeling intimidated, so that he or she will be communicative rather than defensive in responding to you."* The international community has scolded Israel on numerous occasions over the years for its disproportionate use of force. Palestinians must not counter violence with violence. Furthermore, in alignment with this principle, the oppressed would plan their actions and reactions to secure the moral high ground and to make it difficult for the oppressor to escalate the conflict.

8. *"Be proportionate. Determine which issues are trivial and which deserve your time and energy. The basis for judgment is the degree to which life and the quality of life are abused. Mount a campaign with a strength equal to that of the opponent, and appropriate to the issue."* The oppressor obviously hopes to create conditions in the occupied territories that are so bleak and depraved that the oppressed will turn against one another for mere survival. Palestinians of different political parties should focus on their common vision and collective ambition to create an independent state, based

on justice. Working together toward this shared goal, the parties can then work to incorporate the assistance of Arab neighbors and the backing of the international community.

9. *"Be disciplined. Especially when a large number is involved in a collective effort, make certain that your side is committed to a nonviolent approach and that your position is coherent. Consistency is one of your strengths."* This strategy is perhaps more difficult for Palestinians than any other oppressed group, in large part because of the nearly incessant dehumanization and pressure thrust on them. Nonetheless, experience shows that greater discipline yields a greater likelihood for a breakthrough.

10. *"Know when to quit. A deadlocked campaign, or one with negative results, may require that you revise your tactics and perhaps even change your proximate goals. A concession to your side without an agreement on principle is not victory. In a Gandhian fight, you can claim to have won only if your opponent can say the same."* Ultimately, both sides should stridently seek a resolution in which both Palestinian and Israeli leaders can address their respective people—a majority on both sides want just peace for Israel and Palestine—and say that both sides "win." This end must be the constant focus for all who seek a lasting peace in the region. The process may take two steps forward and one step back—yet if truth and justice are the guide, hope always remains for a better tomorrow.

These rules can be more effectively implemented when representatives of the international community are present and fully engaged in the discussions and that the discussions are based on international law, which alone can guarantee the rights and integrity of both sides of the conflict.

PEACE IS NOT ENOUGH

In conflict resolution, whether between individuals or nations, the highest objective is to achieve reconciliation and forgiveness between the conflicting parties. When forgiveness is given and received, healing commences. This constitutes the mountaintop in peaceable relations among people.

At least three different models or paradigms are available for people engaged in resolving a conflict—the subhuman, the human, and the divine.[7] The subhuman level represents a paradigm in which conflicts are not resolved. As the conflict rages or simmers, violence and terrorism escalate. Hate, fear, bloodshed, insecurity, and revenge are always present. Tragically, this paradigm is often present in today's world. People in conflict are not willing to transcend their greed, prejudice, or religious extremism to resolve their differences. They demand absolute justice and seek to crush their enemy.

The Christian faith urges people to abandon this subhuman paradigm because it does not reflect God's purpose for human beings and does not allow them to achieve their God-given potential. However, the New Testament points to two superior levels that can both lead to reconciliation and forgiveness and the restoration of the humanity of the conflicting parties.

Given the human paradigm, repentance is a precondition; it must precede reconciliation and forgiveness. According to Luke, the risen Christ commissioned his disciples to preach repentance and forgiveness of sins in his name to all nations (Luke 24:47). Repentance calls for the admission of guilt, crime, and injustice. When a person expresses remorse and sorrow, the door is opened for forgiveness.

In the conflict between Israel and Palestine, repentance would correspond to an admission by the government of Israel of the injustice it has dealt to the Palestinians in its confiscation of land, its violation of human rights, and its systems of domination and oppression. Such repentance, combined with a willingness to do justice and offer just reparations, could open the way to reconciliation and forgiveness.

Finally, there is the divine paradigm, a radical model embedded in the Christian faith. It is a paradigm of revolutionary forgiveness even when no admission of guilt takes place. Christians are supposed to practice forgiveness of others because it is how God deals with us: as God forgives us continuously, we must forgive others. The letter to the Colossians advised the early church there to "forgive each other; just as the Lord has forgiven you, so you also must forgive" (Col. 3:13).[8] Forgiveness is a grace, a free gift. This type of forgiveness is truly revolutionary, and it reflects the very essence of the Christian gospel. Forgiveness is not earned or achieved. It is not even the consequence of repentance. A person need only receive it with humble gratitude and in the same humble way offer it to others.

This point is well illustrated by two images that emerge in Paul's writings. In Romans, Paul speaks about God who "justifies the ungodly" (Rom. 4:5). The source of this radical form of justification is God (see also Rom. 3:24-26). This means that God treats the criminal as if he had been a good person. God is thus the ultimate paradigm to be imitated and modeled. This was demonstrated by the father's welcome of his rebellious son in the parable of the Prodigal Son (Luke 15:11-32).[9] The father treated his son as if he had never left. This is the meaning of justification as a free gift of God.

A second image is of reconciliation. Paul says that it is through Christ that we have received reconciliation (Rom. 5:11) and in 2 Corinthians: "All this is from God, who reconciled us to himself through Christ and has given us the ministry of reconciliation; that is, in Christ God was reconciling the world to himself, not counting their trespasses against them, and entrusting the message of reconciliation to us" (2 Cor. 5:18-19). In other words, because we have drifted away from God, God takes the initiative and brings us back. Our reconciliation with God is not due to anything we have done, but to what God has done for us in and through the death and resurrection of Christ. It is interesting to observe that the New Testament never speaks of God being reconciled to us, but always of our being reconciled to God. The drifting away and the estrangement are all on our side, while the love of God is forever constant and unceasing.

APPLYING THE HUMAN PARADIGM

Some people are able to transcend the human paradigm to achieve the forgiveness expressed in this divine paradigm. Most of us, however, feel more at home with the human paradigm. It is hard enough to achieve. In fact, many times we live by the subhuman paradigm. Although we must always strive for the divine paradigm, we are thankful when we can practice the human paradigm. Given human weaknesses, it is good to acknowledge that there are six steps that can assist in arriving at peace, reconciliation, and even possible forgiveness.

Step 1: The first step is to confront and analyze the roots of the conflict and its development over the years. The context of any struggle is important because this clarifies how the problem arose or where the original crime was committed. There is a need to listen to, and understand the narratives of, the two conflicting parties, looking for threads that might lead to their possible reconciliation. This must be done with sensitivity, honesty, and objectivity through the lens of international law. Any injustice must be identified.

Step 2: In order to move toward a solution in Israel-Palestine, the illegal Israeli occupation must come to an end and Palestinian violence must stop. The weight of the international community must support the oppressed against the oppressor. Furthermore, it must be clear that the Palestinians were dragged into the conflict by the Zionists' occupation of their land. No matter the influence and power of the oppressor, morality and international law demand that pressure be placed on the aggressive party to end its illegal occupation. Unfortunately, this could take a long time. The Palestine-Israel conflict is already over sixty years old, and the international community has been unsuccessful so far in forcing Israel to comply with international law. There is no hope for any movement toward peace as long as the injustice persists, and injustice is the main source of the violence. Suppressing violence through brutal force only begets more violence. People will continue to resist the oppression and aspire for liberation and peace. Ultimately, freedom will triumph over domination and justice over oppression. But until the injustice is stopped, there is no prospect of peace.

Step 3: Justice is done when international law is implemented, when peace and its derivatives begin to be felt by the two communities. So long as the injustice persists, hate and its derivatives have the upper hand. In essence, justice and peace begin when the oppressor becomes aware of its violation of the other's humanity. Justice is done when the international community, through nonviolent methods, forces Israel to put an end to its injustice. In this case, justice is defined not as strict or absolute, but as justice tempered by mercy and compassion. The doing of justice must not crush the enemy but it must hold the enemy accountable.

However, no hope for change is possible until the occupation ends. Once the government of Israel acknowledges the rights of the Palestinians to their land and shows its willingness to implement the demands of international law, hope may spring alive for all the people of the land. Such action must include willingness on the part of Israel to make amends and offer restitution. The oppressor must accept its responsibility to compensate the oppressed, and the oppressed, in turn, must be open to begin their new lives in freedom without revenge.

Step 4: Once justice is done, peace will not be far off. Once people know that the peace is based on justice, most people on both sides should be willing to accept it, lay down their arms, and end the violence. There is no reason that two states, Palestinian and Israeli, cannot live in peace and side by side as viable states, with both independent, sovereign, and democratically inclusive of all of their citizens. All the people of the land will then stand equal under the law with their dignity and humanity protected. Yet, neither justice nor peace is the final objective: the end goal is healing. In fact, the real work will begin once justice is done and peace has arrived.

Step 5: It is important for people of faith to work for healing, a process that has two important steps: reconciliation and forgiveness. Which action should come first is debatable. Some insist that forgiveness precedes reconciliation, while others argue that forgiveness is the ultimate goal. Others have suggested a model for reconciliation composed of four steps: confession, repentance, reconciliation, and restitution. It begins with an open acknowledgment of the injustice and calls for a change of attitudes and just actions.[10] A Truth and Reconciliation Commission is also essential to review the history of the conflict, hold perpetrators accountable, and reconcile narratives.

Reconciliation is a long process, and sometimes it is never achieved. It is incumbent on Christians, however, to bring about reconciliation between the greatest number of people on both sides. We must use all the expertise in the various fields to address the cumulative residue of hate, bitterness, and resentment that still lie deep in many people's hearts and minds. Moreover, economic development must go hand in hand with the achieved peace. The Palestinians need to have gainful employment in order to end poverty and raise the standard of living. The contributions of social scientists and educators are vital to the process of reconciliation. Although not easily brought about, reconciliation can take place because of the goodness and goodwill in the hearts of many people.

Step 6: Forgiveness, the final step in the process of healing, completes the process of reconciliation and even goes beyond it. Once forgiveness occurs, healing has been effected.

Genuine forgiveness occurs when the forgiven person has been freed from all charges. The slate has been wiped clean. The file for the crime has been closed. The debt has been cancelled, and the accused has a new lease on life. In essence, it is the criminal who is forgiven and not the crime; the crime can still be condemned. Forgiveness, however, has transcended the crime, and there remains no desire or need for revenge.

When forgiveness is offered and received, full liberation takes place and both parties are set free. The forgiver is set free from the burden of revenge, and the forgiven is set free from guilt. Although a forgiver may not be able to forget the injustice, it is still possible to live in forgiveness. To better understand this process, Christians should return to the unconditional loving actions of God described in the New Testament. God took the initiative in forgiving and liberating all people through the death and resurrection of Jesus Christ.

The process of forgiveness is to be initiated by the forgiver, in imitation of God's action. Unfortunately, forgiveness offered does not always mean forgiveness is received. But forgiveness must always be offered, as God has offered it to us. It is our responsibility as children of God to receive it with thanksgiving, to act on it, and to be ready at all times to offer it to others.

CONCLUSION

In the case of Israel-Palestine, the possibility of reconciliation and forgiveness is enhanced when the process is based on justice and nonviolence, and when confession and admission of wrongdoing take place.

The international community has the responsibility to end the conflict and build peace on the basis of justice and fairness as articulated by international law. Once that happens, Israelis and Palestinians need to walk the way of healing, reconciliation, and forgiveness. I believe that many Palestinians, though now experiencing the oppressive measures of Israeli occupation, will live in peace, accept to be reconciled, and even offer forgiveness. As long as the injustice persists, the door to reconciliation and forgiveness is slammed shut. Justice is the key that unlocks the door.

When the door is opened, we might be surprised to find that people who have suffered torture, humiliation, oppression, and the loss of loved ones are open to reconciliation. Indeed, many times those who have suffered most, on both sides, are the first to forgive. They are willing to give and receive forgiveness. When that happens, the process of justice, peace, and reconciliation has been completed and a sense of closure can finally be felt. Former enemies have been reconciled, and they can live together in peace. This is not imaginary or elusive. It can happen. Many people can, by the grace of God, reach their highest human potential and experience reconciliation and forgiveness. They can live with the past and find healing for their emotions and memory. They can positively channel their energy and employ it in the service of others, for the betterment of their community and world. They can live their lives and find meaning and joy. They can gradually dwell less in the past, enjoy the present, and look with a smile and hopeful hearts to the future. Freedom, liberation, and liberty have now triumphed.

This is the justice we demand. This is the peace we seek. This is the reconciliation for which we hope.

Zionist Plan for Palestine 1919

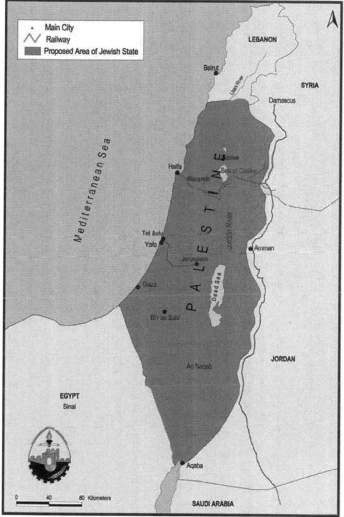

Bethlehem Bible College/Applied Research Institute—Jerusalem (ARIJ)

Appendix B

Balfour Declaration

Foreign Office
November 2nd, 1917

Dear Lord Rothschild,

I have much pleasure in conveying to you, on behalf of His Majesty's Government, the following declaration of sympathy with Jewish Zionist aspirations which has been submitted to, and approved by, the Cabinet.

"His Majesty's Government view with favour the establishment in Palestine of a national home for the Jewish people, and will use their best endeavours to facilitate the achievement of this object, it being clearly understood that nothing shall be done which may prejudice the civil and religious rights of existing non-Jewish communities in Palestine, or the rights and political status enjoyed by Jews in any other country."

I should be grateful if you would bring this declaration to the knowledge of the Zionist Federation.

Yours sincerely,
Arthur James Balfour

Palestinian Loss of Land 1946 to 2005

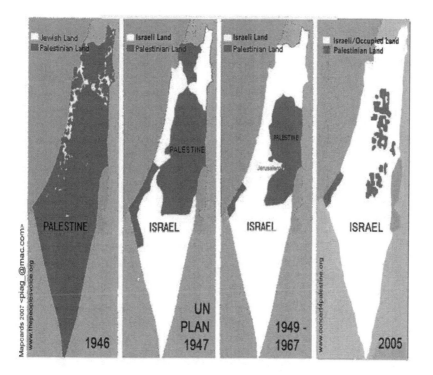

These maps show the loss of Palestinian land from the proposed U.N. Partition Plan of 1947 through to the present day. The third map shows the two-state solution, with Palestinians keeping 22 percent of the land of historic Palestine. The final map shows the loss of Palestinian land due to the structures of the occupation—the Wall, checkpoints, restricted roads, closed military areas, and Israeli settlements.

Appendix D

West Bank Barrier Route—June 2007

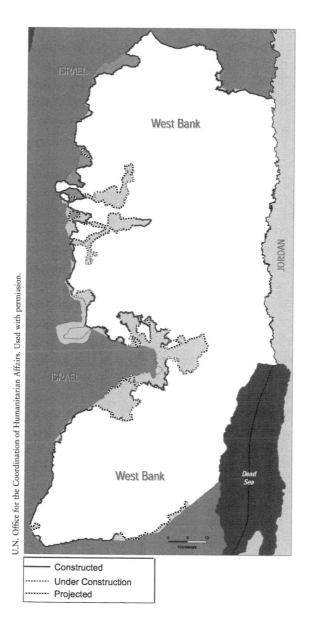

Notes

PREFACE

[1]Naim Ateek, *Justice, and Only Justice: A Palestinian Theology of Liberation* (Maryknoll, NY: Orbis Books, 1989).

CHAPTER 1—THE BIRTH OF SABEEL

[1]For more information on my father and my family's experiences, see my *Justice, and Only Justice: A Palestinian Theology of Liberation* (Maryknoll, NY: Orbis Books, 1989), 7-13.

[2]*Intifada* is an Arabic term meaning "shaking off," "an abrupt wakening," or "uprising." See Naim S. Ateek, "Pentecost and the Intifada," in *Reading from This Place*, ed. Fernando F. Segovia and Mary Ann Tolbert (Minneapolis: Fortress Press, 1995), 69-81.

[3]A number of scholars have written about nonviolence in the first intifada. See, for example, Gene Sharp, "The Intifada and Nonviolent Struggle," *Journal of Palestine Studies* 19, no. 1 (Autumn 1989): 3-13; Peter Ackerman and Jack DuVall, *A Force More Powerful: A Century of Nonviolent Conflict* (New York: Palgrave, 2000), 397-420, and Mary Elizabeth King, *A Quiet Revolution: The First Palestinian Intifada and Nonviolent Resistance* (New York: Nation Books, 2007).

[4]The origins of Hamas and Hamam are further documented in a special issue of Sabeel's newsletter, *Cornerstone* 34 (Fall 2004): 2-4. A recent book by the independent investigative reporter Robert Dreyfuss, *Devil's Game: How the United States Helped Unleash Fundamentalist Islam* (New York: Metropolitan Books, 2005), provides further evidence of Israeli support for the development of Hamas.

[5]The Palestine Liberation Organization, formed in 1964, is made up of a number of Palestinian factions. Fatah is the first and largest of these factions. Many smaller factions, such as the Popular Front for the Liberation of Palestine, have broken off from Fatah over the years.

[6]Ben Kaspit, *Ma'ariv*, May 7, 2006.

[7]Naim S. Ateek, Marc H. Ellis, and Rosemary Radford Ruether, *Faith and the Intifada: Palestinian Christian Voices* (Maryknoll, NY: Orbis Books, 1992).

[8]Against those who might object that Jesus was not an ethnic Palestinian, it is important to realize that "Palestinian" is not an ethnic denotation, but a geographic one. Before 1948, Jews as well as Muslims and Christians living in the same region were all known as Palestinians and carried a Palestinian passport. Furthermore, some might object that this is an anachronism since the land was not officially called Palestine until the second century after Christ. Technically this is true, although Josephus does use the word "Palestine" to refer to the area. In any case, it is also possible to use the term figuratively.

CHAPTER 2—THE GENEROUS OFFER OF THE PALESTINIANS

[1]All texts are from the NRSV unless otherwise indicated.

[2]"Biblically speaking, one cannot talk about justice without referring to righteous-

ness. Both concepts are similar in meaning and are often used as parallels in the Bible. Usually, however, the word *mishpat* (root, *shafat*) is translated 'justice,' and *tsedek* (root, *tsadak*), 'righteousness' (Naim Stifan Ateek, *Justice, and Only Justice: A Palestinian Theology of Liberation* [Maryknoll, NY: Orbis Books, 1989], 142.

[3]In a speech delivered to the Friends of Sabeel North America conference in Boston on October 27, 2007, David Wildman, the executive secretary for Human Rights and Racial Justice for the General Board of Global Ministries of the United Methodist Church, used the parable of the widow and the unjust judge to present a "Biblical Framework for Eroding Apartheid." In his speech, he stated, "When it says the judge has no respect for people that is biblical language for no respect for international law and human rights." The presentation is available at http://www.fosna.org/conferences_and_trips/RemovingLogOfApartheidDavidWildman.htm.

[4]Richard A. Horsley, *Jesus and Empire: The Kingdom of God and the New World Disorder* (Minneapolis: Fortress Press, 2003), 21.

[5]Thomas Merton, *Faith and Violence* (Notre Dame, IN: University of Notre Dame Press, 1968).

[6]See http://www.tiph.org.

[7]Jimmy Carter, *Palestine: Peace Not Apartheid* (New York: Simon & Schuster, 2006), 209.

[8]For more on Christian Zionism, see chap. 6 of this book.

[9]John J. Mearsheimer and Stephen M. Walt, "The Israel Lobby and U.S. Foreign Policy," *London Review of Books* 28, no. 6 (March 23, 2006). This article was subsequently expanded and published in book form as *The Israel Lobby and U.S. Foreign Policy* (New York: Farrar, Straus and Giroux, 2007).

[10]Ibid., 6.

[11]Ibid., 17.

[12]Ibid., 8.

[13]Ibid., 10-11.

[14]Ibid., 11.

[15]Ibid.

[16]Ibid., 7.

[17]William Sloane Coffin, *Credo* (Louisville, KY: Westminster John Knox Press, 2004), 84.

[18]Carter, *Palestine*, 210.

[19]"The United States gives Israel access to intelligence that it denies its NATO allies and has turned a blind eye towards Israel's acquisition of nuclear weapons. . . . It also blocks Arab states' efforts to put Israel's nuclear arsenal on the International Atomic Energy Agency's agenda" (ibid., 3). "[Israel's] conventional forces are far superior to its neighbors and it is the only state in the region with nuclear weapons" (ibid., 8).

[20]The Iraq Study Group, chaired by James A. Baker III, and Lee H. Hamilton, *The Iraq Group Report: The Way Forward—A New Approach* (New York: Vintage, 2006), xv.

[21]Ibid., 44.

[22]Ibid., 57-58.

[23]Carter, *Palestine*, 131.

[24]Ibid., 135.

[25]See the text of Yasir Arafat's letter to President Clinton, January 13, 1998, available online at www.mideastweb.org/arafatwye1998.htm. For the English text of the original Palestinian National Charter, see Walter Laqueur and Barry Rubin, eds., *The Israel-Arab Reader*, 6th ed. (New York: Penguin, 2001), 117-21.

[26]Jeff Halper, "A Most Ungenerous Offer," *The Link* 35, no. 4 (September/October 2002).

[27]In opposition to the World Zionist Organization's plan, several prominent Jewish citizens in America composed "A Statement to the Peace Conference," objecting to a Jewish state in Palestine; see *The New York Times*, March 4, 1919.

[28]Ateek, *Justice, and Only Justice*, 27-28.

[29]Alfred M. Lilienthal, *The Zionist Connection: What Price Peace?* (New York: Dodd, Mead, and Company, 1978), 61-91.

[30]The details of this ethnic cleansing have been documented by Israeli historian Ilan Pappe in his book *The Ethnic Cleansing of Palestine* (Oxford: Oneworld, 2006).

[31]Carter, *Palestine*, 152.

CHAPTER 3—THE BREEDING OF VIOLENCE

[1]Laurens van der Post, *A Walk with a White Bushman* (New York: Penguin Books, 1987), 281.

[2]Chris Hedges, *War Is a Force That Gives Us Meaning* (New York: Public Affairs, 2002), 21.

[3]Moshe Menuhin, *The Decadence of Judaism in Our Time* (New York: Exposition, 1965), 236.

[4]Barbara Tuchman, *Bible and Sword: England and Palestine from the Bronze Age to Balfour* (New York: Ballantine Books, 1984). See pages 224, 279-80, 318.

[5]Naim Ateek, *Justice, and Only Justice: A Palestinian Theology of Liberation* (Maryknoll, NY: Orbis Books, 1989), 27-28.

[6]John W. Mulhall, *America and the Founding of Israel: An Investigation of the Morality of America's Role* (Los Angeles: Deshon Press, 1995), 62-68.

[7]See Woodrow Wilson's "Fourteen Points" speech of January 8, 1918: "A free, openminded, and absolutely impartial adjustment of all colonial claims, based upon a strict observance of the principle that in determining all such questions of sovereignty the interests of the populations concerned must have equal weight with the equitable claims of the government whose title is to be determined."

[8]Joel Kovel, *Overcoming Zionism: Creating a Single Democratic State in Israel/Palestine* (Ann Arbor, MI: Pluto Press, 2007), 150-55.

[9]Ilan Pappé, *The Ethnic Cleansing of Palestine* (Oxford: Oneworld, 2006), 51.

[10]Ibid., 54.

[11]Mulhall, *America and the Founding of Israel*, 120.

[12]Pappé, *Ethnic Cleansing of Palestine*, 56.

[13]Ibid., 58-59.

[14]Mulhall, *America and the Founding of Israel*, 124.

[15]Kovel, *Overcoming Zionism*, 150-53.

[16]George Mendenhall, *Ancient Israel's Faith and History* (Louisville, KY: Westminster John Knox Press, 2001), 36.

[17]Ateek, *Justice, and Only Justice*, 33-36.

[18]Oren Ben-Dor, "Who Are the Real Terrorists in the Middle East?" *The Independent* (UK), July 26, 2006.

[19]Pappé, *Ethnic Cleansing of Palestine*, 78-79.

[20]Ibid., 71.

[21]Ben-Dor, "Who Are the Real Terrorists?"

[22]Ian Lustick, *Arabs in the Jewish State: Israel's Control of a National Minority* (Austin: University of Texas, 1980).

[23]Ilan Pappé notes that this policy of using "settlement belts" in order to gain land actually began in 1947 with the creation of the U.N. Partition Plan (*Ethnic Cleansing of Palestine*, 69).

[24]Jeff Halper, *Matrix of Control* (Israel Committee Against Home Demolitions, February 2000), available at www.icahd.org.

[25]Ben-Dor, "Who Are the Real Terrorists?" (emphasis added).

[26]See chap. 9 of this book for more on suicide bombings.

[27]Hedges, *War Is a Force That Gives Us Meaning*, 84.

[28]Nicholas D. Kristof, *The New York Times*, March 18, 2007.

[29]Akiva Eldar, "The Occupation Corrupts from Above," *Ha'aretz* newspaper, November 24, 2003.

[30]Jimmy Carter, *Palestine: Peace Not Apartheid* (New York: Simon & Schuster, 2007), 131.

[31]Mark Braverman, *Preventing Workplace Violence* (Thousand Oaks, CA: Sage Publications, 1999), 21.

[32]Ibid., 20.

[33]Ibid., 16, 23.

[34]Gilles Kepel, *The Revenge of God: The Resurgence of Islam, Christianity and Judaism in the Modern World* (Boston: Polity Press, 1994), 199. Although early Zionism was a secular movement, its attitude toward Palestinians is reflected in forms of Jewish religion that are exclusive and nationalist. Israel Shahak, in his book *Jewish History, Jewish Religion: The Weight of Three Thousand Years* (Boulder, CO: Pluto Press, 1994), devotes an entire chapter to a critique of those aspects of Jewish religious law that discriminate against non-Jews. A particularly egregious example of the kind of argument that this sort of philosophy can lead to is presented by Rabbi Meir Kahane, *They Must Go* (New York: Grosset & Dunlap, 1981).

[35]The front page of *Al-Quds* newspaper, March 25, 2007, featured a picture of one of these dogs attacking a Palestinian woman. *Al-Quds* is the main daily Palestinian newspaper.

[36]A 2006 report by the Arab Association for Human Rights and the Centre Against Racism, entitled *Suspected Citizens: Racial Profiling Against Arab Passengers by Israeli Airports and Airlines*, documents the abuse and humiliation of Arab travelers at Ben-Gurion Airport.

[37]Herbert E. Thomas, *The Shame Response to Rejection* (Sewickley, PA: Albanel Publishers, 1997), 32.

[38]"Uprising," KPFK Radio, Los Angeles, January 30, 2007. In response to such abuse, Machsom Watch, a voluntary organization of Israeli Jewish women that monitors checkpoints and reports human rights abuses, came into being. They monitor the behavior of soldiers at checkpoints; see http://www.machsomwatch.org/.

[39]Thomas, *The Shame Response*, 34.

[40]Ibid., 32.

CHAPTER 4—THE BIBLE AND THE LAND

[1]George E. Mendenhall and Gary A. Herion, *Ancient Israel's Faith and History: An Introduction to the Bible in Context* (Louisville, KY: Westminster John Knox Press, 2001), 36.

[2]Mustafa Abu Sway, "The Holy Land, Jerusalem and Al-Aqsa Mosque in the Qur'an, Sunnah, and Other Islamic Sources," unpublished, revised from a paper entitled "The Holy Land, Jerusalem and Al-Aqsa Mosque in the Islamic Sources," *Journal of the Central Conference of American Rabbis* (CCAR) (Fall 2000): 60-68.

[3]Sway, "The Holy Land ... Other Islamic Sources," 3.

[4]Ibid., 4.

[5]Study Group of the Church of Scotland, *Theology of Land and Covenant*, May 2003, 2.5.3.

[6]Colin Chapman, *Whose Promised Land?* (Oxford: Lion Publishing, 2002), 297.

[7]Study Group, *Theology of Land and Covenant*, 2.5.2.

[8]Walter Brueggemann, *Theology of the Old Testament: Testimony, Dispute, Advocacy* (Minneapolis: Fortress Press, 1997), 729-33.

[9]Ibid., 729.

[10]Brevard Childs, *Biblical Theology of the Old and New Testaments*, as quoted in Walter Brueggemann, *Theology of the Old Testament*, 730.

[11]Bruggemann, *Theology of the Old Testament*, 730.

[12]Ibid., 732.

[13]Ibid.

[14]Gal. 3:23-29; Eph. 1:9-10; 2:11-22; Col. 3:10-11.

[15]*Alquds*, January 1, 2004.

[16]W. D. Davies wrote one of the first books on this topic: *The Gospel and the Land* (Berkeley: University of California Press, 1974).

[17]Christopher J. H. Wright, *Old Testament Ethics for the People of God* (Downers Grove, IL: InterVarsity Press, 2004), 191.

[18]Tom Wright, "Jerusalem in the New Testament," in *Jerusalem Past and Present in the Purposes of God*, ed. Peter W. L. Walker (Cambridge: Tyndale House, 1992), 67.

[19]For more on the role of the book of Jonah in the development of Old Testament theology, see chap. 5 of this book; see also Miguel De La Torre, *Liberating Jonah: Forming an Ethics of Reconciliation* (Maryknoll, NY: Orbis Books, 2007).

[20]Wright, *Old Testament Ethics for the People of God*, 189.

[21]The Episcopal Church, *The Book of Common Prayer* (Boston: Seabury, 1977).

CHAPTER 5—JONAH, THE FIRST PALESTINIAN LIBERATION THEOLOGIAN

[1]Leon Morris, *The Gospel According to John*, New International Commentary on the New Testament, ed. F. F. Bruce (Grand Rapids: Eerdmans, 1971), 434.

[2]See, for example, Douglas Stuart, *Hosea-Jonah*, Word Biblical Commentary 31 (Waco, TX: Word, 1987), 431.

[3]See the book of Nahum, esp. 1:14-15; 2:11-13; 3:1-7.

[4]Naim Stifan Ateek, *Justice, and Only Justice: A Palestinian Liberation Theology* (Maryknoll, NY: Orbis Books, 1989), 96, 110.

[5]Leslie C. Allen, *The Books of Joel, Obadiah, Jonah and Micah*, New International Commentary on the Old Testament (Grand Rapids: Eerdmans, 1976), 185-88. Although some scholars dispute the linguistic and historical evidence for such a late date for Jonah, neither is there any overwhelmingly persuasive evidence to the contrary. See Phyllis Trible, "Jonah," *The New Interpreter's Bible* 7 (Nashville: Abingdon, 1996), 465-66.

[6]G. Ernest Wright, *The Old Testament against Its Environment* (London: SCM Press, 1962).

[7]*The Interpreter's Bible* 6 (Nashville: Abingdon Press, 1956).

[8]Other references to the expulsion or destruction of the people in the land can be found in Deut. 7:1-2; 9:1-3; 20:16-17; Josh. 6:21. See also T. Desmond Alexander, "Beyond Borders: The Wider Dimension of the Land," in *The Land of Promise: Biblical, Theological, and Contemporary Perspectives*, ed. Phillip Johnston and Peter Walker (Downers Grove, IL: InterVarsity Press, 200), 47-48.

[9]See Rosemary Radford Ruether and Herman J. Ruether, *The Wrath of Jonah: The Crisis of Religious Nationalism in the Israeli-Palestinian Conflict*, 2nd ed. (Minneapolis: Fortress Press, 2002).

CHAPTER 6—THE THEOLOGY AND POLITICS OF CHRISTIAN ZIONISM

[1]Jimmy Carter, *Palestine: Peace Not Apartheid* (New York: Simon & Schuster, 2006), 34.

[2]Naim Ateek, Cedar Duaybis, and Maurine Tobin, eds., *Challenging Christian Zion-*

ism: Theology, Politics, and the Israel-Palestine Conflict (London: Melisende, 2005).

[3]Donald Wagner, "A Christian Zionist Primer, Part II: Defining Christian Zionism," *Cornerstone* 31 (Winter 2003): 12.

[4]Quoted in Stephen Sizer, "The Historical Roots of Christian Zionism from Irving to Balfour," in *Challenging Christian Zionism*, 21.

[5]Gary Burge, "Theological and Biblical Assumptions of Christian Zionism," in *Challenging Christian Zionism*, 51-53.

[6]Sizer, "The Theological Basis of Christian Zionism: On the Road to Armageddon," in *Challenging Christian Zionism*, 60-74.

[7]Ibid., 75.

[8]See the July 27, 2007, letter written by evangelical leaders to President George W. Bush in support of the peace process and the two-state solution. Available from Evangelicals for Social Action at http://www.esa-online.org.

[9]See also Matt. 24:36, 42; Luke 12:39-40; 17:26-30; Acts 1:6-8.

[10]Barbara Tuchman, *Bible and Sword* (London: Macmillan, 1982), 24.

[11]Donald E. Wagner, *Anxious for Armageddon* (Scottdale, PA: Herald Press, 1995), 27.

[12]Doreen Ingrams, *The Palestine Papers: 1917-1922* (New York: G. Braziller, 1973), 73.

[13]*Ha'aretz*, July 17, 2002.

[14]Ibid.

[15]Herb Keinon, "US Christian Leader Bauer: Israel a Priority for Evangelicals," *Jerusalem Post*, July 5, 2002.

[16]Yigal Schleifer, "Newfound Friends," *Jerusalem Report*, July 1, 2002.

[17]Ibid.

[18]Ibid.

[19]Ibid.

[20]Ibid.

[21]Quoted by Stephen Sizer, "The Origins of Christian Zionism," *Cornerstone* 31 (Winter 2003): 4.

[22]"The Gospel According to John," *Ha'aretz*, May 5, 2006.

[23]Some of the following points are based on my introduction to *Challenging Christian Zionism*, 13-19.

[24]Grace Halsell, *Forcing God's Hand: Why Millions Pray for a Quick Rapture—And the Destruction of Planet Earth* (Washington, DC: Crossroads International Publishing, 1999).

CHAPTER 7—SON OF DAVID OR SUFFERING SERVANT?

[1]In 2005, the U.S. military budget was at least $478.2 billion and Israel's defense budget was $9.6 billion. Together, the military spending of the United States and Israel amounts to almost half of the total global defense expenditure of just over $1 trillion (P. Stalenheim, D. Fruchart, W. Omitoogun, and C. Perdomo, "Military Expenditure," *SIPRI Yearbook 2006* [Oxford: Oxford University Press, 2006], 302).

[2]Much has been written about these four groups, but my own ideas have been enhanced by the work of John Yoder and George Mendenhall. I am indebted here to the work of John Yoder in his books, *The Original Revolution* (Scottdale, PA: Herald Press, 1971) and *The Politics of Jesus* (Grand Rapids: Eerdmans, 1972). Also, see the work of George Mendenhall, *Ancient Israel's Faith and History* (Louisville, KY: Westminster John Knox Press, 2001), esp. chap. 8, 203ff.

[3]Even though many scholars believe that it is anachronistic to refer to the violent revolutionaries of Jesus' time as "Zealots," since the term was not used until after the year 66, it is clear that the "zealot option" of violent revolution against Rome did exist

for Jesus' contemporaries, whether or not it went by that name. See Yoder, *Politics of Jesus*, 56-58.

[4]Yoder, *Politics of Jesus*, 47 and 62. Yoder cites Oscar Cullman, *The State in the New Testament* (New York: Scribner, 1956), 8: "The political import of the formation of a group of disciples is heightened if we take seriously Oscar Cullman's suggestion that perhaps as many as half of the twelve were recruited from among the ranks of the Zealots." Yoder also argues that the power struggles among the disciples were a manifestation of the Zealot understanding of the meaning of the kingdom.

[5]Yoder, *Politics of Jesus*, 25.

[6]Mendenhall, *Ancient Israel's Faith and History*, 193.

[7]Ibid., 189-90, 194.

[8]N. T. Wright, *Jesus and the Victory of God* (Minneapolis: Fortress Press, 1997), 509. See also Mendenhall, *Ancient Israel's Faith and History*, 221.

[9]Jon D. Levenson, *Sinai and Zion: An Entry into the Jewish Bible* (Minneapolis/Chicago/New York: Winston Press, 1985), 96.

[10]Barbara R. Rossing, *The Rapture Exposed: The Message of Hope in the Book of Revelation* (Boulder, CO: Westview Press, 2005), 111.

[11]Ibid., 119.

[12]See "Appendix A: The Gospel Passion Narratives as Historical Sources," in Christopher Bryan, *Render to Caesar: Jesus, the Early Church, and the Roman Superpower* (Oxford and New York: Oxford University Press, 2005), 65ff.

[13]See http://www.rachelcorrie.org/.

[14]Rossing, *Rapture Exposed*, 121.

CHAPTER 8—SADDAM, SODOM, AND THE CROSS

[1]Rosemary Radford Ruether, *America, Amerikka: Elect Nation and Imperial Violence* (London: Equinox, 2007), 261.

[2]Gen. 18:16-19:29; Jer. 23:14.

[3]Palestinian leader Mahmoud Abbas (Abu Mazen) officially apologized to the Kuwaiti government for Palestinians' support of Saddam Hussein during the 1990 invasion on December 12, 2004, *BBC News*.

[4]See Ilan Pappé, *The Ethnic Cleansing of Palestine* (London: Oneworld Publications, 2006).

[5]It would be more accurate to refer to the invasion of Kuwait by Iraq and the subsequent invasion of Iraq by the United States as the Second Gulf War, the first being the 1980-1988 war between Iran and Iraq. However, as the focus of this chapter is on the U.S. involvement in Iraq, the First and Second Iraq Wars refer to the Gulf Crisis of 1991 and the 2003 occupation of Iraq, respectively.

[6]Bob Woodward, *Plan of Attack* (New York: Simon & Schuster, 2004), 309-11.

[7]Eric Schmitt, "Threats and Responses: Military Spending; Pentagon Contradicts General on Iraq Occupation Force's Size," *The New York Times*, February 28, 2003.

[8]James A. Baker III and Lee H. Hamilton et al., *The Iraq Study Group Report: The Way Forward* (New York: Vintage Books, 2006), 32. These numbers have obviously continued to rise; as of the writing of this book, more than 4,000 Americans have lost their lives in Iraq.

[9]Rob Stein, "100,000 Civilian Deaths Estimated in Iraq," *Washington Post*, October 29, 2004.

[10]The Iraq Study Group, chaired by James A. Baker III, and Lee H. Hamilton, *Iraq Group Report*.

[11]Ibid., 50. According to the *Report*, the Iraq International Support Group should be established to handle regional diplomacy and should be composed of "Iraq and all the states bordering Iraq, including Iran and Syria; the key regional states, including Egypt

and the Gulf States, the five permanent members of the United Nations Security Council; the European Union" (ibid., 49).

[12]Ibid., 54.

[13]Ibid., 57.

[14]Ibid., 58.

[15]*The Washington Report on Middle East Affairs* 16, no. 2 (March 2007), 9. As this book is published, these figures continue to rise.

[16]Ibid.

[17]An estimated 1.5 million Armenians were killed by the Ottoman Empire or Turkish Nationalists between 1915 and 1928. For more information see the Web site of the Armenian National Institute at http://www.armenian-genocide.org/.

[18]Perpetrated by the Ottoman Empire against Assyrian Christians from 1915 to 1918. Estimates of alleged killings vary from 250,000 to 750,000 but the Turkish government has continued to maintain that the genocide never happened.

[19]Approximately 6 million Jews were murdered by the Nazi regime during World War II.

[20]Although this chapter attempts to interpret the biblical texts as they stand rather than from a critical point of view, it is interesting to note that archeological evidence indicates that Jericho had been destroyed long before Joshua's conquest. Some of the more problematic narratives in the Bible are most likely stories created later and do not represent historical fact. See Bernhard W. Anderson with Steven Bishop and Judith H. Newman, *Understanding the Old Testament*, 5th ed. (Upper Saddle River, NJ: Pearson/Prentice Hall, 2007).

[21]Desmond Tutu makes the claim that civilians account for more than 90 percent of all war casualties today in his "Stop Killing the Children," *Washington Post*, November 24, 1996, C7.

[22]Sabrina Tavernise, "The Scene: A Night of Death and Terror for Lebanese Villagers," *The New York Times*, July 31, 2006.

[23]President George W. Bush's proposed budget for the 2007-2008 fiscal year included $145.2 billion for war efforts in Afghanistan and Iraq as well as $99.6 billion in additional new spending for 2006-2007 (Sheryl Gay Stolberg, "Bush Releases Budget Aimed to Erase Deficit," *The New York Times*, February 6, 2007). Assuming an Iraqi population of around 27 million, that amount of spending is enough to pay each Iraqi citizen a little over nine thousand dollars.

[24]Peter Arnett interview with Saddam Hussein. Originally aired on January 30, 1991, on CNN. Some excerpts from the interview can be found in the January 31, 1991, article in *The New York Times*, "War in the Gulf: Baghdad; Excerpts from Saddam Hussein's Comments on the Gulf War."

[25]"Most Americans Back U.S. Tactics," *Washington Post*, November 29, 2001.

[26]"Most Favor Nuclear Option against Iraq," *Washington Post*, December 18, 2002. The question asked whether Americans would support the use of nuclear weapons against Iraq if Iraq used chemical or biological weapons against U.S. troops.

[27]Dana Milbank and Jim VandeHei, "No Political Fallout for Bush on Weapons," *Washington Post*, May 17, 2003, A1.

[28]Excerpted from the World Alliance of Reformed Churches' statement "An Ecumenical Faith Stance against Global Empire," written in Manila, Philippines in July 2006. The statement can be found at http://warc.jalb.de/warcajsp/side.jsp?news_id=809&part_id=0&navi=6.

[29]Ibid.

[30]George E. Mendenhall and Gary A. Herion, *Ancient Israel's Faith and History: An Introduction to the Bible in Context* (Louisville, KY: Westminster John Knox Press, 2001), 36.

[31]Lincoln Steffens, *Autobiography of Lincoln Steffens* (Berkeley, CA: Heyday Books, 2005), 781-82.

CHAPTER 9—SAMSON, THE FIRST SUICIDE BOMBER

[1]The American State Department defines terrorism as "Premeditated, politically motivated violence perpetrated against noncombatant targets by subnational groups or clandestine agents, usually intended to influence an audience." In the American definition, terrorism can never be inflicted by a state. This is a useful definition because, as Brian Whitaker writes, "it gets the US and its allies off the hook in a variety of situations. The disadvantage is that it might also get hostile states off the hook—which is why there has to be a list of states that are said to 'sponsor' terrorism while not actually committing it themselves." Under the State Department rules, if Palestinians attack a Jewish settlement with mortars it is considered terrorism. If, however, Israeli rockets attack a Palestinian community it is not because Israel is a state and states can never inflict terrorism (www.guardian.co.uk, May 7, 2001). To say that states cannot inflict terrorism betrays a lack of understanding of the depth of evil in our world and the direct involvement of many states in violence and terrorism. One wonders whether there is really a clean and civilized "terrorism" committed by states and a dirty and barbaric "terrorism" perpetrated by militant groups. Palestinian daily experience has shown that it is the injustice of the Israeli state perpetuated through violence and terrorism against the Palestinians that has created and prompted its Palestinian counterpart. Ultimately, the issue boils down to whose definition is used. Brian Whitaker wrote in the same article that a more honest definition of terrorism is as follows: "Terrorism is violence committed by those we disapprove of."

[2]By 2005, out of 165 suicide bombers, eight have been women (Palestinian Human Rights Monitoring Group [PHRMG], "Suicide Attacks: A Case for an End to an Egregious Means," available online at www.phrmg.org).

[3]"Analysis: Palestinian Suicide Attacks," *BBC News*, January 29, 2007, http://news.bbc.co.uk/2/hi/middle_east/3256858.stm.

[4]Suzanne Goldenberg, "A Mission to Murder: Inside the Minds of the Suicide Bombers," *The Guardian* (UK), June 11, 2002.

[5]PHRMG, "Suicide Attacks." See also the PHRMG press release on suicide attacks at www.phrmg.org/pressrelease/2007/Suicide%20Attacks.htm.

[6]www.btselem.org/english/statistics/Casualties.asp. According to B'tselem, 4,676 Palestinians have been killed by the Israeli military since the beginning of the second intifada, while a total of 1,045 Israelis have been killed by Palestinians in the same period.

[7]*The Phenomenon of Collaborators in Palestine* (Jerusalem: PASSIA Publications, March 2001).

[8]Khaled Abu Toameh, "Love and Hate," *Jerusalem Report*, May 20, 2002, 27.

[9]"Open Debate," Al Jazeera TV, June 29, 2002, with Khaled Mash'al.

[10]Akiva Eldar, "Ask Clinton What He Thinks about Camp David," *Ha'aretz*, August 21, 2001. In an unpublished paper, Dr. Mustafa Abu Sway of Alquds University maintains that the reference to the "seventy virgins" is neither mentioned in the Qur'an nor in the most authentic compendia of Hadith. It is, however, found in Mu'jam Al-Tabarani.

[11]Arno J. Mayer, professor emeritus of history at Princeton, has written in the wake of September 11, "In modern times, acts of individual terror have been the weapon of the weak and the poor, while acts of state and economic terror have been the weapons of the strong." Quoted by Gore Vidal, *Perpetual War for Perpetual Peace: How We Got to Be So Hated* (New York: Nation Books, 2002), xi.

[12]http://www.imamyahyahendi.com/. See especially Imam Hendi's article "Islam, the Myth and the Real," available at http://www.imamyahyahendi.com/library_articles_6.htm.

[13]"Save a Life, Save All Humanity—Take a Life, Kill All Humanity," April 1, 2006, 2. Available at www.beliefnet.com/story/87/story_8753_1.html?rnd=69.

[14]Ibid., 6.

[15]Ibid., 7.

[16]Ibid.

[17]Ibid., 8.

[18]Ibid.

[19]Eldar, "Ask Clinton What He Thinks about Camp David."

[20]Alexandra Williams, "Our Daughter Was Killed by a Suicide Bomber," *The Mirror* (London), June 25, 2002. Many families who have lost loved ones in this conflict have come together to work for reconciliation. See http://www.theparentscircle.org/.

[21]Shamai Leibowitz, "An Israeli Officer's Response to President Bush," June 27, 2002, www.zmag.org. See also "The Ethics of Revenge," a moving speech of Yitzhak Frankenthal, chairman of the Families Forum, given at a rally in Jerusalem on Saturday, July 27, 2002, outside Prime Minister Sharon's residence (magazine@tikkun.org). Frankenthal's son Arik was killed by Palestinians. He also blames the Israeli occupation. He writes, "We lost sight of our ethics long before the suicide bombings. The breaking point was when we started to control another nation." He adds, "The Palestinians cannot drive us away—they have long acknowledged our existence. They have been ready to make peace with us; it is we who are unwilling to make peace with them. It is we who insist on maintaining our control over them; it is we who escalate the situation in the region and feed the cycle of bloodshed. I regret to say it, but the blame is entirely ours."

[22]One of the criticisms voiced by Israel against the Palestinians and some Arab countries, especially Saudi Arabia, regards the payments given to the families of the martyrs. Every family receives twenty-five thousand dollars. Israel considers this payment an encouragement to young men to become suicide bombers and maintains it must stop. Most Palestinians, however, consider the money received not an encouragement to suicide bombers but support for their families. One wonders whether Israel's condemnation of these payments implies that the families of the suicide bombers should be penalized. In fact, Israel has on numerous occasions mercilessly demolished their homes. Indeed, many times the family is not even aware of what their son or daughter is going to do. It is wrong, therefore, to inflict further pain and suffering on the family by starving them to death, or destroying their home. In the history of the church, a baby born out of wedlock was not penalized and thrown outdoors to die because he or she was born in sin. The baby was baptized and received as a child of God. It is right to support and comfort the family in spite of what its son or daughter has done. If Israel is so anxious to stop the suicide bombings it must consider stopping its oppressive occupation and giving them justice.

[23]It is interesting to point out that some Christians have argued that the classic definition of a martyr should be expanded to include those who have been killed as a result of taking a prophetic stand against injustice and oppression, including Dietrich Bonhoeffer, Martin Luther King Jr., Oscar Romero, and others. These are people who have borne witness and committed themselves to the struggle for justice and peace and consequently suffered for it (see Rowan D. Crews Jr., "Martyrdom," in *Dictionary of the Ecumenical Movement*, ed. Nicholas Lossky, Jose Miguez Bonino, John S. Pobee, Tom F. Stransky, Geoffrey Wainwright, and Pauline Webb [Geneva: World Council of Churches Publications, 1991], 660).

[24]The Philistines are not racially or ethnically related to today's Palestinians. Some scholars believe that they were a sea people originating from the Aegean Islands and Crete. Others say that they came from the south and west coasts of Asia Minor between the twelfth and thirteenth centuries BCE and settled in the southern coast of Palestine. During Roman rule, the entire area was known, using a slight variation of their name, as Palestine.

[25]It is interesting that Samson's name is not mentioned among those who committed suicide in the *Interpreter's Bible Dictionary*. Although the word "suicide" does not appear in the Bible, there are people who committed the act. See, for example, 1 Sam. 31:4-5; 2 Sam. 17:23; and 1 Kgs. 16:18.

[26]The issue of suicide in today's world is not black and white. It is a complicated phenomenon. There are people who due to terminal illness or deep psychological sickness

and derangement attempt to or, indeed, take their life. Ultimately, it is only the merciful God who can judge. This is an important point in the context of our focus on suicide bombings.

[27]Dorothee Sölle, "Suffering," *Dictionary of the Ecumenical Movement*, ed. Lossky et al., 963.

[28]From a sermon preached at Eutaw Alabama Church during the 1966 Alabama Tour. Poster produced by Community Printers and the Resource Center for Nonviolence in Santa Cruz, California.

[29]See highlights of Archbishop Tutu's address at a conference cosponsored by Friends of Sabeel and the Episcopal Diocese of Massachusetts in Boston on April 13, 2002 (*Cornerstone* 24 [Spring 2002]: 3). Available online at http://www.sabeel.org/old/news/cstone24/frontpage.html.

[30]An eyewitness once told me that at a meeting between Israeli officials and representatives of American Christian Zionist leaders a request was made to the Christians to purchase arms for Israel. The Christian Zionists agreed to do that. When we hear such stories, we wonder whether we believe in the same God of love and peace.

[31]At Sabeel, we have always condemned collective punishment in any form. See the Sabeel statement, "A Human Tragedy Called Gaza," at http://www.sabeel.org/etemplate.php?id=69.

CHAPTER 10—DANIEL OR JUDAH MACCABEUS

[1]In many ways this system continues to operate even today. In a world in which the United States exists as the sole superpower, its military, economic, and cultural hegemony has resulted in an American empire. Israel continues to rely on its military and political alliance with the United States. See Jack Nelson-Pallmeyer, *Saving Christianity from Empire* (New York and London: Continuum, 2005).

[2]George Mendenhall, *Ancient Israel's Faith and History* (Louisville, KY: Westminster John Knox Press, 2001).

[3]Ibid., 186.

[4]Ibid.

[5]Ibid., 188.

[6]Ibid., 189.

[7]Ibid., 190.

[8]Ibid.

[9]Ibid., 193.

[10]Wes Howard-Brook and Anthony Gwyther, *Unveiling Empire: Reading Revelation Then and Now* (Maryknoll, NY: Orbis Books, 1999), 51.

[11]Ibid., 50.

[12]Ibid., 52.

[13]Walter Wink, *Engaging the Powers: Discernment and Resistance in a World of Domination* (Minneapolis: Fortress Press, 1992), 175-93.

[14]Walter Wink, *Jesus and Nonviolence: A Third Way* (Minneapolis: Augsburg Fortress, 2003), 16.

[15]Ibid., 21-22.

[16]Ibid., 25.

[17]Ibid., 27-28.

[18]This document is available on the Sabeel website at http://www.sabeel.org/pdfs/mri.htm.

[19]See www.cpt.org.

[20]See http://eappi.org/.

[21]See http://www.palsolidarity.org/.

[22]See http://www.icahd.org/eng/.

[23]See http://www.bilin-village.org/.

[24]See http://www.palestinesolidarityproject.org/.

CHAPTER 11—WHOSE JERUSALEM?

[1]Karen Armstrong, from a presentation at the University of Chicago, May 21, 1996.

[2]*Kingdom of Heaven,* 2005, dir. Ridley Scott.

[3]Leslie Susser, "The Carrot of Statehood," *Jerusalem Report,* June 5, 2000, 18-19.

[4]George E. Mendenhall, *Ancient Israel's Faith and History: An Introduction to the Bible in Context* (Louisville, KY: Westminster John Knox Press, 2001), 191.

[5]Ibid., 196-97.

[6]J. David Pleins, *The Psalms: Songs of Tragedy, Hope and Justice* (Maryknoll, NY: Orbis Books, 1993), 117.

[7]Ibid., 126.

[8]Peter Walker, "Jerusalem in the Early Christian Centuries," in *Jerusalem Past and Present in the Purposes of God,* ed. Peter Walker (Grand Rapids: Baker Book House, 1994), 79-97.

[9]W. D. Davies, *The Gospel and the Land* (Berkeley: University of California Press, 1974), 302.

[10]Wes Howard-Brook and Anthony Gwyther, *Unveiling Empire: Reading Revelation Then and Now* (Maryknoll, NY: Orbis Books, 1999), 157-58.

[11]Ibid., 184.

[12]Ibid., 192.

[13]Martin Luther King Jr., "I See the Promised Land," April 3, 1968, as quoted in Barbara Rossing, *The Rapture Exposed: The Message of Hope in the Book of Revelation* (Boulder, CO: Westview Press, 2004), 165.

[14]Ibid., 166.

[15]Howard-Brook and Gwyther, *Unveiling Empire,* 166.

[16]John Dominic Crossan, *God and Empire* (San Francisco: Harper, 2007), 25.

[17]See www.newamericancentury.org. This document serves as "an unabashed proclamation of the Imperial intentions of its writers, many of whom were or are currently in power in the Bush administration. This document is a clearly defined theology of empire and is warmly embraced by many people in government and in the business communities which stand to benefit financially from an American Empire without limits of time or space" (*God and Empire* book review, www.bpleland.wordpress.com, April 12, 2007).

[18]David C. Korten, *When Corporations Ruled the World* (West Hartford, CT: Kumarian Press, 1995), 69, quoted in Howard-Brook and Gwyther, *Unveiling Empire,* 238.

[19]Howard-Brook and Gwyther, *Unveiling Empire,* 176-77.

[20]Ibid., 185.

[21]Ibid., 190.

[22]Churches for Middle East Peace, "Christians Call for a Shared Jerusalem," www.cmep.org, September 1996.

[23]Karen Armstrong, *Jerusalem: One City, Three Faiths* (New York: Ballentine, 1996), 427.

CHAPTER 12—ISRAEL'S PREDICAMENT

[1]The full text of the Arab League Proposal is available at http://www.al-bab.com/arab/docs/league/peace02.htm. For a more detailed list of Arab peace proposals that have

been rejected, see Jeff Halper, *An Israeli in Palestine: Resisting Dispossession, Redeeming Israel* (London: Pluto Press, 2008), 89-96.

[2]For a detailed description of the demographic situation in Israel-Palestine as it relates to the conflict, see Bernard Wasserstein, *Israel and Palestine: Why They Fight and Can They Stop?* (London: Profile Books, 2004), 5-30.

[3]See Naim Ateek, "Who Is My Neighbor?" *Interpretation* 62, no. 2 (April 2008): 156-65.

[4]According to Wasserstein, in March 2002 as much as 42 percent of the Jewish population of Israel was in favor of population transfer for Arabs (Wasserstein, *Israel and Palestine*, 28-29).

[5]Quoted in John Mahoney, "Avraham Burg: Apostate or Avatar?" *The Link* 40, no. 4 (October-November 2007): 2. For more on Avraham Burg and other Israeli Jews who have the courage to speak out, see the entire issue of *The Link*.

[6]Ibid., 11.

[7]Ibid., 10.

[8]Avraham Burg, *Victory over Hitler* (Tel Aviv: Chemed Books, 2007). At the time of this writing, the book was only available in Hebrew.

[9]Mahoney, "Avraham Burg," 12.

[10]Halper, *Israeli in Palestine*, 74.

[11]Ibid., 74.

[12]Ibid., 75.

[13]Ibid., 76.

[14]Joel Kovel, *Overcoming Zionism: Creating a Single Democratic State in Israel/Palestine* (Ann Arbor, MI: Pluto Press, 2007).

[15]Ibid., 161-64.

[16]Ibid., 165.

[17]For the whole report, see http://www.acri.org.il/pdf/State2007.pdf. See especially the section, "The Rights of Palestinian Citizens of Israel," 14-25.

[18]Ibid., 14.

[19]Ibid.

[20]Farid Esack, "Exclusive Identity and the Struggle Against Apartheid," *Cornerstone* 48 (Spring 2008): 10.

[21]John Dugard, "Occupation, Apartheid, and Colonialism in International Law," *Cornerstone* 48 (Spring 2008): 13.

[22]Ibid.

[23]United Nations Office for the Coordination of Humanitarian Affairs (OCHA)—occupied Palestinian territory, "East Jerusalem: The Humanitarian Impact of the West Bank Barrier on Palestinian Communities," June 2007, 14. Available online at http://www.ochaopt.org/documents/Jerusalem-30July2007.pdf.

[24]Ibid.

[25]For the full text of the advisory opinion, see the ICJ Web site at http://www.icj-cij.org/docket/index.php?p1=3&p2=4&code=mwp&case=131&k=5a.

[26]Ibid. The domination and control of the United Nations by the United States has obstructed the exercise of justice by the world body. Israel stands in violation of many U.N. resolutions and has been protected continuously by the United States. In his speech before the Israeli Knesset on May 15, 2008, President Bush mentioned the United Nations only once, and in a decidedly negative way. He said, "We believe that democracy is the only way to ensure human rights. So we consider it a source of shame that the United Nations routinely passes more human rights resolutions against the freest democracy in the Middle East than any other nation in the world" (George W. Bush, speech to the Knesset, Jerusalem, May 15, 1008; full text available at: http://www.whitehouse.gov/news/releases/2008/05/20080515-1.html).

[27]Kovel, *Overcoming Zionism*, 204-7.

[28]Mahoney, "Avraham Burg," 2.

[29]"State of Israel: Proclamation of Independence," in Walter Laqueur and Barry Rubin, eds., *The Israel-Arab Reader: A Documentary History of the Middle East Conflict*, 6th ed. (New York: Penguin, 2001), 82-83.

[30]Bush, speech to the Knesset, Jerusalem, May 15, 2008.

[31]See chap. 5.

CHAPTER 13—THE TWO-STATE SOLUTION IS NOT ENOUGH

[1]Adeed Dawisha, *Arab Nationalism in the Twentieth Century: From Triumph to Despair* (Princeton, NJ: Princeton University Press, 2003), 13.

[2]John W. Mulhall, *America and the Founding of Israel: An Investigation of the Morality of America's Role* (Los Angeles: Deshon Press, 1995), 49. See also Michael Prior, ed., *Speaking the Truth about Zionism and Israel* (London: Melisende, 2004), 27.

[3]Menahem Ussishkin, chairman of the Jewish National Fund (in the early twentieth century) and president of the twentieth Zionist Congress, on April 28, 1930, in an address to journalists in Jerusalem (Nur Masalha, *Expulsion of the Palestinians: The Concept of "Transfer" in Zionist Political Thought, 1882-1948* [Washington, DC: Institute for Palestine Studies, 1992], 178).

[4]Sabri Jiryis, *The Arabs in Israel* (New York: Monthly Review Press, 1976), 76.

[5]Michael Prior, "Confronting the Bible's Ethnic Cleansing in Palestine," *The Link* (New York: Americans for Middle East Understanding, December 2000).

[6]See Joel Kovel, *Overcoming Zionism: Creating a Single Democratic State in Israel-Palestine* (Ann Arbor, MI: Pluto Press, 2007), esp. 197-221. See also Jeff Halper, *An Israeli in Palestine: Resisiting Dispossession, Redeeming Israel* (Ann Arbor, MI: Pluto Press, 2008), esp. 15-35.

[7]"The June 6, 2004 Israeli Government decision #1996, stated: 'As a rule, residential areas and sensitive structures, including synagogues, will not remain' (Appendix A, Clause 7)." Lara Friedman, "Settlements in Focus," Americans for Peace Now, www.peacenow.org.

[8]Al-Awda: The Palestinian Right to Return Coalition: www.al-awda.org. This figure includes 750,000 who were forced to become refugees, and 32,000 who were internally displaced.

[9]See www.unrwa.org.

[10]See www.al-awda.org.

[11]United Nations "Universal Declaration of Human Rights," adopted by U.N. General Assembly Resolution 217 A, December 10, 1948, art. 13.

[12]U.N. General Assembly Resolution 194, December 11, 1948, para. 11.

[13]See www.unrwa.org.

[14]Adaptation of a Talmudic legend, by Rinah and Leon Sheleff, 2001. Available online at http://www.laurasimms.com/CrisisStories.html.

CHAPTER 14—FROM JUSTICE TO FORGIVENESS

[1]In 2007, the Association for Civil Rights in Israel released a report documenting trends of racism in Israeli society. Fifty-five percent of the Israeli Jews surveyed supported the idea that the government should encourage Arab emigration; 75 percent of those surveyed stated that they would not agree to live in the same building as Arabs. For the whole report, see http://www.acri.org.il/pdf/State2007.pdf.

[2]Martin Luther King Jr., "Dreams of Brighter Tomorrows," *Ebony*, March 1965.

[3]M. K. Gandhi, *The Essential Gandhi: An Anthology of His Writings on His Life, Work, and Ideas*, ed. Louis Fischer (New York: Vintage, 2002).

[4]Obery M. Hendricks, *The Politics of Jesus: Rediscovering the True Revolutionary Nature of Jesus' Teaching and How They Have Been Corrupted* (New York: Doubleday: 2006), 172.

[5]Mark Jürgensmeyer, *Gandhi's Way: A Handbook of Conflict Resolution* (Berkeley: University of California Press, 2005), 63-64.

[6]Ibid., 39-40.

[7]What follows is based on my article that appeared in the *Ecumenist* 42, no. 4 (Fall 2005): 3-5; this journal of theology, culture, and society is published by Novalis-Saint Paul University, Ottawa, Ontario, Canada.

[8]See also Col. 2:13; Eph. 4:32; and Matt. 18:21-33, the parable of the Unforgiving Servant.

[9]For further treatment of the parable of the Prodigal Son, see Kenneth E. Bailey, "Cultural Understanding of the Parable of the Prodigal Son," in *Forgotten Faithful: A Window into the Life and Witness of Christians in the Holy Land*, ed. Naim Ateek, Cedar Duaybis, and Maurine Tobin (Jerusalem: Sabeel, 2007), 156-67; and Kenneth E. Bailey, *Jacob and the Prodigal* (Downers Grove, IL: InterVarsity Press, 2003).

[10]John Dawson, *What Christians Should Know about Reconciliation* (Lancaster, UK: Sovereign World, 1998), 226.

Bibliography

Abu Sway, Mustafa. "The Holy Land, Jerusalem and Al-Aqsa Mosque in the Islamic Sources." *Journal of the Central Conference of American Rabbis* (CCAR) (Fall 2000): 60-68.

Alexander, T. Desmond. "Beyond Borders: The Wider Dimensions of the Land." In *The Land of Promise: Biblical, Theological and Contemporary Perspectives*, edited by Philip Johnston and Peter Walker, 35-50. Leicester, UK: Apollos, 2000.

Allen, Leslie C. *The Books of Joel, Obadiah, Jonah, and Micah*. In New International Commentary on the Old Testament. Grand Rapids: Eerdmans, 1976.

Anderson, Bernhard W., with Steven Bishop and Judith H. Newman. *Understanding the Old Testament*. 5th ed. Upper Saddle River, NJ: Pearson/Prentice Hall, 2007.

Applied Research Institute, Jerusalem. "The Growing Hardships of Traveling in the West Bank." Jerusalem: ARIJ, 2002.

Armstrong, Karen. *Jerusalem: One City, Three Faiths*. New York: Ballentine, 1996.

Atack, Ian. *The Ethics of Peace and War*. Edinburgh: Edinburgh University Press, 2005.

Ateek, Naim. *Justice, and Only Justice: A Palestinian Theology of Liberation*. Maryknoll, NY: Orbis Books, 1989.

———, Cedar Duaybis, and Marla Schrader. *Jerusalem: What Makes for Peace!* London: Melisende, 1997.

Ateek, Naim, Cedar Duaybis, and Maurine Tobin, eds. *Challenging Christian Zionism: Theology, Politics, and the Israel-Palestine Conflict*. London: Melisende, 2005.

———. *The Forgotten Faithful: A Window into the Life and Witness of Christians in the Holy Land*. Jerusalem: Sabeel, 2007.

Ateek, Naim S., Marc H. Ellis, and Rosemary Radford Ruether. *Faith and the Intifada: Palestinian Christian Voices*. Maryknoll, NY: Orbis Books, 1992.

Bailey, Kenneth E. "Cultural Understanding of the Parable of the Prodigal Son." In *Forgotten Faithful: A Window into the Life and Witness of Christians in the Holy Land*, edited by Naim Ateek, Cedar Duaybis, and Maurine Tobin, 156-67. Jerusalem: Sabeel, 2007.

———. *Jacob and the Prodigal*. Downers Grove: InterVarsity Press, 2003.

Baker, James A., and Lee H. Hamilton, et al. *The Iraq Study Group Report: The Way Forward—A New Approach*. New York: Vantage Books, 2006.

Braverman, Mark. *Preventing Workplace Violence*. Thousand Oaks, CA: Sage Publications, 1999.

Bruce, F. F., ed. *New International Commentary on the New Testament*. Grand Rapids: Eerdmans, 1971.

Brueggemann, Walter. *Theology of the Old Testament: Testimony, Dispute, Advocacy*. Minneapolis: Fortress Press, 1997.

Bryan, Christopher. "Appendix A: The Gospel Passion Narratives as Historical Sources." In *Render to Caesar: Jesus, the Early Church, and the Roman Superpower*. Oxford/New York: Oxford University Press, 2005.

Burge, Gary M. *Whose Land? Whose Promise? What Christians Are Not Being Told about Israel and the Palestinians*. Cleveland: Pilgrim Press, 2003.

Carter, Jimmy. *Palestine: Peace, Not Apartheid*. New York: Simon & Schuster, 2006.

Chacour, Elias, with Mary E. Jensen. *We Belong to the Land: The Story of a Palestinian Israeli Who Lives for Peace and Reconciliation.* San Francisco: Harper, 1990.

Chapman, Colin. *Whose Promised Land? The Continuing Crisis over Israel and Palestine.* Oxford, UK: Lion Publishing, 2002.

Churches for Middle East Peace. "Christians Call for a Shared Jerusalem." www.cmep. org. September 1996.

Coffin, William Sloane. *Credo.* Louisville, KY: Westminster John Knox Press, 2004.

Cragg, Kenneth. *Palestine: The Prize and Price of Zion.* London and Washington, DC: Cassell, 1997.

Crews, Rowan D., Jr. "Martyrdom." In *Dictionary of the Ecumenical Movement*, edited by Nicholas Lossky et al. Geneva: World Council of Churches Publications, 1991.

Crossan, John Dominic. *God and Empire.* San Francisco: Harper, 2007.

Davies, W. D. *The Gospel and the Land.* Berkeley: University of California Press, 1974.

Dawisha, Adeed. *Arab Nationalism in the Twentieth Century: From Triumph to Despair.* Princeton, NJ: Princeton University Press, 2003.

Dawson, John. *What Christians Should Know about Reconciliation.* Lancaster, UK: Sovereign World, 1998.

Dreyfuss, Robert. *Devil's Game: How the United States Helped Unleash Fundamentalist Islam.* New York: Metropolitan Books, 2005.

Ellis, Marc H. *O, Jerusalem! The Contested Future of the Jewish Covenant.* Minneapolis: Fortress Press, 1999.

———. *Reading the Torah Out Loud: A Journey of Lament and Hope.* Minneapolis: Fortress Press, 2007.

———. *Revolutionary Forgiveness: Essays on Judaism, Christianity, and the Future of Religious Life.* Waco, TX: Baylor University Press, 2000.

———. *Toward a Jewish Theology of Liberation.* Maryknoll, NY: Orbis Books, 1987.

Episcopal Church, The. *The Book of Common Prayer.* Boston: Seabury Press, 1977.

Gish, Arthur. *Hebron Journal: Stories of Nonviolent Peacemaking.* Scottdale, PA: Herald Press, 2001.

Halper, Jeff. "End of the Road Map: Preparing for the Struggle Against Apartheid." *Counterpunch*, September 2003.

———. *An Israeli in Palestine: Resisting Dispossession, Redeeming Israel.* Ann Arbor, MI: Pluto Press, 2008.

———. "A Most Ungenerous Offer." *The Link* 35, no. 4 (September/October 2002): 1-13.

Halsell, Grace. *Forcing God's Hand: Why Millions Pray for a Quick Rapture—And the Destruction of Planet Earth.* Washington, DC: Crossroads International Publishing, 1999.

Hedges, Chris. *War Is a Force That Gives Us Meaning.* New York: Doubleday/Anchor Books, 2002.

Hendricks, Obery M. *The Politics of Jesus: Rediscovering the True Revolutionary Nature of the Teachings of Jesus and How They Have Been Corrupted.* New York: Doubleday, 2006.

Horsley, Richard A. *Jesus and Empire: The Kingdom of God and the New World Disorder.* Minneapolis: Fortress Press, 2003.

Howard-Brook, Wes, and Anthony Gwyther. *Unveiling Empire: Reading Revelation Then and Now.* Maryknoll, NY: Orbis Books, 1999.

Ingrams, Doreen. *The Palestine Papers: 1917-1922.* London: G. Braziller, 1972.

Jiryis, Sabri. *The Arabs in Israel.* New York: Monthly Review Press, 1976.

Johnston, Philip, and Peter Walker, eds. *The Land of Promise: Biblical, Theological, and Contemporary Perspectives.* Leicester, UK: Apollos, 2000.

Jürgensmeyer, Mark. *Gandhi's Way: A Handbook of Conflict Resolution.* Berkeley: University of California Press, 2005.

————. *Terror in the Mind of God: The Global Rise of Religious Violence.* 3rd ed. Berkeley: University of California Press, 2003.

Kahane, Meir. *They Must Go.* New York: Grosset and Dunlap, 1981.

Kepel, Gilles. *The Revenge of God: The Resurgence of Islam, Christianity, and Judaism in the Modern World.* Cambridge, UK: Polity Press, 1994.

Kimball, Charles. *When Religion Becomes Evil.* San Francisco: HarperSanFrancisco, 2002.

King, Martin Luther, Jr. "Dreams of Brighter Tomorrows." *Ebony*, March 1965.

Kovel, Joel. *Overcoming Zionism: Creating a Single Democratic State in Israel/Palestine.* Ann Arbor, MI: Pluto Press, 2007.

Kushner, Tony, and Alisa Solomon, eds. *Wrestling with Zion: Progressive Jewish-American Responses to the Israeli-Palestinian Conflict.* New York: Grove Press, 2003.

LaHaye, Tim, and Jerry Jenkins. *Left Behind: A Novel of the Earth's Last Days.* Carol Stream, IL: Tyndale House, 2000.

Levenson, Jon D. *Sinai and Zion: An Entry into the Jewish Bible.* Minneapolis/Chicago/ New York: Winston Press, 1985.

Lilienthal, Alfred M. *The Zionist Connection: What Price Peace?* New York: Dodd, Mead & Company, 1978.

Lindsay, Hal. *The Late Great Planet Earth.* Grand Rapids: Zondervan, 1970.

Lossky, Nicholas, et al., eds. *Dictionary of the Ecumenical Movement.* Geneva: World Council of Churches Publications, 1991.

Lustick, Ian. *Arabs in the Jewish State: Israel's Control of a National Minority.* Austin: University of Texas Press, 1980.

Masalha, Nur. *Expulsion of the Palestinians: The Concept of "Transfer" in Zionist Political Thought, 1882-1948.* Beirut: Institute for Palestine Studies, 1992.

Mearsheimer, John J., and Stephen M. Walt. "The Israel Lobby and US Foreign Policy." *London Review of Books*, March 2006.

————. *The Israel Lobby and US Foreign Policy.* New York: Farrar, Straus and Giroux, 2007.

Mendenhall, George E., and Gary A. Herion. *Ancient Israel's Faith and History: An Introduction to the Bible in Context.* Louisville, KY: Westminster John Knox Press, 2001.

Menuhim, Moshe. *The Decadence of Judaism in Our Time.* New York: Exposition, 1965.

Morris, Leon. *The Gospel According to John.* In New International Commentary on the New Testament, edited by F. F. Bruce. Grand Rapids: Eerdmans, 1971.

Mulhall, John W. *America and the Founding of Israel: An Investigation of the Morality of America's Role.* Los Angeles: Deshon Press, 1995.

Nelson-Pallmeyer, Jack. *Saving Christianity from Empire.* New York and London: Continuum, 2005.

Pappé, Ilan. *The Ethnic Cleansing of Palestine.* Oxford, UK: Oneworld Publications, 2006.

The Phenomenon of Collaborators in Palestine. Jerusalem: PASSIA Publications, 2001.

Pleins, J. David. *The Psalms: Songs of Tragedy, Hope, and Justice.* Maryknoll, NY: Orbis Books, 1993.

Prior, Michael. *The Bible and Colonialism: A Moral Critique.* Sheffield, UK: Sheffield Academic Press, 1997.

————. "Confronting the Bible's Ethnic Cleansing in Palestine." In *The Link.* New York: Americans for Middle East Understanding, December 2000.

————. *Zionism and the State of Israel: A Moral Inquiry.* New York: Routledge, 1999.

————, ed. *Speaking the Truth about Zionism and Israel.* London: Melisende, 2004.

Raheb, Mitri. *I Am a Palestinian Christian.* Minneapolis: Fortress Press, 2004.

Rantisi, Audeh, and Ralph Beebe. *Blessed Are the Peacemakers: A Palestinian Christian in the Occupied West Bank.* Grand Rapids: Zondervan Books, 1990.

Rossing, Barbara R. *The Rapture Exposed: The Message of Hope in the Book of Revelation*. Boulder, CO: Westview Press, 2004.

Ruether, Rosemary Radford. *America, Amerikka: Elect Nation and Imperial Violence*. Oakville, CT: Equinox, 2007.

———, and Herman J. Ruether. *The Wrath of Jonah: The Crisis of Religious Nationalism in the Israeli-Palestinian Conflict*. 2nd ed. Minneapolis: Fortress Press, 2002.

Said, Edward W. *The Politics of Dispossession: The Struggle for Palestinian Self-Determination, 1969-1994*. New York: Vintage Books, 1994.

———. *The Question of Palestine*. New York: Vintage Books, 1992.

Segovia, Fernando F., and Mary Ann Tolbert, eds. *Readings from This Place: Social Location and Biblical Interpretation in Global Perspective*. Vol. 2. Minneapolis: Fortress Press, 1995.

Shahak, Israel. *Jewish History, Jewish Religion: The Weight of Three Thousand Years*. Boulder, CO: Pluto Press, 1994.

———, and Norton Mezvinsky. *Jewish Fundamentalism in Israel*. Sterling, VA: Pluto Press, 1999.

Sizer, Stephen. *Christian Zionism: Road-map to Armageddon?* Leicester, UK: InterVarsity Press, 2004.

———. "The Origins of Christian Zionism." *Cornerstone* 31 (Winter 2003): 4-8.

———. *Zion's Christian Soldiers? The Bible, Israel, and the Church*. Leicester, UK: InterVarsity Press, 2007.

Sölle, Dorothee. "Suffering." In *Dictionary of the Ecumenical Movement*, edited by Nicholas Lossky et al. Geneva: World Council of Churches Publications, 1991.

Stalenheim, P., D. Fruchart, W. Omitoogun, and C. Perdomo. "Military Expenditure." *SIPRI Yearbook 2006*. Oxford: Oxford University Press, 2006.

Steffens, Lincoln. *Autobiography of Lincoln Steffens*. Heyday Books, 2005.

Stohlman, Nancy, and Laurieann Aladin. *Live from Palestine: International and Palestinian Direct Action against the Israeli Occupation*. Cambridge, MA: South End Press, 2003.

Stuart, Douglas. *Hosea-Jonah*. Word Biblical Commentary 21. Waco, TX: Word, 1987.

Study Group of the Church of Scotland. *Theology of Land and Covenant*. May 2003.

Susser, Leslie. "The Carrot of Statehood." *Jerusalem Report*, June 2000.

Thomas, Herbert E. *The Shame Response to Rejection*. Sewickley, PA: Albanel Publishers, 1997.

Trible, Phyllis. *Jonah. New Interpreter's Bible* 7. Nashville: Abingdon Books, 1996.

Tuchman, Barbara. *Bible and Sword: England and Palestine from the Bronze Age to Balfour*. New York: Ballentine Books, 1984.

Tutu, Desmond. *God Has a Dream: A Vision of Hope for Our Time*. New York: Doubleday, 2004.

———. "Injustice and Oppression Will Never Prevail." *Cornerstone* 24 (Spring 2002): 3.

Vidal, Gore. *Perpetual War for Perpetual Peace: How We Got to Be So Hated*. New York: Nation Books, 2002.

Wagner, Donald. *Anxious for Armageddon*. Scottdale, PA: Herald Press, 1995.

———. "A Christian Zionist Primer, Part II: Defining Christian Zionism." *Cornerstone* 31 (Winter 2003): 12-13.

Walker, Peter W. L., ed. *Jerusalem Past and Present in the Purposes of God*. Cambridge, UK: Tyndale House, 1992.

———. *Jesus and the Holy City: New Testament Perspectives on Jerusalem*. Grand Rapids: Eerdmans, 1996.

The Washington Report on Middle East Affairs 26, no. 2 (March 2007).

Wink, Walter. *Engaging the Powers: Discernment and Resistance in a World of Domination*. Minneapolis: Fortress Press, 1992.

———. *Jesus and Nonviolence: A Third Way*. Minneapolis: Fortress Press, 2003.

————. *The Powers That Be: Theology for a New Millennium*. New York: Doubleday, 1998.

————, ed. *Peace Is the Way: Writings on Nonviolence from the Fellowship of Reconciliation*. Maryknoll, NY: Orbis Books, 2000.

Woodward, Bob. *Plan of Attack*. New York: Simon & Schuster, 2004.

Wright, Christopher. *Old Testament Ethics for the People of God*. Downers Grove, IL: InterVarsity Press, 2004.

Wright, G. Ernest. *The Old Testament against Its Environment*. London: SCM, 1962.

Wright, N. T. *Jesus and the Victory of God*. Minneapolis: Fortress Press, 1997.

Yoder, John Howard. *The Original Revolution*. Scottdale, PA: Herald Press, 1971.

————. *The Politics of Jesus*. Grand Rapids: Eerdmans, 1994.

Index

not allowing narrow theology of
the land, 64-65
Christianity: Middle Eastern, loaded
with Trinitarian faith, 11; roots of,
54; theology of, lifting up justice
and peace, 90
Christian-Muslim relations, 13-14
Christian Peacemaker Teams (CPT),
139
Christians: choosing theology of violence and exclusion, 92; committing to ministry of reconciliation,
65; following Jesus' model, 101-2;
theology of the land grounded in
the New Testament, 64-65
Christians United for Israel (CUFI),
28, 88
Christian Zionism: antisemitism of,
89; basic tenets of, 79-80; challenging, 88-91; distinguishing from
Jewish Zionism, 89; early major
players in, 83-84; as exclusive form
of theology, 78-80; growing understanding of, 79-81; predating Jewish political Zionism, 81; promoting violent theology, 90; translated
into political agenda, 80-81; variety
of terms for, 81
Christian Zionists, 26, 27-28; basic
beliefs of, 82; becoming Israel's ally,
85, 89-90; linked with U.S. right-
wing conservatives, 76; not relating
to Palestinian Christians, 90-91;
reaching out to, 79; uniting with
Jewish Zionists, 86-88
churches, avoiding justice themes, 21
Church of Scotland, 52
Clemenceau, Georges, 113-14
Clinton, Bill, 85, 86
Coffin, William Sloane, 28-29
collective punishment, by Israeli government, 127-28
confederation, of two states, 175
Conference of Presidents of Major
Jewish Organizations, 27
confession, 186
conflict resolution: paradigms for, 183-
87; ten basic rules for, 181-83
conflicts, finding non-war solutions
for, 112
Constantine, 92
Consultancy, the, 40-41, 43
Cooper, Anthony Ashley. *See* Shaftesbury (Lord)

cooptation, 43
corpus saparatum, 172
Corrie, Rachel, 102
cross, as paradigm for human condition, 111-12
Crossan, John Dominic, 148
Cyril of Jerusalem, 147

Daniel, book of, 135-36
Darby, John Nelson, 83
David, lineage of, 96-97
Dawisha, Adeed, 165
Declaration of Independence (Israel),
162
Declaration of Independence (Palestin-
ian), 31
Declaration of Principles (1993), 25, 32
DeLay, Tom, 86
dependence, 43
dispensationalism, 83
Dome of the Rock, 174
Dugard, John, 159, 160

early church: combining messianic
strands of thought, 98-100; faith
centers of, 146; meaning of discipleship for, 100; rejecting Davidic
strand, 100
East Jerusalem, occupation of (1967),
85
Eckstein, Yeheil, 87
Ecumenical Accompaniment Program
in Palestine and Israel (EAPPI), 139
Edict of Milan, 92
Egypt, peace treaty with Israel, 5-6
Elhanan, Nurit, 121
Elhanan, Rami, 121
Ellis, Marc, 9, 28
empire, characteristics of, 113-14,
148-49
Ephesians, letter to, as exemplary
expression of New Testament theology, 62-63
Esack, Farid, 158-59
Essenes, 94
ethnic nationalism, 155-56
ethnocracy, 156-57
Eusebius, 146
exile, prophets' responses to, 131-34
Ezra, emphasizing purity of Jewish
blood, 72
Ezra, book of: exclusivist text in, 143;
xenophobia in, 131
Ezra, Gideon, 121